UNRULY
CINEMA

UNRULY CINEMA

History, Politics, and Bollywood

RINI BHATTACHARYA MEHTA

UNIVERSITY OF
ILLINOIS PRESS
Urbana, Chicago, and Springfield

Library of Congress Cataloging-in-Publication Data
Names: Mehta, Rini Bhattacharya, author
Title: Unruly cinema: history, politics, and Bollywood /
    Rini Bhattacharya Mehta.
Description: Urbana: University of Illinois Press, [2020]
    | Includes bibliographical references and index.
Identifiers: LCCN 2020001591 (print) | LCCN 2020001592
    (ebook) | ISBN 9780252043123 (cloth) | ISBN
    9780252084997 (paperback) | ISBN 9780252052002
    (ebook)
Subjects: LCSH: Motion pictures—India—History—
    20th century. | Motion pictures—Political aspects—
    India—History.
Classification: LCC PN1993.5.18 M415 2020 (print) |
    LCC PN1993.5.18 (ebook) | DDC 302.23/430954—dc23
LC record available at https://lccn.loc.gov/2020001591
LC ebook record available at https://lccn.loc.gov/
    2020001592

for
Ayesha

Contents

Acknowledgments

This book comes at the end of six years of labor, during which time advice and encouragement from peers, colleagues, and friends kept me going. Without their support, I would not have dared to pick up a new project for my first monograph. I am grateful to the University of Illinois at Urbana-Champaign for providing me the intellectual home that is every academic's dream. My two home departments—the Program in Comparative and World Literature and the Department of Religion—have nurtured me through the years of my tenure track; the collegiality and warmth of both is what every assistant professor hopes for.

A fellowship from the Unit for Criticism and Interpretive Theory at UIUC in 2014–16 and support from the Campus Research Board provided time and funds needed for research and travel for the book. I am grateful to Susan Koshy, director of the Unit for Criticism, for organizing a review of the manuscript in 2015. Antoinette Burton, Priya Joshi, Lilya Kaganovsky, Robert Rushing, and Julie Turnock read a very early and rough version of the manuscript and offered crucial insight. Estibalitz Ezkerra-Vegas proofread an early version of the manuscript. Harriet Murav was the kindest mentor when I was preparing to submit my sample chapters to the press. Antoinette Burton always found time whenever I needed advice. I am grateful to Matthew E. Nelson for carefully proofreading the final version of the manuscript.

At home, Prashant and Ayesha showed extraordinary patience and continued to cheer me on; they showered me with love when I was at my crankiest worst.

My family in Kolkata, Atmaja Sen, Barnali Sen, and Soumyajyoti Sen, have been a source of strength and unconditional affection. My baba and my ma always believed in me; losing Ma in 2015 was the darkest moment in my life.

This book was written during the period I began teaching a course on Indian cinema at UIUC. The course, designed by me, has grown to become a large lecture class of three hundred students every year. The experience of teaching this course has shaped the argument I present in *Unruly Cinema*; I am grateful for all the difficult questions students from diverse backgrounds and from different majors asked me. A faculty fellowship from the National Center for Supercomputing Association has opened up a world of possibilities for me to connect the study of Indian cinema with digital humanities. Donna Cox's work and vision at the NCSA will continue to inspire my research in that direction. Finally, I thank Daniel Nassett at the University of Illinois Press for his encouragement and advice at every step. It really takes a village to accomplish a task such as this, and much more so when an impractical assistant professor writes her first book on something completely different from her doctoral dissertation. Here goes the verdict: it can be done.

UNRULY CINEMA

INTRODUCTION

Indian Cinema against the Currents of History

The history of Indian popular cinema is a long saga of contrariness. Since indigenous cinematic production began in British India in 1899, every state-led attempt to control, reform, and refine popular cinema, by the British as well as by their postcolonial successors, has failed. Popular Hindi cinema—the progenitor of Bollywood and the focus of this book's case studies—has strangely thrived not only through political turbulence and economic downturns but also against claims of competing cinemas to aesthetic and technical superiority, not least in the case of Hollywood imports and Indian art house films. Bollywood's current global ascendance and national prominence can be understood only through the long and circuitous history of Indian popular cinema. Despite its belated naming, Bollywood—as a kind of Indian cinematic "event"—has happened before, as a riposte to historical disruptions in the Indian media, market, and governance. *Unruly Cinema* picks four such moments of disruption to trace the long and conflicted genealogy of Bollywood. The guiding idea of *Unruly Cinema* is that the history of Indian popular cinema—including Bollywood, its latest avatar—must be approached through the conflicts, frictions, and fissures in Indian cinema's past. It is only by accentuating and then analyzing key historical moments that we can arrive at the meaning of Bollywood as an event. Hence the subtitle: *History, Politics, and Bollywood.*

It is necessary to begin this book by reminding readers of a fact that students of Indian cinema have long known: the seemingly new phenomenon of global Bollywood is rooted not only in the complexities of colonial and post-colonial history but also in India's multilingual and multilayered film industry. Although indigenous Indian efforts at film production had begun in 1899, it was only after the introduction of sound in 1931 that the national output of films began steadily to increase. By 1971, that output reached levels high enough to surpass the United States and Japan, establishing India as the largest national film producer in the world.[1] Throughout the Cold War era, India's prodigious film output was primarily for national consumption. The various regional language cinemas catered, as they still do, to discrete linguistic communities, organized along state borders within India.[2] The only significant outlier has been Bombay-produced Hindi cinema. Even in Bombay (now officially named Mumbai), Hindi cinema coexists with the regional language cinema of Maharashtra, the state in which Mumbai sits (and whose official language is Marathi). Hindi cinema, Bollywood's precursor, was thus an anomaly, the only cinema distributed and exhibited nationally other than imports (which mostly came from Hollywood).[3] Outside of its own national market, Indian cinema's limited international distribution during the Cold War era was largely divided into two broad categories. Parallel cinema—or "art cinema," as it was commonly known—in various languages was officially selected for film festivals and "panorama" events, mostly in Europe and North America. Popular Hindi films, by contrast, were exported to the USSR as well as to parts of Asia and Africa.[4] While Bollywood has continued to maintain Hindi cinema's market in Asia and Africa, its crucial departure from the Cold War era is that it is now the dominant Indian cinematic form in the West, replacing Indian art cinema. The departure occurred memorably in 2002, when Sanjay Leela Bhansali's big-budget melodrama *Devdas* premiered at Festival de Cannes. In 2007, Sony Pictures Entertainment became the first Hollywood studio to finance a Bollywood film directed by Bhansali, *Saawariya* (My Love), starring two scions of prominent Bombay film families, Ranbir Kapoor and Sonam Kapoor.

Bollywood's debut on the twenty-first-century global media market has had a cascading effect on Indian cinema, both nationally and globally. The success of the Telugu two-part film *Baahubali* (2015–17), for example—which set a new benchmark for success at the box office in India with gross sales exceeding INR 8 billion with its Tamil and Hindi dubbed versions—is a post-Bollywood phenomenon. All three versions of *Baahubali* were made available for sale on iTunes, in the special eponymous subcategory "Indian cinema." In 2017, the year in which *Baahubali: The Conclusion* was released throughout India in the original Telugu and the dubbed Hindi and Tamil versions, the total output of Indian cinema rose to its highest, at 1,986 films in forty-three languages. The count in the following year, April 2017 to March 2018, fell to 1,813 but rose to new heights in the next year, April 2018 to March 2019, at 2,446 films in fifty-five languages. Each year in the twenty-first century, the total has nearly equaled the combined output of the second and the third highest film-producing nations, China and the United States. From 1971, when India became the highest film-producing nation, to this day, the linguistic diversity of Indian cinema has been unparalleled in world cinema. How did such copious and diverse film production continue despite numerous authoritative attempts to control, reform, and refine the industry? The key to this complicated, compelling narrative behind the "Bollywood phenomenon" is a set of nonintuitive turns in the trajectory of Indian popular cinema. These turns protected it from the turbulence of shifting political and cultural climates between 1931 and 2000 and propelled Bollywood's global emergence.

The four chapters of this book present an analysis of four discrete moments in the history of Indian cinema. The first of these breakthrough moments was the market-driven yet almost accidental triumph of Indian talkies over Hollywood and other imports in the 1930s. The second was the emergence of the nationalist social melodrama, a genre that outwitted the nation-state with cinematic-lyrical manifestos in the 1950s. The third breakthrough came via the co-optation of the voice of the oppressed in the action genre, which in the 1970s was centered on the "angry young male." Finally, there was Indian cinema's discovery of the global neoliberal, self-consciously "Indian" aesthetic that engendered Bollywood. These shifts are well-documented and acknowledged in government reports, news media, and histories of Indian cinema. *Unruly Cinema* uses these turns to organize the teleology of popular Indian cinema, from its beginnings to Bollywood. Organized thus, Indian cinema's history of contrariness exposes the unevenness of Bollywood's historical progression from colonial origins to the post-global present. That history reveals a complex popular-cultural flow growing within and in spite of an equally complex national cultural drift.

Unruly Beginnings: The Colonial Sounds of Indian Cinema

Indigenous cinema in British India, restricted as it was by colonial rule, was until 1930 an impoverished cinema with an uncertain future. It became a viable entity only after sound technology was implemented in the 1930s.[5] As sound film production steadily grew, the percentage of films imported from Hollywood significantly declined. Official and popular histories of Indian cinema have emphasized the role played by Indian films' innovative, hybrid musical form in overcoming Hollywood's dominance.[6] The "all talking, singing, and dancing" films (as the poster for *Alam Ara* [Beauty of the World], the first "Hindustani" talkie, advertised in 1931) are understood as having sealed Indian cinema's advantage over Hollywood imports. While the coincidence of Indian sound cinema and the retreat of Hollywood from India lends plausibility to that narrative, the real story is more complex, involving a confluence of causes and precipitating events.

In 1927, when sound technology was introduced to cinema, Hollywood dominated the market within Britain as well as throughout its global empire. The British strategy for dealing with Hollywood's organized production and global marketing was to subsidize and promote British cinema through regulation. Such was the history that led to the Quota Act (1927) for Britain's domestic market, an act that had only limited success. British India's counterpart of the Quota Act was a push for *empire cinema*, a hypothetical category of British colonial cinema that would supplement British filmmaking with some token colonial labor and resources. That cinema would then be marketed in the colonies to compete with Hollywood. While the government appointed a committee to study the market for empire cinema, no concrete measures or efforts were undertaken.[7] The indigenous films had a market share of 20 percent in the late 1920s, with the remaining 80 percent consisting mostly of Hollywood films. But the weakening of Hollywood's international market following the Great Depression in 1929, combined with the increase in the popularity of cinema in India, created the perfect storm for the Indian "talkie" to wrest the market away from Hollywood, so much so that 40 percent of films shown in India in 1936 were now Indian.

Indian cinema's first seemingly insurmountable problem—making films with imported technology in an oppressive colonial economy and competing against the marketing might of the Hollywood studios—was therefore overcome only after 1931. The unequal participation of Indians in the economy due to limits set by the colonial government makes the cinema's triumph nearly incredible. How was it that a colonized population not allowed to manufacture salt for daily use without paying revenue to the British government could manage to mechanically produce and reproduce the most technology-dependent art form of the early twentieth century?[8] The answer lies in the disorganized and diverse world of Indian silent cinema produced between 1913 and 1930. An exploration of this world in chapter 1 helps explain the inherent scatteredness that conditioned the birth of the Indian talkie. What emerged in the 1930s was a hybrid cinema with hybrid music in the three port towns—Bombay, Calcutta, and Madras—that served as India's colonial metropolises. That hybridity was as much a by-product of colonial modernity as it was the progenitor of a national modernity.

Tracing the hybridity in an actual corpus of the early Indian films, unfortunately, has been made impossible by the paucity of available films. Without a sizable archive, early Indian film history is unavoidably stymied. Most silent films have been lost or destroyed, and secondary literature discussing lost films remains our only way of accessing, however indirectly, the work of such pioneers as Baburao Painter and Dhirendra Nath Ganguly.[9] The absence of an archive during the transition to sound was detrimental to the growth of an organic cinematic tradition as well. According to Shyam Benegal, auteur and one of the pioneers of the "New Cinema" of the 1960s, the arrival of sound in Indian cinema ended the "stylistic development in the silent film" and the "organic evolution of the cinema" as "cinema took its entire form from the urban theatre."[10] Benegal interprets cinema's wholehearted adaptation of the largely melodramatic, complete entertainment packages of the hybrid form of urban theater as the "traditionalisation of the Indian cinema."[11]

What Benegal critiqued as the "traditionalisation of the Indian cinema" has been the preferred triumphal narrative in nationalist historiographies of Indian cinema adopted during the colonial era and after independence. The nationalist history of Indian cinema—made official through government-produced pamphlets from 1954 onward—ignored the modernity and hybridity of early Indian cinema and developed a linear approach to Indian cinema's national trajectory. It took D. G. Phalke's idea of "swadeshi cinema" (Indian images for and by Indians) quite literally, ignoring Phalke's and others' use of swadeshi as a business strategy. In so doing, this history privileged the mythological and the social genres over action and fantasy, thus creating a familiar straight line from the arrival of cinema in British India through Phalke's swadeshi intervention to postcolonial Indian cinema.[12] As I elaborate in chapter 1, the linear growth of a coherent national cinema was not possible even in the era of Indian nationalism, owing to a gap between art form and its mechanical production, which was further augmented by the uneven participation of Indians in the colonial economy. There was no direct correspondence between ideology and the use of technology among those in the colonized strata who had access to the chain of supply. My analysis borrows from Someswar Bhowmik, who has explored in *Indian Cinema: Colonial Contours* how the growth of early Indian cinema was facilitated by capitalists of the lower strata.[13] Their contribution to the popular bent of cinema has been largely glossed over by official histories that emphasize a handful of educated middle-class individuals who align more easily with the vision of a national cinema. Ashish Rajadhyaksha, in his discussion of cinema's "modernist realism," has also questioned the viability of the term *swadeshi* in the context of cinematic production, since the term served the purpose of extending bourgeois value in Indian society.[14]

Following the 1903–8 swadeshi movement in Bengal, the "swadeshi idea" was widely used as a marketing and advertising tool by manufacturers small and large, including filmmakers such as Phalke. Thus, it was not swadeshi, in the nationalist sense of the term, that made Indian cinema a battleground between economic and cultural interests. Apart from the heterogeneous and hybrid body of film production, there was a hitherto untapped body of consumers spread over Britain's Indian empire that defied narrow definition or delimitation by identity. The subaltern masses (following Dipesh Chakrabarty's use of the term in *Provincializing Europe* as the opposite of *bourgeois*), which formed the majority of the viewing public, symbolized both a market to be manipulated and a force to fear.[15] The 1928 *Report of the Indian Cinematograph Committee* documents various articulations of British and Indian bourgeois anxiety of the nonliterate public's gaze. Even as the melodramatic Indian cinematic form of the 1930s was less hybrid and more stylized than its silent predecessor, it provided the right product at the right time: a cinema that could hold the bourgeois and subaltern attentions alike in the name of "culture" and rescue the Indian film market from Hollywood's dominance.

Chapter 1 highlights the heterogeneity of the milieu (as opposed to the national unity underscored in received histories) inhabited by the studios of Bombay and Calcutta, and later Madras. This turbulent environment produced various genres under the umbrella of melodrama through the 1930s and the early 1940s. Imperial Studios and Bombay Talkies in Bombay and New Theatres Studios in Calcutta nurtured a generation of stars who become the most significant players in the business after World War II, when wartime economic unrest caused an influx of illegal funding into the film industry. This influx had profound consequences as the studio system was gradually replaced by an ad hoc, independent, star-centric system of production. The independent growth of cinema and film song popularity buoyed each other through the political and economic tribulations caused by World War II and the 1947 partition.[16] The hybridity inherent in colonial Indian cinema as well as the hybrid film culture that bound the bourgeois and the subaltern as consumers was naturalized as "Indianness" in Indian cinema. The non-diegetic song, itself a hybrid product, is one such naturalized "essence" of Indian cinema that carried over the legacy of the studio-era productions such as *Devdas* (1936) and *Achhut Kanya* (The

Untouchable Girl, 1936) through the breakdown of the studios during World War II to postindependence productions.

Whose Cinema? Struggle for Legitimacy in a Nation-State

When India became independent in August 1947, the Indian film industry, even in its scattered post-studio state, was too immense for the Indian government either to ignore or to suppress. Notwithstanding the lack of a strong capitalist base or organization, India on the cusp of political independence in 1947 was the third largest producer of cinema, after the United States and Japan.[17] The next protracted disruption for Indian cinema, explored in chapter 2, was not caused by extraneous factors like foreign cinemas or governments. It was the result, rather, of the postcolonial state's adverse attitude and its repeated paternalistic attempts to acculturate popular cinema, especially Hindi cinema produced in Bombay in the 1950s. The postcolonial government approached cinema as neither an industry nor an art but as a problem that required bureaucratic and ideological solutions. In a small irony, popular cinema in India carried the idea of the nation and later the nation-state to the masses far and wide, accentuating the task that print technology had begun in the nineteenth century of imagining a national community. Throughout the 1950s, Hindi films produced in Bombay (simultaneously with Bengali films produced in Calcutta and Tamil films in Madras) deployed the melodramatic form of the early talkies to engage the ideologies of the nation-state in ways more effective than anything designed or approved by the government. Nationalism was perpetuated much more efficiently by popular formulations in cinema than it was by the documentaries that the government's Films Division produced and that all theaters were obligated to screen before their main feature presentations.

In retrospect, it is easy to surmise how such switching of roles could happen. Commercial cinema did not carry the political burden of the state's documentary wing. The contradictions between the progressive, developmental claims of the state's ideology and the vestiges of "premodern" creeds—religion, patriarchy, or caste—were resolved effectively in popular cinema through melodramatic narratives that emphasized emotion over narrative logic and deployed non-diegetic music to conflate love, devotion, and patriotism. Hindi cinema from the 1950s, the most recognizable precursor of Bollywood, became the (unofficial) ideological apparatus of the nation-state, so much so that national cultural memory of the 1950s and 1960s came to be embodied in that era's stars and visualized film songs. Both in Salman Rushdie's novel *The Satanic Verses* (1988) and in Mira Nair's *Mississippi Masala* (1992), "Mera Joota Hai Japani" (My Shoes Are Japanese), a song from Raj Kapoor's *Shree 420* (The Gentleman Fraud, 1955), is deployed as performative and mnemonic nationalism in a global context.[18] In Rushdie's novel, Gibreel Farishta, a middle-aged actor strongly reminiscent of Amitabh Bachchan, falls from the sky singing this song when his plane explodes midair over Scotland. In Nair's film, an Indian Gujarati family carries an audiocassette recording of the song in their sparse luggage as they are forced out of Idi Amin's Uganda. Through life, death, and exile, Indians are projected as imagining their community through the audio-visual-lyrical medium of Indian cinema.

Still, Indian cinema struggled for legitimacy in newly independent India. Cinema was the only form of artistic production that was not supported by the "Akademis" (official academies) created under Jawaharlal Nehru's government.[19] Official events, such as the National Film Awards, fell under the Ministry of Information and Broadcasting's jurisdiction. Nehru—India's first prime minister, the leader of the Indian National Congress, and the political descendant of Mahatma Gandhi—created or oversaw most of the bureaucratic support systems in the nascent Indian state, and Indian popular cinema repeatedly failed to earn state support. While Nehru intervened on behalf of Satyajit Ray for *Pather Panchali*'s (Song of the Road, 1955) entry into Festival de Cannes in 1956 (there were objections raised by a section in the government against Ray's "depiction of poverty"), he considered popular cinema an inferior art form in need of government's tutelage. When the Indian government replaced the British-Indian Cinematograph Act of 1918 with its own version in 1952, it reasserted the government's power over certification and taxation. A quasi-socialist state's regulatory policies became a financial and artistic burden for the film industry. Apart from direct government control, secondary entities such as the state-run All India Radio could be easily manipulated to disrupt the normal functioning of the industry. Film music's disappearance from radio transmission between 1952 and 1957 manifested the state's indirect control. Paradoxically, the National Film Awards and National Film Festivals that began in 1954 under the Ministry of Information and Broadcasting presented a united front by pretending that cinema's ideological world was in complete harmony with that of the nation-state.

Thus, despite the overwhelming popularity of commercial films, the film industry had little standing in the face of the state's regulatory power. In chapter 2, I explicate how the dominant genre(s) of popular cinema—especially a carefully crafted nationalist social genre initiated by populist directors such as Raj Kapoor—survived the Nehruvian regime of control and regulations by adopting and modulating a nation-statist ideology that could smooth over the contradictions between the progressive stance of the state and the regressive inertia of tradition and patriarchy. In the immediate aftermath of India's political independence, postcolonial Indian cinema weathered these adversities by projecting a stronger nationalist sentiment than the nation-state's official apparatus ever could.

People's Cinema versus the People's Hero

As cinema's aesthetic and ideological merits continued to be questioned by the state and the press, popular cinema faced its third disruption in the wake of an organized media policy initiated by the government to support and nurture the production of "art" films. The argument for fostering a "better" cinema was easy to pitch, as there were few critical arguments "for" commercial Hindi films in the Cold War era.[20] Incidentally, most of the charges made against the formulas used in postcolonial Hindi cinema continue to be true for contemporary Bollywood's most successful productions. In the first two postcolonial decades, while the disorderly musical form of Hindi cinema kept reprising a strategic combination of a melodic nationalism and the family drama, the government began endorsing art cinema, often referred to as "New Cinema" or parallel cinema, after the "Manifesto of the New Cinema Movement" (1968) by Arun Kaul and Mrinal K. Sen.[21] Sen's *Bhuvan Shome* (1969) and Kaul's *Uski Roti* (His/Her Bread, 1970) were in the first generation of films to be funded and promoted by the Film Finance Corporation, the government's agency for funding innovative cinema. By 1973, the corporation had assumed control of distribution of all raw film stock.[22] Producers of Hindi cinema, with their unofficial finances and their dependence on imported equipment and stock, saw the state's new role as unnecessary and incomprehensible antagonism toward the industry. The triumph of the nationalist social genre was never allowed a moment without a sense of precariousness, once New Cinema became an adversary armed with government support. It is only in the *longue durée* that the power of the nationalist social genre as the state's unofficial ideological apparatus has become recognizable.

In the 1970s, the nationalist social genre gave way to a newly configured "action genre" centered usually on an "angry young man" played by Amitabh Bachchan. Drawing from British postwar realism and cinema of the British New Wave, the Indian mutation of the "angry young man" was the perfect foil for retaliatory action that could still be couched in melodrama. This was the genre that would revitalize Bombay cinema and produce an unruly counter-discourse to both the state's normalizing attempts and New Cinema's aesthetic superiority. I approach this third unruly turn in Indian cinema's history in chapter 3 through the prism of contemporary critical discourses on cinema. The conflict between the two forms of cinema—entertainment and art—was fought in the public sphere through the 1960s and 1970s, thus triangulating the erstwhile "cinema versus state" dynamic. Critics, directors, and artists alike expressed and defended their views in print media, and the first generation of writing on Indian cinema was born. Indian art cinema or New Cinema, in conjunction with the government-sponsored Film and Television Institute in Pune, had a cascading long-term effect on Indian cinema. Directors from outside the mainstream, such as Ritwik Ghatak, were invited to teach at the institute, and directors who trained there, such as Ketan Mehta, made films that were critically acclaimed at home and abroad. But in the short term and in the economic context of filmmaking, New Cinema worked exactly how art cinema could be expected to work in a developing country in the Cold War era: it was self-conscious and sophisticated, made with a discerning viewership in mind, and was thus unable to attract viewers away from mainstream melodrama. While films by Ray, Benegal, and Sen were screened at Cannes, Berlin, Paris, and New York, they had a negligible presence in the markets where popular Hindi cinema dominated.[23]

From the perspective of Bombay-based cinema, the rise of art cinema was a disruption that could have pushed the stagnation and repetition of the commercial melodramatic form to the point of irrelevance. But by the time state-run television and state-sponsored art cinema attained a critical mass, Bombay cinema had undergone a new configuration of stardom and genre. Hindi film slid slowly away from the melodic nationalist family drama toward cinematic narratives of revenge and retribution, influenced by British New Cinema of the 1960s, among others. While the Indian art cinema movement of the 1960s and 1970s reinvigorated the medium to the excitement of a section of the educated middle class, the Hindi mainstream industry in Bombay reoriented the national imaginary to focus on physical violence and cathartic revenge, thus rallying the urban poor viewership as a stepping stone to national popularity. By the time Indian art cinema had established itself and television had begun to reach the remotest corners of the nation with the help of a satellite-based network, popular cinema had responded with a restructuring of the male star-text. It broke out of the bourgeois nationalist mold and adopted a new mythology of a simulated revenge carried out within the bounds of the legal system (the villain is not killed but subdued by the hero, to be arrested by the police who arrive to reaffirm the state's power over all). Films such as *Zanjeer* (Chains, 1973) and *Sholay* (Embers, 1975) rescripted the role of the male protagonist vis-à-vis the nation, validating the pursuit of social or personal justice by extrajudicial and violent means.

Amitabh Bachchan's "angry young man" star-text, from *Zanjeer* to *Deewar* (The Wall, 1975) and beyond, resonated with the surging urban blue-collar viewers in a way "art cinema," which often claimed to represent the dispossessed, could never do. The action genre also spoke to the national viewership under Indira Gandhi's increasingly autocratic government with the same intensity that Raj Kapoor's nationalist social films had in Nehruvian India. These films were not entirely novel. They simply entered the national mainstream from the realm of B movies, where they had lived since the early years of Indian cinema.[24] Once violence—however orchestrated and choreographed—was engrafted in popular formula films, it persisted as the preeminent cathartic force across genres well into the late 1980s, through the early careers of such twenty-first century stars of Bollywood as Aamir Khan and Shah Rukh Khan.

If the nationalist social genre had powered through the 1950s, maintaining its equilibrium, it was partly because of a stalemate between the state and cinema in their protracted bureaucratic battle. The Nehruvian state taxed and regulated, while the film industry fought back with an image of national unity that could not be matched by any existing political ideology, let alone that of the nation-state. But the rise of art cinema and the counter-rise of the popular revenge and retribution genre unsettled that equilibrium. Chapter 3's focus on the post-Nehruvian period, under Indira Gandhi's leadership, illuminates a different kind of complexity, which was caused by the government's proactive measures. By financing and supporting "art cinema" and sponsoring alternate modes of "better" entertainment through television, the government played a role in exacerbating the plebeian, unruly image of popular cinema. This is the era that saw a clear bifurcation between two distinct cinemas—the popular commercial cinema and the new art cinema—existing in almost every Indian language. Exploring the adversarial interface between the two cinemas, which erupted in ad hominem attacks by Nargis Dutt, who played the title role in *Mother India* (1957), on Satyajit Ray, whom she accused of selling images of Indian poverty to the West, I follow the trajectory of the popular national imaginary, whose manifestation in the action genre of the 1970s and early 1980s was punctuated by violence in India's political life through the 1980s and merged almost seamlessly with the televised Hindu epics in 1987–89.[25]

Cinema on the Cusp of Globalization: The Emergence of Bollywood

Hollywood—with its ever-widening pool of artists and filmmakers, its quick adaptation of the latest technology, and its mighty advertising budget—was kept at bay in postcolonial India by government regulation.[26] As India initiated globalization in 1991 by opening its domestic market to foreign investment and commerce, Hollywood studios got a historic opportunity to wrest back the market they had lost in the 1930s. The unlikely emergence of Bollywood in the era of Hollywood's return to India is the subject of the fourth and final chapter. Between 1973—the release year of *Zanjeer*, the first film featuring Amitabh Bachchan as the "angry young" hero—and the 1980s, the motifs of anger and revenge achieved their own equilibrium within the melodramatic form, so much so that action sequences were routine even in a love story or in the story of an impoverished disco dancer's struggle for recognition.[27] Anger and revenge, once normalized, had become endemic to all genre conventions. The handful of Hollywood films that were released in pre-globalization India were mostly of the action/adventure genre, with cinematography and special effects far superior to their Indian equivalents. The only barrier to imports was the "foreign" language and limited marketing. That barrier would be easily demolished in the 1990s by aggressively marketing and by dubbing Hollywood films into Hindi. Under such renewed pressure from outside, a new configuration of Hindi cinema emerged in Bombay, buoyed by the next generation of film and song stars, a sea change in film music marketing caused by the audiocassette industry, and the creation of a new cinematic nationalism that joined the diaspora's nostalgia for a homeland left behind with a rejuvenated nation-state's global ambitions. Bollywood had arrived.

There is nothing intuitive or familiar about Bollywood's reinvigoration of Indian Hindi popular cinema. Chapter 4 takes the reader through the unruly period of transition that rose from the decay of the 1970s revenge and retribution films. Although micro-variations mattered little within the all-consuming star-centric system, extrinsic factors engendered a cohort of films starring a new generation of actors. Films such as *Qayamat Se Qayamat Tak* (From Doom to Doom, 1988) and *Tezaab* (Acid, 1988) projected a generation of youth who could neither continue to live with the nationalist social genre's compromises nor exact the action genre's fantasy of revenge. The adversaries of these youth—standing in the way of their heterosexual couple formations—were ingrained in the fabric of the familial-social-political reality. A vicious multigenerational family feud in *Qayamat Se Qayamat Tak* causes the young protagonists' untimely death. In *Tezaab*, the heroine's father lives off her earnings as a dancer and does nothing to protect her from a Muslim gangster. The suffering protagonists in these films were predictive of the neoliberal Indians whose ties with the idealist secular Nehruvian nation-state had unraveled.

Transitional films such as these, which would become the foundation for Bollywood, were resonant with extrinsic factors such as the rise of the audiocassette industry, which broke free from the selective coterie of playback singers for films; the rise of a political Hindu nationalism; and the no-less-significant rise of a caste-based electoral polity. Matters of ethnicity, religion, and caste, avoided carefully in articulations of conflict in earlier films, were now seen and heard in films. Voices never heard before on state-controlled radio and television networks (All India Radio and Doordarshan) were marketed through audiocassettes on private startup labels. T-Series, one such label that provided the platform for young playback singers for films (including songs in both *Qayamat Se Qayamat Tak* and *Tezaab*), had begun by copying songs previously released on vinyl records by HMV/GramCo, which had held a virtual monopoly on recorded music through most of the twentieth century. The success of Super Cassette Industries—the parent company of T-Series Cassettes—was premised on a loophole in the Indian copyright law, which demonstrated the limits of a regulatory governance at a time of pro-capitalist rhetoric of economic reform and rapid modernization from Rajiv Gandhi's government, even before the actual onset of globalization.[28] The decay of the Nehruvian nation-state without any clear direction toward an alternative combined with the rise of a political Hindu nationalism constituted the Indian predicament at the end of the Cold War era. The transition ended in India's induction into globalization in 1990–91, when it had to deregulate its markets as per the conditions of a crucial loan from the World Bank.

The onset of economic liberalization in 1991 ended India's isolation from the images and products of advanced capitalist economies, as private cable channels were introduced and Hollywood's reach to India's viewership was (re)facilitated. The transitional films discussed above were not enough to reach a critical mass to match earlier momentums (the nationalist social genre of the 1950s or the revenge and retribution wave of the 1970s). They were also not equal to the unprecedented gush of television programs from the United States and beyond that were available via cable from 1991 onward. This transitional cinema faced an insecure future in 1994, when Steven Spielberg's *Jurassic Park*, the first Hollywood film to be dubbed in Hindi, towered above every other film in India in ticket sales, a feat followed by Jan de Bont's *Speed* later that year. This fourth challenge, generated by the return of Indian cinema's adversary (Hollywood) from the 1920s, was as global in nature as the first. For the last three decades of the Cold War, Hindi cinema produced in Bombay had an international market spreading over Asia and Africa, particularly in those regions where Hollywood circulated less successfully. With the dissolution of the Soviet Union and the Eastern Bloc, a major share of that international market was now gone, and the prospect of dubbed Hollywood films penetrating the global market was a serious threat, especially for Bombay-based Hindi films that had to compete with Hollywood films dubbed in Hindi across the nation.

If Indian indigenous cinema's precarious existence in the early twentieth century was ultimately transformed by the birth of the "all talking, singing, and dancing" sound film, the challenge in the late twentieth century was overcome by the simultaneous rise of Bollywood and the neoliberal Indian state. A neoliberal supernational imaginary united the globalization-era Indian nation-state with the Indian diaspora. The role of Bollywood in giving powerful expression to the key ingredients of that supernational imaginary—Hindutva, a muscular ethnocentric nationalism based on militarization; and a pro-corporate, amoral nation-state—can hardly be overemphasized. This will form the core of my analyses of films in the fourth chapter.

The denouement of the long narrative of this book boils down to two simultaneous reinventions. The first is Indian cinema's reinvention of the nation, as defined by a hegemonic Hindu nationalism on the one hand and the diaspora as an extended national family on the other. The second is Bombay-based Hindi cinema's reinvention of itself as Bollywood, adopting the name that was previously used only sarcastically and almost always within scare quotes. Both reinventions invigorated popular Indian cinema, both inside and outside of Bollywood. The first reinvention changed the paradigmatic nationalism so far represented in popular cinema through Nehruvian ideals of secularism and unity into an aggressive expression of violence and hatred toward dissenting others. This was inaugurated memorably in *Roja* (1992), a Tamil film dubbed into Hindi, the first national film that typecast Kashmiri Muslims as Islamic terrorists. Predating the crucial 2001 "war on terror" moment, *Roja's* depiction of the inherently violent Muslim mujahideen uncannily predicted the post-9/11 turn in global media. The spectacle of violence shifted from the realm of class struggle (the "angry young man" of the 1970s action genre fought for some form of social justice) into the interface between the nation and its enemies. The corollary of this defense of the nation was an unquestioned show of loyalty and faith toward tradition, redefined by a politicized form of Hinduism. These reinventions, by replacing the social justice–based action genre, created a new paradigm for cinematic Indianness. The national "self" that was born out of the process was in equal parts right-wing nationalist and neoliberal globalist, manifested in the star text of Shah Rukh Khan from *Dilwale Dulhaniya Le Jayenge* (The Brave Heart Will Win the Bride, 1995) to *Kabhi Khushi Kabhie*

14

Gham (Sometimes Happiness, Sometimes Sorrow, 2001) and beyond. One of the significances of Bollywood lay "in its self-positioning as an unofficial ideological apparatus."[29]

Unruly Cinema: One Way (Out of Many) to Theorize

The title *Unruly Cinema* is inspired by Carol Vernallis's 2013 book, *Unruly Media*, a study of the "swirl" of contemporary pervasive media forms such as YouTube, music videos, and digital cinema. Indian popular cinema's indomitability—alternating between sources of pride and frustration to the Indian nationalist worldview—emerged in sporadic bursts in the *longue durée* without any linear dependence on technological advancements (with an exception of the coming of sound).[30] By scrutinizing the earlier crises, my study seeks to demystify and illuminate the "Bollywood phenomenon" in Indian cinema, in part by rematerializing the economies, symbolic and political, in and through which it took shape. In so doing, I elaborate the long and complex history of the "popular cinema" and illustrate the very real frictions at the heart of its emergence and its self-representations. Between the official induction of "Bollywood" into the *Oxford English Dictionary* in 2001 and the widely reported centenary of Indian cinema in 2013, discourses on Indian "popular cinema" that was suddenly identified as "Bollywood" have spun out of narrow academic and official control. Information flowing out of books, articles, and databases has spilled onto vast new territories of dialogue, ranging from the popular levels of social media to the expanded media studies curricula in American universities. A noteworthy feature of these emergent discourses—in websites, periodicals, and social media as well as in many academic journals—has been an almost unconscious conflation of Bollywood with Indian cinema. Global news media ranging from the *Wall Street Journal* to *The Telegraph* (UK) and *The Guardian* reported the 2013 centenary as Bollywood's, with brief asides on the multilinguality and multilocality of Indian cinemas that exist beyond Bollywood. The temporal dimension of the naming—since "Bollywood" was sparsely used before the late 1990s to describe Bombay cinema—was mostly excluded from the media reports. Most scholarly volumes published in the last ten years have focused more on the here and now of Bollywood than on the historical background. This book's elucidation of how Indian popular cinema has mitigated the earlier crises will situate "Bollywood" in the larger and longer context of Indian cinema, thus facilitating a better understanding of popular cinema's mutation and survival in India.

In lieu of a linear and continuous narrative, a history of Indian cinema is more likely to embody contradictions that have always existed in the idea of "Indian cinema," as represented by various contenders. The conflation of Bollywood with Indian cinema is only the latest and most popular example in a long line of such contradictory and ultimately unstable claims to the mantle of a "national cinema." The meaning and identity of a pan-Indian cinema have never been constant, and it is possible to interpret each of the four crises from multiple standpoints. The idea of an "Indian" cinema has been represented by unique clusters of films to discrete viewerships. Himanshu Rai's collaborative efforts with Germany's Emelka Studios and UFA—films such as *Light of Asia* (1925) and *A Throw of Dice* (1929), both directed by Franz Osten—represented Indian cinema in Europe in the 1920s while they were virtually unknown to viewers in the Indian subcontinent. An alternative future of such films was possible if the British campaign for promoting empire cinema had succeeded. In the decade in which Satyajit Ray's Apu trilogy (1955–59) placed India on the map of world cinema as imagined by West European and American critics, Soviet viewers of the post-Stalinist cultural era responded to and accepted *indiiskie melodramy* as represented by Raj Kapoor's films such as *Awaara* (The Vagabond, 1951) and *Shree 420* as quintessential Indian cinema.[31] Ray's films ran in empty theaters in the USSR while *Awaara* held a box office record among all foreign films exhibited there. The parallel lives of Ray's and Kapoor's legacies were framed by both their receptions outside India and their alignments with discrete forms of regionalism. The problem of identity of a "national cinema" for the nascent postcolonial state in the 1950s was never resolved.

Nor can an assessment of Bollywood's unruly past ignore the transnational audiences of the wider third world, where Indian cinema had more currency than Hollywood films, owing to an unequal and complicated flow of materials and products in the pre-global world. Hindi films of the 1970s action genre, including those starring Amitabh Bachchan, were popular in the Middle East and North Africa, so much so that videocassettes of films ranging from *Sholay* to *Shahenshah* (Emperor, 1988) were produced with Arabic subtitles for export, long before English subtitles became available. Popular and recognizable in the above regions as an Indian film star, Bachchan was virtually unknown in the West beyond the Indian diasporic viewership until he was rebranded as a Bollywood star in 2001. The Middle Eastern and African viewers watched and received Bachchan's "angry young man" persona in the 1970s and 1980s outside the Indian sociopolitical context that created the market for it. In the absence of centralized or even organized marketing such as that by Hollywood's Motion Picture Export Association of America, Indian cinema's representations depended on its various modes of "reach," which in turn were coincidental and beyond the simple control of either the film industry or the government. Within India, non-Hindi linguistic groups with a strong cinematic tradition, such as Bengali, Marathi, Malayalam, and Tamil, had distinct and separate collective experiences of Indian cinema. In the Bengali cultural memory, for example, the 1950s and 1960s are more likely to be recalled as the era of the stars Uttam Kumar and Suchitra Sen than the era of Raj Kapoor and Nargis Dutt, while the history of Tamil cinema in the same era would be dominated by the rise of Dravida cultural politics and its counterpoints, embodied in the films with M. G. Ramachandran and Sivaji Ganesan in the lead roles. Telugu cinema's engagement with the "mythological" genre continued through the 1970s, its influence stretching even longer to fuel the political career of N. T. Rama Rao in 1982, an actor of the mythologicals who successfully campaigned for his own political party in the costumes of his most popular roles, including the Hindu deities Rama and Krishna. And within all major linguistic groups there has been, since the 1960s, a sensibility toward the separation between "art" and "commercial" cinema.

While all these details belong in an encyclopedic history of Indian cinema, they are also elements relevant to a genealogy of Bollywood. The ascendance of Bollywood, far from overshadowing the other Indian cinemas, has paralleled reconfigurations within those regional industries as well. Bollywood's past is more connected to than disjointed from the various other Indian cinemas. Produced by a star-centric system and subject to the same national rules of certification and taxation since 1952, all Indian popular cinemas—irrespective of the language or region of origin—share a common history that is neither cacophonous nor harmonic. At all times, each cinema has been incontrovertibly unruly from any normative perspective, be it official or hegemonic, and there has been an inexplicable Indian national popular character shared by all regional popular cinemas. The uncomplimentary characterization "all-India film" (used frequently by Chidananda Dasgupta from the 1960s onward, evoking the standardized programming of All India Radio) applied to Hindi, Tamil, Telugu, Malayalam, and Bengali cinema alike.[32] Thus, while the currency of Bollywood in the global era of digital and online media is a function of multiple converging factors within a global present, it is also a logical outgrowth of the cumulative pasts of Indian cinemas and exists in a continuum with them.

A Tamable Future?

Imagining the destiny of an unruly object like Bollywood has proved to be the most difficult part of this book. Once Bollywood has happened, whither lies the future? An op-ed article in the *New York Times* in 2007 asked, "Can Hollywood Make a Bollywood Movie?"[33] It was a timely question, as the first Bollywood film produced by Sony/Columbia Studios had just been released, and more than one Indian production company was teaming up with Hollywood studios. In the decade following that moment, a majority of the top-grossing Bollywood films have been funded in full or part by a Hollywood studio. What does this mean, beyond complicating the ever-evolving, flexible historiography of Indian cinema? The reason why Hollywood studios' productions of Indian films are not construed as a "fifth" contingency in this book is the continuity that exists between Hollywood-produced films and those that came before. The star-centric system, augmented by dynastic holds on film careers, has remained unchanged, and Hollywood studios have so far only financed ventures without exerting any other form of influence. Recent volumes that have illuminated different aspects of the current position of Bollywood vis-à-vis the Indian economy and global capital are Adrian Athique's *Indian Media*, Aswin Punathambekar's *From Bombay to Bollywood,* and Ajay Gehlawat's *Reframing Bollywood* and *Twenty-First Century Bollywood.*[34] How will the evolving role of global capital in Bollywood production change the scholarship on Indian cinema and vice versa? Books on or related to Bollywood belong to a field that has seen extraordinary expansion in the last fifteen years. That expansion in turn corresponds to a broader expansion occurring in global media studies. As the most significant cultural production system to emerge out of the world's largest democracy, Indian popular cinema is now increasingly in demand as a subject in literature, cultural studies, and film and media studies curricula. The number of doctoral dissertations submitted on the subject has been rising steadily in the last twenty years. But the significance and reach of Bollywood cinema has been evolving, in conjunction with the ebb and flow of global media. Since the time Bollywood has been incorporated into the curricula of media studies in the Anglo-American academia in the late 1990s, the idea of national cinema itself has changed radically. International corporations, including media streaming networks such as Netflix and Amazon Studios and platforms such as YouTube, have substantial power to sway the configurations of star-centric systems such as Bollywood's. The unruly, contrary nature of Bollywood has been so far evaluated in the context of national cinemas. What will become of such evaluations when the national cinematic framework ceases to be useful? *Unruly Cinema* foresees that cinema and media studies will need to actively incorporate digital methods and advanced visualizations in their presentations of the global flows in the present and near future.

CHAPTER 1

Colonial Indian Cinema

A Peripheral Modernity

Cinema went through two major transformations in the first four decades of the twentieth century. The first was the emergence of America as a global presence in the film industry, replacing France as the foremost producer and distributor of films worldwide.[1] This emergence was driven by American studios' sustained campaign to capitalize on cinema's universal appeal. The global success of the campaign was bolstered by the First World War, which had depleted Europe's manufacturing power. As the United States became the foremost exporter of manufactured goods during the war, the cargo of American films found easy passage to Europe and beyond. As early as 1916, New York replaced London as the global hub for film export, and by 1921 American films captured a majority share of the market in every country except Germany. The second transformation, however, proved a decisive check on Hollywood's overwhelming dominance and led to the diverse growth of other national cinemas. This transformation came around 1930, when sound film production exceeded that of silent film worldwide.[2] The arrival of sound coincided with a critical moment in American and global capitalism. With American manufactures and exports affected by the Great Depression, Hollywood was forced to face the linguistic diversity of its global viewership. Between 1929 and 1934, various national quotas on film imports, coupled with the cost of film dubbing, led to a steep downslide in Hollywood's foreign market. Though the slide ended in 1934 and recovery began in 1935, that half-decade weakening was enough to allow major film-producing nations in Europe to start battling for control of their domestic markets. While the far reach and prominence of Hollywood remained part of the global human experience, the 1930s proved that the world wanted more from cinema than Hollywood had to offer. Other industries of the world were ready to step in.

Outside Europe, only India and Japan were able to overcome Hollywood's hold on their film markets.[3] Both countries had developed their affinity for movies through used "junk" films routed through Europe. India was an outlier yet, as a colonized territory subject to British imperial control over imports, licensing, and exhibition—that is, every aspect of production and consumption of cinema. As Hollywood's exports took a brief tumble, Japanese and Indian cinemas mapped out their own distinct courses.[4] In the Indian scenario, the agent of transformation was what Kristin Thompson has called "a unique native version of the musical genre," a composite form of cinema that has since become the mainstay of Indian popular film across regions, genres, and languages.[5] While the vast majority of silent films exhibited in British India in the 1920s were imports from Hollywood, the Indian talkie with songs soon wrested the market away, so much so that in 1937, Hollywood's share of the market had dropped to 46 percent (from 90 percent in 1922 and 80 percent in 1929), with Indian films now at 38 percent and British films at 12.[6] By 1939, the output of Indian films had grown enough to claim over half of the market, with Hollywood as the only significant foreign import at 45 percent.[7] By 1947, at its birth as a sovereign nation-state, India was the third highest film-producing nation in the world, with films in ten languages serving 80 percent of the domestic market. Although the Cold War–era global dynamic of various national cinemas mostly worked out in Hollywood's favor, in India Hollywood remained a minority cinema, with exhibition limited to select theaters in the metropolises.[8]

The world's largest national industry since 1971, Indian cinema is a multilingual, multilocal entity, wrongly treated in popular imagination as an extension of Bollywood. The cinema of "Bollywood" (a sobriquet for the Hindi-language film industry based in Bombay or Mumbai) constitutes less than 15 percent of Indian cinema's total output in the twenty-first century. It is also, however, the only domestic film industry with nationwide distribution in India, and it is currently the best-known global cultural product out of India. To make sense of these facts and the industry they describe, we need to return to the beginnings of Indian cinema. Why? The answer lies in the single formal element that connects the first sound films produced in Bombay and Calcutta in the 1930s to twenty-first-century Bollywood: the use of non-diegetic songs, played at a uniform tone and volume, generally interrupting the flow of the narrative, and, at least after the first few years, almost never catching the habitual Indian viewer by surprise. In a way, what makes Bollywood unique was already germinating in the first Indian talkie, *Alam Ara,* directed by Ardeshir Irani. Released in March 1931, the Hindi/Urdu/Hindustani film *Alam Ara* was followed by eleven other films within the same calendar year—all had non-diegetic music, songs sung by actors interspersed throughout the body of visual narrative. Playback music—music recorded separately and inserted in the film during editing—was introduced in 1935, introducing song recordings as an important subdomain of the film market. Film songs remained the majority product of the Indian recording industry for the next seven decades.[9]

Accepting non-diegetic songs as an integral part of the Indian cinematic tradition, we must also be wary of essentialist reduction. While influences from pre-cinematic theatrical traditions—both the urban proscenium and open-air folk categories—flowed into cinemas throughout South Asia, there was nothing inevitable about the de rigueur Indian adaptation of non-diegetic songs. Notwithstanding its roots in other live performative arts, songs in India's early sound cinema were novelties that refused to conform to cinematic rules, producing a discrete art form encased in another art form. Such encasing was present from the beginning, when, between 1931 and 1935, music and dialogue had to be recorded simultaneously with the filming. This could be accomplished only by "tight frame composition" of "one-shot" songs that required suspension of all action. The line between actor and singer was fluid, as was the line between the cinematic narrative and the song sequence. Shankarrao Damle, chief sound engineer for Prabhat Film Company in Pune, describes one such sequence from a film he had watched in his youth:

> A couple of horsemen are seen riding furiously through a forest—it was a hunting expedition. One of the horsemen is the king. . . . Suddenly his horse comes to a halt underneath a big tree and we see the king dismounting. . . . In the next shot we see the king taking deliberate and determined steps towards the camera. Apparently, he has something on his mind and before one can wonder what it might be, the king has stopped and burst into a song. The song goes on for about three minutes. . . . Neither the camera nor the king has moved. After the song is over, the king goes back to this horse and resumes the hunt.[10]

Though Damle does not name the film, we can assume it was made in the early 1930s, before playback music was introduced.[11] For a relevant parallel in the era of playback music, let us turn to a fictional but entirely plausible film scene described in Salman Rushdie's novel *Midnight's Children:*

Pia kissed an apple, sensuously, with the rich fullness of her painted lips; then passed it to Nayyar, who planted, upon its opposite face, a virilely passionate mouth. This was the birth of what came to be known as the indirect kiss—and how much more sophisticated a notion it was than anything in our current cinema; how pregnant with longing and eroticism! The cinema audience (which would, nowadays, cheer raucously at the sight of a young couple diving behind a bush, which would then begin to shake ridiculously—so low we have sunk in our ability to suggest) watched, riveted to the screen, as the love of Pia and Nayyar, against a background of Dal Lake and ice-blue Kashmiri sky, expressed itself in kisses applied to cups of pink Kashmiri tea; by the foundations of Shalimar they pressed their lips to a sword . . . as they *mouthed* to *playback music*.[12]

In both Damle's recollection and Rushdie's imagination, the non-diegetic song is an aberration and a cultural curiosity: absurd to the outsider and a staple to the accustomed viewer. The formal strangeness that the song added to cinematic diegesis from the early years was enhanced further after 1935, when the actors increasingly broke into song in the voice of playback singers, the playback singer's voice easily distinguishable from that of the actor.[13] But others have offered more nuanced views. In 1967, the Indian auteur Satyajit Ray referred to his coming across an American film magazine that interpreted the Indian film song as a device similar to "Brechtian alienation" in theater, and Ray himself maintained that the song, even in its non-diegetic form, could be understood as a "cinematic device" only if it had some resonance with other devices or styles used in the same film.[14] In the same essay, Ray draws out a more material justification: in the absence of the "music halls, revues, plays, concerts" that the middle class in advanced stages of capitalism had, cinema in India was the only affordable entertainment for the masses, thus offering the perfect platform for songs that had no ontological reason to be in films. Caryl Flinn, in her essay on screen musicals on a global scale, finds such a materialist function of songs quite plausible for Indian audiences who "traditionally return to musicals for the purpose of re-experiencing the songs, with the movies functioning as a sort of visualized iTunes or radio."[15]

Writing forty years apart, Ray and Flinn both locate the place of songs in Indian film in the material conditions of cinematic production, a position strongly advocated in this book. The "song in film" thus offers the perfect segue to this chapter's contextual history of early Indian cinema, which will trace the arc of the medium from the first Indian screenings of silent films in 1896 to the moment of Indian talkies' prevailing over Hollywood in the 1930s. In contrast to France, Germany, and Japan—countries with significant national cinema bodies that fostered monolingual film industries through nation-statist policies in opposition to Hollywood and that were aided by capitalist advancement—India gained control of its domestic film market while still a colony at the bottom end of capitalist development. India's unparalleled linguistic and cultural diversity only heightens the contrast. What makes the history of Indian cinema unique is that its many commercial cinemas sprouted and evolved *despite* so many forces and opinions aligned against it throughout the twentieth century, from the disapproval of the British imperial state to the resistance of the anticolonial nationalists, and then from the apathy of the regulatory nation-state to the perpetual condescension of informed film critics.

The odds were stacked against Indian cinema from the beginning. Indian filmmakers who co-opted the new filmic technology belonged to a population shorn of its manufacturing abilities by colonialism. The "age of empire"—the last phase in what Eric Hobsbawm has called the long nineteenth century—saw an unprecedented acceleration in the flow of technology on a global scale, but that flow had a directional politics that is particularly relevant to the history of cinema in India.[16] The British East India Company's trade and conquest model—as different from the discovery and conquest of the Spanish conquistadores—engendered the earliest phase of globalization. And cinema from the very beginning was embedded in the intensely mobilized flow of things and ideas bearing mechanical modernity out of metropolitan Europe into the colonies. Cinema arrived in India to cater to the largest mass of colonial captives in global capitalism. There was little scope in a regulated but messy economy for entrepreneurship or technological experimentation. But cinema's unusual nexus of art, technology, and business, combined with its new, inchoate nature, made it a perfect medium. While the immediate popularity of cinema across the subcontinent may not be extraordinary, the circumstances of indigenous film production ended up exploding the "captive consumer model" for colonized Indians. This chapter journeys through the messy, overlapping interchange between consumption and production experienced by the first post-cinematic generation of Indians.

The Colonial Prosumers

The opening of the Suez Canal in 1869 had established an efficient sea route from Europe to Asia. The canal, eulogized by Walt Whitman in "A Passage to India," facilitated transport of manufactured goods as well as the latest technology from Europe to Britain's territories in India and Burma.[17] Bombay and Calcutta, the two port cities that became the first Indian centers of cinema production, were colonial creations, built by the East India Company in the seventeenth century. These cities were India's first modern metropolises, but they were also distinct colonial fabrications of haste, profit, and progress, which made their landscapes different from that of London or Paris. Populations thrust together by the machinery of the East India Company inhabited a shared space that nevertheless had discrete niches for each group. Single-screen theaters built in the 1930s through the 1960s had comfort and film selections tailored to distinct localities, easily visible in the mid- to late twentieth-century maps of these two cities. In the late nineteenth and early twentieth centuries, as the flow of technology from the West accelerated, the consumption of new gadgets coexisted with innovative uses of the old throughout a broad spectrum of the population. Sudhir Mahadevan's research on consumers of photography in colonial Calcutta reveals a hybrid lot: there were "elite and poor Europeans, amateur and commercial photographers, and elite and poorer Indians."[18] This observation held true for colonial Bombay too. In the scattered, hybrid world of colonial consumption, photography was as much part of the elite milieu as it was of the commonplace market or the "bazaar" scene.

Mahadevan's research on the circulation of photography and photographic equipment in colonial India reveals a paradox that is particularly relevant to early cinematic technology. Photography studios had existed in India from the 1840s onward; "Bourne and Shepherd" of Calcutta, one of the oldest existing studios, began selling and renting photographic equipment in 1868.[19] As early as 1854, the East India Company had officialized the use of photographs in its archeological and topographical surveys.[20] Even a handful of photographic images from the 1857 Indian soldiers' rebellion against the East India Company have survived, making it the first photographed Indian war. In the 1870s, a "colonial market" emerged for ready-made and mass-manufactured media, fueled by the development of the dry gelatin plate, which was significantly more durable and portable than the material used in the earlier wet-collodion process. As imported goods flowed in, they made local manufacturing redundant, precluding any organic or native-driven change in the paradigm of photographic media. Due to the widely variant financial capabilities of Indians, all older machines, methods, and raw material remained in use, creating a strange diversity in levels of technology and sophistication. In Mahadevan's detailed study, this model of coexistence between outdated machines and the latest media equipment is traced from the early days of cinema to a post-globalization India, where roaming bioscope-wallahs still use century-old viewing boxes to show strips from recent films.[21]

Hands-on technology experience varied widely along the broad spectrum of colonial consumers. The purchasing power of the colonial Indian middle classes was more limited than that of their counterparts in the global north. Photography, for instance, would remain limited on the level of individual consumption well beyond India's independence in 1947. Innovative products such as the Kodak camera that allowed consumers in the metropolitan West to partake in the production of photographs had an extremely limited sphere of influence in early twentieth-century India. On the other hand, technological novelties that could be incorporated into small-scale commercial enterprises and recycled endlessly gained quick currency.

One such novelty was the magic lantern, a contraption that projected still images onto a wall or screen. Several versions of the magic lantern coexisted with the earliest moving projectors all over the world. In Kalyan, a suburb of Bombay, a certain Mahadeo or Madhavrao Patwardhan created his own version in 1892 and named it Shambharik Kharolika. His sons traveled to different parts of India with a variety of slides depicting narratives from the Indian epics, "thus anticipating the mythologicals of early silent Indian cinema by a decade."[22] In terms of function, the "magic lantern" was an innovative extension of the painted scrolls that wandering performers of stories from the epics and the mythologies often used in their shows throughout South Asia. Patwardhan had introduced and perfected "the technique of multiple and simultaneous projection of slide-strips": he used three separate projectors—one to project the background scenery and the like while the other two concentrated on the main event.[23] Patwardhan's modified and technologized shows retained the composite entertainment packages that the scroll artistes had been using for more than a century: dialogue, third person narration, and live music.

While the Shambharik Kharolika was a product of a new projector-based technology, the rolling movement of a scroll mounted either on a wall or between two poles had existed in different parts of the subcontinent as early as the seventeenth century. A pre-technological experience of frontality had been a part of the Indian experience well before the figures projected on the screen began exhibiting motion. The majority of the scroll-based shows were based on mythological tales derived from the two major Indian epics, the *Ramayana* and the *Mahabharata*, or from the Puranas, the most significant source for all premodern Hindu mythology. Early Indian cinema's connection with and dependence on epic and Puranic sources is an important detail. Although comedy, action, and stunt films were as or even more popular than mythological titles, it is from mythological sources that Indian filmmakers inherited the use of frontality that came to be featured to varying degrees in every genre of Indian cinema. Frontality is a convention that pre-cinematic images in India, especially those that were similar to the scroll paintings, used to depict the characters—deities and mythological heroes alike—as facing the viewer. Complex scenarios from mythology were traditionally presented in two dimensions, flattened out and placed systematically on the canvas. Recent film scholars such as Babli Sinha have used Diana Eck's theories of *darśana*, or "seeing," in Hindu theological practices to make sense of the pronounced frontality in Indian cinema. Whatever the intention of the filmmakers was, it could be said that the Indian viewers' pre-cinematic experience of frontality made for a seamless transition to the enjoyment of cinema. Innovations or improvisations such as the Shambharik Kharolika helped in the transition between scroll paintings and cinema. In the years leading up to the arrival of cinema, Indians were compelled to such innovations, since repurposing older imports was more economical than buying the newest technology.

It was in this heterogeneous colonial, semi-capitalist milieu that cinematic exhibition made landfall. The obligatory beginning for any history of cinema in India is the arrival of the Lumière brothers' "Cinématographe" on July 7, 1896, in Watson's Hotel in Bombay, where Mark Twain had stayed in January of the same year during his visit to India.[24] Marius Sestièr, who made a monthlong stop in Bombay on his way to Australia, was the first agent of the Lumières in India. He was soon followed by others, representing various companies. By the end of 1896, Calcutta, the capital of the British Indian Empire, had its own shows, and in 1897, Madras became the third Indian city to be visited by the Lumières' agents. Following the Lumière Cinématographe, several other exhibitions such as Stewart's "Vitagraph," Hughes's "Moto-photoscope," Anderson's "Andersonoscopograph," and the "Biurnal Optical Diorama" toured Bombay, Calcutta, and Madras.[25] The French company Pathé Frères, which established a worldwide network of distribution centers in the first two decades of global domination of cinema by Europe, opened an office in Calcutta in 1907.

The initiation of India into the twentieth century's essential art form was successfully completed within the decade. Among all technological innovations meant for mass production and consumption, the silent moving image reached farther pockets of the Indian subcontinent and catered to the masses more rapidly and successfully than photography, print, or the telegraph could ever do. The agent of this fast spread was the "traveling cinema." This Indian business phenomenon complemented and slowly replaced the wandering performers of indigenous arts. It consisted of the barest projection equipment: a screen, an optional tent, a team of as few as two or three technicians, and so-called junk films. Eusoofally Abdoolally, one of the earliest studio and theater owners, began his career as such an exhibitor. Madan Studios—the largest exhibition and production enterprise in the 1920s—had an extensive set of traveling cinemas that crisscrossed the subcontinent. The traveling exhibitors used any available mode of conveyance—from trains to bullock carts and mules—to transport their tents and equipment. They kept screening their repertoire of three or four programs until the films disintegrated from overuse and exposure to heat and humidity. Frames from discarded films would then be recycled for use in magic lantern–type shows. In Yves Thoraval's account, the exhibition business was completely ad hoc in nature in terms of payment and services rendered.[26] The history of this early spread, gleaned from unofficial records, consists mainly of anecdotal information, such as that segments on the Boer War and coverage of Queen Victoria's funeral were among the biggest draws in the traveling cinema circuits.[27] Permanent movie theaters, referred to in British Indian newspapers as "picture palaces," made their appearance after 1906. J. F. Madan's Elphinstone Picture Palace in Delhi and Bioscope Hall in Calcutta opened in 1906 and 1907 respectively, and Electric Theatre was built on Mount Road in the city of Madras in 1909–10. Picture palaces catered to the urban resident and migrant viewers. Their surging numbers are aptly demonstrated by the growth of permanent movie theaters: "from 30 in 1909 to 51 in 1920, 85 in 1927, and 126 in 1931."[28] Still, the traveling cinemas continued to supplement permanent theaters throughout British India, making the growth of viewership distinct from that in the United States, where a comparable number of American viewers watched films mostly in theaters.

The Lumière brothers' ingenious business model—packaging the functions of the movie camera and the projector together in a single piece of equipment ready to circulate on a global scale—facilitated the dissemination of cinema as a universal medium. It also created an opportunity for the first generation of creative and technical cinema enthusiasts to become filmmakers and entrepreneurs on a global scale. But in the beginning, Indians, like colonized populations elsewhere, were exclusively imagined as prospective consumers. Once the novelty was introduced, major European and American entertainment companies stepped into the business of regular distribution in India. Pathé Frères' entry into the Indian market in 1907 was followed by Gaumont, Éclair, Vitagraph, the American Bioscope, and the Danish Nordisk. Most films imported for exhibition in India came from France; the secondary source countries were America, Italy, England, Denmark, and Germany.

Well into the early 1910s, it was difficult for Indians to learn and develop the craft of film production in a systematic and professional manner. There was no way of learning it in India, and even if aspirants traveled to Europe or the United States, a significant deposit of money was required to become an apprentice at one of the few companies that even accepted apprentices.[29] Indian enthusiasts therefore had to train themselves. They did so by tinkering with the equipment, modifying the settings, and adding accessories that they developed themselves, just as Patwardhan did with his Shambharik Kharolika. A Hindi word that several recent books on creative entrepreneurship in India have featured in their titles— *jugaad*—is perfectly suited to early Indian cinema.[30] It refers to a quick fix, a way of solving problems with limited resources. Going from an early position of passive consumption to a landscape teeming with creative experiments required many an act of *jugaad*. Often, early experimenters were already acquainted with photochemical production of images. Not all, however, had the requisite training or ability in aesthetic presentation. Early studio production in India hinged on the combination of the science of the moving image and the art of presentation and was additionally constrained by the regulation and control of raw material, such as equipment and raw film stock, within a colonial economy. It is fair to say that cinema in India grew both within and beyond the bounds of an essentially unequal colonial economy. It did not have, as Mahadevan explains, evoking Ravi Sundaram's discussion of "recycled modernity," a "self-defined political stance, and had scant regard . . . for the modernist premium on originality."[31] Mechanically reproduced art was as bound by space, time, and socio-polity as any art was before mechanization; the colonized masses lived in a different historical time zone and responded to different necessities.

The consequences were complicated, to say the least. The social history of Indian cinema—a field of inquiry that has grown exponentially since the 1990s—offers an important perspective on cinema's propagation in the subcontinent, emphasizing its position in uneven colonial space. Some scholars have characterized early cinema in India as functioning in discrete niches, growing or shrinking as the niches did, instead of in a widespread planar diffusion. The sociopolitical, cultural, and religious niches in the Indian subcontinent that remain relevant today provide a roadmap to the compartmentalized viewership in the early decades of cinema in India.[32] Two studies offer us fresh insight into the diffusion differentials of early Indian cinema. Sudhir Mahadevan in his 2015 book explains the rifts that existed "in the consumption of a cosmopolitan, mechanically reproduced mass culture" and emphasizes the need to pay attention to the "varying scales of film enterprise provoked by differential access to the mainstays of the film business."[33] On the other hand, Manishita Dass has argued for the democratizing function of cinema in India by positing how cinema undermined the limits of the "public sphere shaped and dominated by elite cultural and political discourses and practices—a domain of power and privilege that was not only urban for the most part but urbane, largely restricted to a print-literate public, and fully accessible only to an elite minority of the Indian population."[34] These two complementary views of early cinema's sphere of influence in India give us a sense of the complexities that any history of Indian cinema must face.

What lies behind the overwhelming popularity and success of cinema in India? Such a query is complicated by two major transformations that Indian cinema underwent before India became an independent nation-state: the rise of the studio system in the 1920s and its eventual displacement in the 1940s by star-centric production. Beyond configuring markets and audiences, each transformation also coincided with shifts in the conception of popular, public, and mainstream culture. These shifts were both vertical and horizontal, given the complexities of micro-class divisions and the enormous diversity of language and culture across the Indian subcontinent. Cinema's ability to traverse classes and cultures on a global scale is well known. As Dudley Andrew has noted, "Cinema distinguished itself as the twentieth century's genuinely international medium. Far more than literature, so dependent on translation, films from the outset were watched by peoples in the most far-flung areas."[35] The Indian subcontinent, as the epitome of linguistic diversity, provides a particularly salient example of this kind of wide transmission within a single geopolitical expanse. This was a transculturation distinct from mainstream Indian colonial nationalism that had a more vertical descendance and that remained an intellectual enterprise until the peak of Gandhian mass mobilization and the rise of the Pakistan movement in the 1930s and 1940s. Indian viewers of cinema partook in the imagination of a community that was based on assemblages of values, costumes, and customs produced in an ad hoc fashion that assumed an aura of familiarity in its endless circulation. The Indianness of Indian cinema had more to do with cinema than with India. Much more than any other national cinema, Indian cinema resonated with the Gramscian idea of the national-popular (culture produced in an interface between intellectuals and the broader masses), the strategic coagulation of identity and interests that simply makes sense in a given historical moment.[36] In the absence of a single national culture and language, Indian cinema had anticipated early on the multicultural, multilingual world of global media that came to exist in the twenty-first century. At the center of the multifocal burst of cinema in India was what Kaushik Bhaumik has called "the cultural leadership of the young" in the 1920s, when the young embraced the new work regimes of an emerging modern megalopolis like Bombay and set out to innovate: "Cinema, more than any other cultural medium of the time, came to be associated with the ways of the young."[37]

Trade, Art, and Origins

The early history of Indian experiments with the movie camera, reconstructed largely from secondary sources, features diverse interests and styles, such as those of Hiralal Sen in Calcutta and Harishchandra Sakharam Bhatavdekar in Bombay. Records of Hiralal Sen's work reveal his interest in shooting indoors. Sen's first short, *Dancing Flowers from the Flowers of Persia*, was screened in 1898. He continued to film plays staged in commercial theaters in Calcutta and screened them on different occasions in the same theaters after stage performances. An advertisement appeared in February 1901 in the Calcutta daily, *Amrita Bazaar Patrika*, announcing the first of these stage films by Sen's "Royal Bioscope": "Series of Superfine Pictures from Our World Renowned Plays—*Alibaba, Buddha, Sitaram* etc.—will be produced to the Extreme Astonishment of Our Patrons and Friends."[38] Bhatavdekar, after watching the Lumières' show in Bombay, briefly became an agent for the Lumières until he procured his own movie camera. In 1901, he filmed the "first Indian newsreel," *Return of Paranjpye*, a recording of the Indian mathematician Paranjpye's return from Cambridge. In 1903, he filmed the Delhi coronation of Edward VII, and he continued to film shorts for the rest of his career. In contrast with Sen's work, Bhatavdekar's films were mostly shot outdoors.

Another pioneer was F. B. Thanawala, who named his show "Grand Kinetoscope" and held exhibitions primarily of his own films, including newsreels under the title of *Splendid News of Bombay*.[39] Jyotish Sarkar filmed the protest rallies against the partition of Bengal; he was recruited by J. F. Madan's Elphinstone Bioscope Company, founded in 1905.[40] Significantly less information has been available on early uses of the movie camera outside of Bombay and Calcutta, and it is only recently that S. Theodore Baskaran has compiled such a history focusing primarily on the Madras Presidency. In *History through the Lens*, Baskaran describes several examples of early filmed events and "actuality material": the landing of an airplane in Madras filmed by Maruthamudu Moopanar of Thanjavur in 1910 and the burning oil tanks of Madras after being hit by shells from the German destroyer *Emden*.[41] According to Baskaran, the Mapla Rebellion of 1921 and the Salt March led by Gandhi in 1931 were two filmed events that revealed the imperialist archival politics that guided the shooting of actuality material.[42]

The majority of films from the silent era had already disappeared before the National Film Archives was established in the 1960s. While the censor boards kept records of every film that was licensed from 1920 onward, the lacunae in the archives of pre-1920s silent films prevent systematic study of early cinematic experiments. Consequently, we have been largely dependent on a received nationalist historiography, in which Dhundiraj Govind Phalke's name remains intricately linked to the story of the "birth" of Indian cinema. Phalke's *Raja Harishchandra* (King Harishchandra, 1913) has been widely renowned as the first full-length feature film in India, following Phalke's own advertisements, articles, and his proclamation to the Indian Cinematograph Committee of 1927 that he "created" the film industry in India. Only recently has Ram Chandra Gopal Torney's *Pundalik*, a full-length recording of a play released in 1912, begun to be cited as the first Indian feature film. However, Torney's occasional supplanting of Phalke as the first Indian filmmaker in the recent histories has not affected the mythology and the aura that surround Phalke as the great innovator. In retrospect, Phalke seems to be a convenient choice for the role of a pioneer for Indian national cinema, itself a convenient construct. Phalke belonged to an educated Brahmin family; his father taught Sanskrit for some time at Wilson's College in Bombay. He received training in art, drawing, and photography and was a semiprofessional magician (his magician background has incited a comparison with the work of Georges Méliès in several histories). After studying drawing and painting at the J. J. School of Arts, Phalke trained in photography and the photochemical printing process at Kalabhavan in Baroda. In British India at the turn of the twentieth century, he represented the upper-caste bourgeois with just enough privilege: his caste, class, and access to education, combined with his intellectual curiosity and love for technology, provided him with the edge needed to embark on his bold venture.

The oft-repeated story of that venture begins in 1910, when a somewhat unhappy Phalke, suffering from a downturn in his photography business, wandered into the America-India Cinema. He saw his first movie, *The Life of Christ*, twice in the same evening, the second time with his wife. Within a short period, he was in the grip of what his friends called an obsession: the making of a movie, in India, with Indian characters, based on an Indian subject. There were enough elements and narratives in the epic and Puranic mythologies to make cinema *Indian*, and Phalke seemed to have found a vocation that suited his talents. He saw his training and experience as an asset: "I was well up in all the arts and crafts that go to make a motion picture—drawing, painting, architecture, photography, drama, magic—I was fully convinced that it CAN be done!" he wrote in a 1917 memoir.[43] His friends, who were also his financiers, had less faith in the future of filmmaking in India and were convinced only after Phalke created from scratch his first short simulation, *The Birth of the Pea Plant*, photographing one shot every day with a still camera. It consisted of photographs shown in rapid sequence, which gave the target audience—the financiers—a sense of watching a pea plant's growth condensed in time. Securing a loan for training and equipment, Phalke set sail for England in February 1912, and after a weeklong crash course in filmmaking with Cecil Hepworth he returned with a camera, a film perforator, processing and printing machines, and enough raw stock to start production. Saraswati "Kaki" Phalke, his wife, pawned her jewelry to raise funds for the film. Phalke recruited a motley cast of actors, technicians, and workers; set up his studio in Bombay's Dadar Main Road; and developed most of the film in the kitchen with Saraswati's help. After one year, *Raja Harishchandra* opened on April 21 at Bombay's Olympic Cinema and then was exhibited at Coronation Cinema, with Hindi and English titles.

Raja Harishchandra "integrated different styles and influences from the paintings of Raja Ravi Varma to the conventions of trick films to celebrate religion as a source of political renewal."[44] The protagonist Harishchandra, a king from the *Mahabharata*, is one of the ideal epic characters: he loses his kingdom, following which he and his family are tested to the limits of endurance by the gods but are eventually restored to their original state. Babli Sinha in her recent volume on early Indian cinema offers a condensed view of the various readings of Phalke's use of frontality:

> The tableau style is central to the integration of the religious and political narratives in *Raja Harishchandra*. Rachel Dwyer and Divia Patel argue that the tableau style promotes *darshan*, "a feature that has long been seen in such forms as the jhanki or tableau of the gods, which devotees view in the north Indian raslila and the Ramlila." *Darshan* references "seeing and being seen by the divine, [and] involved a process of divine contiguity between seer and seen in which the benefits of the viewing event would be the outcome of the physical visual 'contact' with the image . . ." The integration of the seer and the seen and the spiritual and the material requires an integrative aesthetic element. The tableau style in which characters appear to be immobile and which feature the pictorial effect of centred long shots is one of the ways in which Phalke reconciled "the perceptive opposition between 'Indian images' and 'industrial technology,'" according to Ashish Rajadhyaksha.[45]

Though the bourgeois elite and the British Indian press ignored Phalke's history-making venture, *Raja Harishchandra* was successful enough to allow Phalke to build a studio in Nasik—equipped with woods, open space, and sets—which became the birthplace of several films on similar themes: *Bhasmasur Mohini* (Bhasmasur and Mohini, 1913), *Lanka Dahan* (The Burning of Lanka, 1917), and *Satyavan Savitri* (Satyavan and Savitri, 1914). In 1917, his own enterprise—Phalke Film Company—was incorporated into Hindustan

Film Company, where he joined five other partners. He continued making films, including documentaries on the process of filmmaking, such as *How Films are Made* and *The Magic of Prof. Kelpha* (*Kalphanchya Jadu* in Marathi, with Phalke's name with the syllables in reverse order). The exclusive focus of these documentaries was his own pioneering work, avoiding any reference to the larger context of filmmaking in India. Apart from these documentaries, his oeuvre remained limited to a narrow repertoire of mythological tales from the Hindu Puranas. Meanwhile, social and historical narratives had begun to be produced by the new studios that had cropped up in Bombay and Calcutta, and Hollywood stunt films had also begun inspiring new spectacles, producing effects far beyond the naive thrills of Phalke's mythic miracles. In 1932, he made his last silent film, *Sethu Bandhan* (The Building of the Bridge), and at the age of sixty-four, Phalke made the first talkie and the last film of his life: *Gangavataran* (The Descent of Ganga), for Kolhapure Cinetone. In retrospect, his success and his days of glory lasted for barely one and a half decades, and he spent the last few years of his life in poverty, his work all but forgotten at a time of phenomenal growth for Indian cinema.

Phalke's short-lived success (contra the nationalist mythology of him as pioneer) makes it difficult to gauge the actual nature of his contribution to the medium. In recent years, the aura that surrounds Phalke's name has been deconstructed, giving rise to a more complicated picture of a smart entrepreneur with artistic inclinations. Someswar Bhowmik's study of colonial Indian cinema projects Phalke as "more an astute schemer than anything else."[46] Phalke was in the right place at the right time and was equipped with training and a business in mechanical reproduction of images. He also had the facility to tap into the mythological-cultural archives, owing to his orthodox Brahmin background. Phalke understood rightly the need to capture the semi- and nonliterate market with images that would incite adulation, with the filmmaker poised as the mediator who facilitated *darśan*. As Bhowmik stipulates, "Phalke's choice was vindicated by the popularity that his films enjoyed among the ordinary people. But the urban educated took little interest in his mythologies, not to speak of the Europeans. The real significance of Phalke's contribution is reflected in the course of silent film production for the next ten years: it was completely dominated by the mythologicals."[47] Whether or not the rise and dominance of the "mythological" genre—as narrated in most official histories—resulted directly from Phalke's (and Torney's) early successes is a complicated question. The mythology surrounding D. G. Phalke has largely been his own creation. He saw himself as "making history," creating an industry out of nothing, and he frequently wrote and spoke on his legendary contribution to the art form.

But did the mythological remain popular for the next ten years because of the accident of Phalke's choice? Or did the mythological speak to a preexisting cultural inclination or even imperative?

Sumita S. Chakravarty reads in the mythological genre "an alternative feminized space carved out of the dominant semantic universe of Western technology as colonial imposition" and gives Phalke credit for it: "If colonialism had succeeded in denigrating Hindu culture and the bulk of the Indian people as effeminate and weak, Phalke's privileging of the mythological as a completely indigenous form of signification that returns meaning to the feminine realm may be taken as a bold decolonizing gesture."[48] Decades before Chakravarty offered her nuanced reading of Phalke's filmmaking as discursive resistance, his legendary status was already sealed with the Indian government's Phalke Award, instituted in 1969. A 2009 film based on Phalke's life directed by Paresh Mokashi—*Harishchandrachi Factory* (Harishchandra's Factory)—reaffirmed the legend. (The film went on to become India's official entry for that year's Academy Awards.) What is more, despite an obligatory nod to Torney and his 1912 feature *Pundalik*, the Indian film industry chose the year 1913 as its centenary, further cementing Phalke's privileged place in historical imagination.

It is possible, however, to think of Phalke's idea of an Indian creating an Indian industry for the consumption of Indians as neither novel nor subversive. By the time Phalke watched *The Life of Christ* in 1910 and dreamed of "India's sons" seeing Indian images on the screen, the concept of swadeshi was thoroughly integrated in public discourse. The term, meaning *indigenous*, gained political currency following the swadeshi movement in Bengal (1903–8), the agitation against the viceroy of India Lord Curzon's proposed partition of Bengal in 1905. What began as the subversive concept of resisting consumption of British goods and promoting indigenous production became a catchphrase for businesses to assert their fledgling identities in a market dominated by British or British-controlled enterprises. Phalke picked up on the catchphrase and aggressively proclaimed his own pioneering status.

The latest historical challenge to Phalke's pioneering status comes from Ranita Chatterjee and Rosie Thomas, who have proposed that Hiralal Sen's full-length feature *Alibaba and the Forty Thieves* (1903), based on the popular Persian narrative, may have been the first feature film. Citing a 1917 report from the *Times of India* that seemed oblivious of Indian filmmakers before 1917 and mentioned J. F. Madan (misspelled as "Madon") as the first Indian ever to make a film, Chatterjee and Thomas have argued that Phalke's achievement was not nearly as well known as he himself claimed. A case can indeed be made regarding the political and cultural logic behind legitimizing Phalke's mythology. It was perhaps more expedient to champion a "mythological" film based on *Mahabharata*, a Hindu epic, rather than a fantasy entertainment extravaganza based on *The Thousand and One Nights* as India's first feature film.[49] Whatever the general business dynamic that existed between mythologicals and the politics of swadeshi, Phalke's success was premised upon its skillful mobilization.

Not everyone needed the catchphrase. The first business empire in the history of Indian cinema, Madan Theatres Limited, was eclectic in its fare and approached production and distribution of movies as an aggressive business venture, testing out new markets and demands, willing to supply the choice of the best and the most. J. F. Madan, the founder of the empire, was an importer of beverages, food, and pharmaceutical products and a dealer in insurance and real estate who was quick to pick up on entrepreneurial possibilities in the field of movie production and exhibition.[50] His first venture was a "bioscope" that opened in a tent in Calcutta in 1902. He acquired distribution rights to both foreign films and equipment on a massive scale and built one of the first cinema chains in the world, a business empire that spread all over India, Burma, and Ceylon. Madan gauged the necessity of indigenous production and set up Madan Theatres Limited as a production company to supply his chain of cinemas with local films as well. Most of these indigenous films were recordings of plays. The first original Madan film, *Bilwamangal,* was produced in 1919. It is the first known feature to be produced in Calcutta. For *Nala and Damayanti* (1920), a narrative from the *Mahabharata*, Madan recruited technicians from France and Italy; he also hired European actors for the lead roles.[51] The large number of theaters and show houses that Madan owned gave the company significant control over the chain of supply, the kind of control that the W. Evans report of 1921 would call a threat to the opening up of a free market in India.[52] At the height of its power, Madan Theatres seemed to be doing everything right, holding unassailable sway over every trend in the business. The first talkie film imported to India—Universal Studios' *Melody of Love*—was screened in theatres owned by Madan: Excelsior and Elphinstone, in Bombay and Calcutta respectively. Madan had watched *The Jazz Singer* (1927) on his visit to Hollywood and "had realized the significance of the revolution that sound in movies had ushered in."[53] Along with the sound projection system that had to be installed in Excelsior and Elphinstone for the talkie show, Madan had also imported the latest equipment for production of talkies and produced several short talkies before Imperial Studios in Bombay beat him to the release of the first full-length talkie feature in March 1931.

Madan's unassailable dominance in the Indian film industry ended abruptly when the family's business empire dissipated beyond redemption in the 1930s.

From 1932 onward, Calcutta's studio scene came to be dominated by New Theatres Studios, founded by B. N. Sircar. Madan's fare had consisted mostly of imports from America, and after his death, his son J. J. Madan began negotiations with Universal Studios for sale of the business. But the plan was thwarted partly by the onset of the Great Depression.[54] Madan had employed an aggressive business model but was spread too thin in terms of production and distribution through both his permanent theaters and traveling cinemas. According to Suresh Chabria, Madan's productions faced criticism from peers for their regular use of international actors and their lack of effort to integrate the foreignness of the medium with local content. For their "international involvement and the consistent use of a strongly Westernized theatrical form the Madans were accused by their Calcutta rivals of merely making films in Bengal and not Bengali films."[55] Of all the regional (non-Hindi/Hindustani) cinemas, Bengali cinema drew the most from its own modern literary texts, and a cultural identity was already in place even before the voices of characters from the Bengali literary masterpieces could actually be heard on-screen. Under the banner of Taj Mahal Company of Calcutta, Sisir Bhaduri, one of the notable directors of the stage in Calcutta, directed a film based on *Andhare Alo* (A Glimmer in the Dark, 1922), a novel by Saratchandra Chattopadhyay. Following the success of this film, "Bengali filmmakers frequently began to draw from their rich stage and literary traditions in a conscious effort to create an indigenous cinematic idiom different from the foreign influenced idiom of Madan Theatres."[56]

The influence and impact of Madan's business empire—while it lasted—remain integral to the history of early Indian cinema. It is worthwhile to examine Madan's legacy in the broader context of ventures—both artistic and entrepreneurial—in the early decades of Indian cinema, especially those ventures that did not endure. While J. F. Madan was a consummate businessman who could translate the development and control of a chain of supply into commercial success with remarkable dexterity, individuals such as Dhirendra Nath Ganguly and Baburao Painter contributed to the formal innovations in the products through their deep artistic engagement with the medium itself. Ganguly, often referred to as D. G., was trained as an artist at Rabindranath Tagore's University at Santiniketan. After his graduation, he began teaching at the Nizam's College in Hyderabad and continued to train himself in the production of photographic images. In 1915, he published *Bhaber Abhibyakti* (Expressions of Emotions), a seminal volume of photographs of himself in different personas, moods, and poses, carefully edited to form intriguing collages. He sent a copy of the volume to J. F. Madan, who offered Ganguly his first break in filmmaking through his company. The alliance between Ganguly and Madan could have yielded interesting results, but Ganguly decided to collaborate with the newly formed Indo-British Company instead, for which he directed his first film, *Bilet Ferat* (Returned from England, 1921), appearing in the lead role. Ganguly's talent at impersonation made the film a success, and he went on to collaborate with various other studios, such as Dominion Films. He appeared in and worked on a number of Calcutta productions and cofounded with P. C. Barua the British Dominion Film Studio in 1929.

Baburao Painter, born Baburao Krishnarao Mestri, was a painter and craftsman by profession who had a gift for technology. With the limited opportunities available to him, he redesigned old cameras, used artificial lights, painted sets to get a particular shade of gray on film, and devised and used filters with tinted glass for the first time.[57] He founded the Maharashtra Film Company in Kolhapur in 1917 and directed his share of "mythologicals" and "historicals" before making arguably one of the best-known "socials" of its time: *Savkari Pash* (The Moneylender's Snare, 1925). With his protégé V. Shantaram in the title role—a peasant rendered landless by an oppressive moneylending system and eventually transformed into an urban laborer—Painter captivated peers and contemporary critics with a powerful poetic realism hitherto unseen in Indian cinema. In 1936, he remade the film with sound. He also created posters for his films, in a style distinct from his contemporaries. J. B. H. Wadia, the founder of Wadia Movietone, would later recall the experience of watching the sound version of *Savkari Pash*, noting in particular a "long shot of a dreary hut photographed in low key, highlighted only by the howl of a dog."[58] Sarojini Naidu, a poet who would become the first woman governor of a state in independent India, called it "a remarkable film that portrays with perfect art the moving and tragic story of Indian peasant life. It is a more eloquent plea on behalf of the villager than a hundred speeches made from public platforms."[59]

Most of the films by Ganguly and Painter are lost, their traces left only in the contemporary writings about them. And in spite of their illustrious protégés and peers who went on to make films (K. Damle and V. Shantaram were Painter's protégés; Debaki Bose and P. C. Barua were Ganguly's), neither Ganguly nor Painter had any immediate artistic legacy. The fact that they experimented with scant technology, mixing technologies and methods in acts of brilliant manipulation of the cinematic form, would largely be forgotten until the National Film Archives in Pune, instituted in the 1960s, began cataloging and restoring the few remaining fragments of their work.

The mostly forgotten legacy of Dhirendra Nath Ganguly and Baburao Painter presents an interesting contrast with Phalke's oft-recalled history. Both Ganguly and Painter managed to use their talent in technology and art to usher in new content and presentation in their films, while Phalke never outgrew his almost childlike fascination with mythological characters and narratives and used every trick he devised for the screening of miracles. Although they occasionally applied Phalke's frontal style to "mythologicals" and "historical costume-dramas," most studios in the 1920s, especially those in Bombay, preferred a Hollywood model for their "modern" treatments: "The popular actors and actresses of the time modeled themselves in appearance and mannerisms on their Hollywood counterparts. The leading ladies, most of them fair-skinned Anglo-Indians, fluttered their eyelashes, set their rosebud mouths in pretty pouts and swooned into the arms of dashing young Parsees in sharkskin suits and soft hats. The villain arched his eyebrows, twirled his moustache and shook with silent laughter."[60]

Mimicry of Hollywood by Indian filmmakers followed from overwhelming exposure of Indian viewers to Hollywood after the outbreak of the Great War in Europe, when the "manufacture of raw film became restricted and equipment harder to come by [in India]. . . . Less affected by the Great War of 1914–18, America moved with alacrity into this vacuum, flooding the market in India with American films."[61] B. D. Garga has observed that "the imitation of Hollywood permeated most aspects of Indian film production." In 1917, as "most of the cinemas were showing American and European films," films such as the Pearl White serials, *The Exploits of Elaine*, *The Fatal Ring*, *Barcelona Mysteries*, and *Grey Ghost* produced an immediate trend in imitations: "Action packed thrillers [were] complete with the gangster and his moll in ever-increasing numbers. A typical example was the Imperial Film Company's *Wild Cat of Bombay* in which the beautiful Sulochana played a kind of lady Robin Hood and changed into nine different kinds of make-up to dodge the police—a clever gimmick which paid off at the box office."[62] Hollywood was thus the dominant foreign source of films screened in India in the 1920s, with France and Britain following distantly behind. Indian mimicry and reproduction of Hollywood might have endured for several decades if an unexpected turn—the coming of sound in 1931—had not ushered in the "indigenous modern." The genre that defined the turn was the "social," variants of which remained dominant in all Indian cinemas until the advent of the action genre in the 1970s. The vestiges of Phalke's frontal spectacle would persist in the occasional historical and mythological films, but they and the Hollywood model of 1920s Bombay studios would metamorphose over the next two decades into an essentially Indian form founded primarily on the social genre, a motley entertainment package described in 1993 by Ashish Rajadhyaksha as the "epic melodrama."[63] Long before Rajadhyaksha coined that term, however, reporters and critics in Soviet Russia used the phrase *indiiskie melodramy* to refer to Indian films in general, beginning around the time of the first Indian Film Festival in the USSR in 1954.

Cinema and Governance: 1918–1928

Even before the advent of sound and melodrama, Hollywood imports account for only part of the quotidian history of cinema in India. Indian fascination with the moving image was also a political problem for India's British rulers, and the imperial machinery posed as big a problem for Indian cinema as Hollywood did. The 1920s—that crucial decade in silent Indian cinema's rise—was marked by persistent efforts by the British colonial government to influence, control, and alter the course of that cinema. Whether Indians were crowding to watch Hollywood productions or trying to make their own films, the administration did not like it. The first official measures—the Indian Cinematograph Act (1918) and the establishment of the regional censor boards in 1920—attempted to subject all aspects of India's interface with cinema to government scrutiny. But even those measures were unable to match the level of control and exploitation that characterized British control over India. The fast growth of the Indian market for cinema fueled the government's economic ambitions. The British hoped to leverage the situation to extract yet further material advantage from their colony. The worrying encroachment of Hollywood into England's market at home and in its colonies was therefore a recurring theme in all British discourse on cinema and trade. Cinema in India was caught right in the middle.

The British approach to cinema in India was pulled by two contending sets of political anxiety. On the one hand were Britain's national-economic concerns that were part of a wider British concern about Britain's place in the post–World War I world. On the other hand were racially charged fears that the masses could unsettle the balance of governance and control in India at any time. Such a disruption had already happened once, during the 1857 rebellion of Indian foot soldiers of the East India Company's army—the event that had precipitated the transfer of India's governance from the East India Company to the Crown. Victoria of England was declared the queen of India in 1858 and empress of India in 1877. The 1857 rebellion—variously called the "Mutiny" by the British and the "first war of independence" by late Indian nationalists—left an enduring anxiety at all levels of British-Indian administration, culminating (in the context of our study) in the paranoid attempt to control all cultural production and expression. Cinema-related laws and regulations in the twentieth century, for example, may have found their blueprint in the Indian Press Act of 1867, which enforced stringent control over print media.

Having inherited the ownership of India from the East India Company, the British colonial government held all indigenous enterprises, whether in business, culture, or education, to be a threat to the fine balance of political control. The precariousness of that balance became increasingly apparent in the aftermath of World War I and the Russian Revolution, specifically owing to the growth of bourgeois Indian nationalism. The Indian Cinematograph Act of 1918—amended in 1919 and 1920—reflected a sense of foreboding about an uncertain future. While the act's concern with safety and operational measures echoed England's Cinematograph Act of 1909, the Indian act was primarily about government's approval of the content of every film distributed in India. The 1918 Indian Cinematograph Act was closer in ideology and rhetoric to the 1867 Press Act than it was to its historical precursor, the 1909 Cinematograph Act of England, and not unreasonably. The 1857 mutiny was only one of several organized rebellions throughout the nineteenth century that brought the colonial power face to face with the disruptive potential of its governed masses. From the 1870s onward, bourgeois nationalism consolidated itself as a force to reckon with. The Indian National Congress was founded in 1885 to interface politically between the government and the colonial bourgeoisie. The swadeshi movement in Bengal had seen an unprecedented mobilization of the masses by bourgeois leaders. Jyotish Sarkar, a filmmaker hired by J. F. Madan, had filmed the swadeshi agitations in Bengal. An indigenous public sphere, however vague and limited, was therefore engendered when Indian viewers watched Sen and Phalke's films on Indian subjects. Further access to cinema portended unlimited expansion of that sphere. Literate consumers of print media were but a small percentage of the total population in India, but even they were worrisome to the government. The potential consumers of cinema were, in comparison, an ominous indeterminate mass that the British could neither recognize as such—for that would refute their denial of India's emergent nationalist identity, however imagined—nor categorize into discrete socioeconomic units. The 1918 Indian Cinematograph Act therefore decreed cascading layers of control from the top down. It preemptively accorded unlimited powers to the governor-general in section 7—he could "constitute as many authorities as he might think fit for examining and certifying films"—anticipating a crisis in governance that could be neither ignored nor acknowledged officially.[64] It might not have been clear what the moving image was capable of, but it had to be kept under surveillance nevertheless.[65]

A "system of provincial censorship" was the next logical step.[66] Censor boards were set up in 1920 in Bombay, Calcutta, Madras, and Rangoon. These comprised both administrative officials and native bourgeoisie who were to represent the various local religions and ethnicities.[67] The distinct composition of each board reflects on the one hand the uneasiness with which the government undertook the surveillance of the new medium and on the other hand the recurring British policy of "communalization," that is, insisting on and nurturing the fault lines between religious communities. More than any other factor, religious identity was a contentious marker and divider of the governed Indian population used by the British throughout the colonial period. In the aftermath of the crushed rebellions of the nineteenth century and the powerful organizing spectacle of the swadeshi movement, the government systematically fostered and enlarged every possible chasm, including religious, between different communities to its own advantage. The possibility of any trans-religious unity remotely resembling nationalism was undesirable for the government, and cultural politics was more vulnerable to manipulation than socioeconomic policies. Ignoring linguistic and regional differences among various Indian groups when it proved expedient, the British administration otherwise emphasized religious divisions, especially between Hindus and Muslims. It was only a matter of time before those different religious communities would be politicized.[68]

The anxieties of governance that Indian cinema caused first the British and later the postcolonial Indian governments form a lengthy narrative that concerns the artistic medium as much as the circulation of capital. A mechanically produced object consumed by the general populace had unlimited possibilities in a heavily populated Indian subcontinent. Beyond the licensing and censorship of cinema, an early manifestation of the government's curiosity in the trade was the appointment of an investigative agent. The appointee, W. Evans, was assigned by the British government of India the task of evaluating the state of the film industry in India and thus providing advice and suggestions for future policy. Much shorter in length and less extensive in scope than the 1927–28 *Report of the Indian Cinematograph Committee*, the Evans report reads more like a white paper on trade policy. The document is unenthusiastic, utilitarian, and devoid of any understanding of the nuances of the market. The only indigenous company mentioned by name was that run by J. F. Madan (referred to as "Messrs. Madan"), who at the time of Evans's investigation owned studios and theaters in Calcutta and in Bombay, along with several other outfits for mobile or otherwise temporary exhibitions. According to Evans, the urgent need of the day was to free the Indian film industry from the dominance of the Madan Theatres, which the report called a "monopoly" that threatened to "slowly strangle" the Indian film industry. The point of contention was not monopoly itself but the ownership of that monopoly. If there were to be a monopoly, it must be British, with absolute government oversight. Evans wrote,

I would first urge the Government of India to control absolutely the trade in films. They should make the traffic in films a Government monopoly, arranging to purchase outright through High Commissioner selected films for importation, and then to rent out these films at equitable rates to exhibitors in India. In other words, they should arrange to supply the Indian market with films and should forbid the importation of films except through themselves. They may also buy up and rent films produced in India. This course of action has been followed already in certain countries.

This will give that small and new exhibitor an equal chance with larger existing companies.

It will also give the Government of India absolute control over the type of film imported, and considerable profit. [. . .]

Should this for any reason be considered impracticable, I recommend that the purchase and distribution of films for India should be exercised for Government by one of the large English renting houses whose world connection would ensure not merely the utmost publicity but also more advantageous terms than could be secured by any purely Indian house. Needless to say, such a firm would utilize as many existing Indian firms as possible for local distribution.[69]

The report was received by the government in 1922 without any discussion, and there is no evidence that any of Evans's suggestions was taken seriously about the government assuming a sweeping control of production and distribution of motion pictures. The issue of Madan Theatres' monopoly was not paid much heed either. The most relevant suggestion that the report made was already in place, which was the empowering of local boards to enact their censorship rules: "The local Indian Boards should be left to pronounce upon the suitability of given films for exhibition in their particular area."[70] In retrospect, W. Evans's report remains a valuable historic documentation of a top-down economic view of the Indian film market, growing in the shadow of global expansion of capital.

There was, however, some overlap between Evans's anxiety regarding Madan's monopoly and the general British anxiety regarding Hollywood's robust capitalist infrastructure and international popularity. The nuanced political and cultural anxieties of imperial control surfaced several years later in 1927, when the Cinematograph Films Bill, also known as the Quota Act, was introduced, aimed at proposing a quota for exhibition of British films in the United Kingdom. Regulation of trade within the empire with an eye on British interest was a contentious issue, and Priya Jaikumar has described the 1927 bill as "drawing both enthusiastic applause and sharp criticism in the British House of Commons."[71] As British political opinion continued to sway between protectionism and free trade, cinema in various parts of the empire came under scrutiny and evaluation. A key piece in the Quota Act was empire cinema, interpreted by Jaikumar in her influential study as a product of fuzzy colonial-imperial logic:

> The [Quota] act stipulated guidelines by which the BT [Board of Trade] could identify a film as British. Among other factors, a film could be registered as British if it was made by a British subject or a British company, if its studio scenes were shot in a studio in the British Empire (unless otherwise authorized by the BT), if the author of the original scenario for the film was a British subject, or if 75 percent of the wages were paid to British subjects or domiciles of the British Empire. According to this act, then, films made anywhere in the empire could be categorized as "British," and by this definition films from British dominions and colonies were eligible for a quota in Britain. This was the regulatory birth of the "British Empire film," a confusing, changeling term that appears in various documents to refer to films made with British or empire resources and, quite contrarily, to describe films originating from colonies and dominions. The imperial push for British cinema's preferential treatment within empire markets rested on the Quota Act's definitional ambiguity between British and British Empire film, which was claimed as a basis for a similar ingress of British films into imperial markets.[72]

India, the largest imperial market, already had a steady annual indigenous production of cinema; the combined number of certificates issued by the censor boards in Bombay, Calcutta, and Madras was eighty-six in 1925 and ninety-four in 1926.[73] To test the Indian ground for empire cinema, the British government of India instituted the Indian Cinematograph Committee, following a resolution dated October 6, 1927. The committee was composed of three British and three Indian individuals and an additional secretary, with one of the three Indians—Diwan Bahadur T. Rangachariar—as the chairman of the committee. In one of the earliest comprehensive histories of Indian cinema, Erik Barnouw and Subrahmanya Krishnaswamy interpreted Rangachariar's appointment as a political gesture that "gave Indian members a preponderant dignity without a majority."[74] In the official resolution, the reason stated for the formation of the committee was that the question of the "adequacy of censorship over cinematograph films in India" was considered by the government as "of sufficient importance and complexity to demand a thorough enquiry by a special committee."[75] The charge of the committee was threefold: (1) to examine the organization, principles, and methods of the censorship of cinematograph films in India; (2) to survey the organization of the exhibition of cinematograph films and the film-producing industry in India; and (3) to consider whether it was desirable that steps be taken to encourage the exhibition of films produced within the British Empire generally and the production and exhibition of Indian films in particular and to make recommendations. In retrospect, it is easy to read in this charge a cautious political tone. India, being both a consumer and producer of cinema, seemed poised to be a crucial piece or player or both in the possible future of empire cinema. Apart from the total number of films certified each year, the government had very little data on the depth and expanse of the film market. In spite of the censor boards' efficient operation, the multitude of traveling cinemas and ad hoc production studios on a small scale was impossible to track. In the shadow of the agitations against the Rowlatt Act, the Jallianwala Bagh massacre, and the noncooperation movement of 1920–22, the political environment in 1927 was such that any little mistake in political maneuvering could ignite political outrage in India.

After more than a year of surveying, interviews, and research, the voluminous *Report of the Indian Cinematograph Committee* was published in 1928. Given the fact that the linguistic implosion of Indian cinema following the advent of sound was yet to happen, the sheer number of layers of investigation that the committee employed is astounding. The 226-page tome offers more insight into the business, economic, and cultural dimensions of the Indian film industry than any contemporary historical or critical study on the subject. The report begins with a preamble on the principle of censorship:

> The object of censorship is strictly limited, namely, to preclude that which is definitely undesirable or unsuitable for public exhibition. Rules and principles may be laid down for the guidance of the censor, but it is in the application of these rules and principles to particular cases that the difficulty arises; and therefore much must be left to the discretion of the censor. Ultimately, the criterion to be adopted by the censor must be based on what he conceives to be the enlightened public opinion on the subject. He is the interpreter of public opinion, and ultimately his decisions derive their sanction from public opinion. It is arguable, as it has been argued before us, that censorship is unnecessary and that it should be left to public opinion to decide what is suitable or unsuitable. Without entering into the merits of this argument as a general proposition, we may say that, as far as India is concerned, public opinion is not sufficiently organised or articulate to make it possible to dispense with censorship. On the other hand, it has been proposed in some quarters that the scope of censorship should be extended and that films should be censored not only on moral and social grounds but on artistic grounds as well; and that films which do not come up to the

required standard of artistic excellence should be debarred from exhibition. We are aware that such practice is in vogue in certain countries, but we do not consider it is either practicable or justifiable to make one man or one body of men the arbiter of taste for a whole population, nor is it desirable in the present condition of the trade in this country.[76]

The quote, in the familiar style of colonial-bureaucratic eloquence, represents well the overall tone of the report. The functional aspect of the report, however, turned toward fresh inquiry, with a massive scale of investigation (4,325 surveys circulated) and similarly impressive qualitative ethnographic detail.[77]

It is difficult to say whether the British government was interested in the report's spirit of fresh inquiry and the rigorously classified data that Rangachariar and his colleagues assembled. None of the report's findings figured in subsequent official discussion on cinema. It would be impossible to guess today if Rangachariar actually went above and beyond his call of duty to produce an incisive and objective report when he was probably recruited to figure out the opportunities for the promotion of "empire cinema" on the basis of three factors: (1) what (in the British view) the Indians deserved and would comprehend, (2) what could be safe for the colonial authority to hand over to the subjects, and (3) how to beat the American competition. The British Empire had—according to the dominant official and public rhetoric—an imperial-moral prerogative, and the Indians' access to visual images from all over the Western world threatened to demolish it. For example, an article published in the *Westminster Gazette* on November 17, 1921, caught the attention of Edwin Montague, secretary of state for India, who sent a copy of it to the British authorities in India, demanding a report on the workings of the censor board. The anxiety of governing a nascent mass of viewers is palpable in the article:

One of the great reasons for the hardly veiled contempt of the native Indian for us may be found in the introduction and the development of "moving pictures" in India. A visitor to an average cinema show in England will be treated to a more or less sensational drama in which somebody's morals have gone decidedly wrong, a thrilling but impossible cowboy film, and, of course, will be afforded an opportunity to appreciate (or not) our marvelous sense of humour as displayed by Charlie Chaplin squirting soda-syphons or breaking innumerable windows.

Now imagine the effect of such films on the Oriental mind. Like us, the Indian goes to see the "movies," but is not impressed by the difference in dress, in custom, and in morals. He sees our women on the films in scanty garb. He marvels at our heavy infantile humour—his own is on a higher intellectual level. He forms his own opinion of our morals during the nightly unrolled dramas of unfaithful wives and immoral husbands, our lightly broken promises, our dishonoured laws. It is soaking into him all the time, and we cannot be surprised at the outward expression of this absorption.

It is difficult for the Britisher in India, to keep up his dignity, and to extol, or to enforce, moral laws which the native sees lightly disregarded by the Britons themselves in the "picture palace."[78]

Rangachariar was not unaware of such rhetoric and specifically the British official attitude toward Hollywood. A British bishop is quoted in the first section of the Indian Cinematograph Committee report as proclaiming, "The majority of the films, which are chiefly from America, are of sensational and daring murders, crimes, and divorces, and on the whole, degrade the white women in the eyes of the Indians."[79] After having heard several white men complain about the Indian public's visual access to white private space via cinema, Rangachariar was convinced of neither the demoralizing effect of American films nor any redemptive value of empire cinema. In chapter 6 of the report, titled "The Resolution of the Imperial Conference Concerning the Exhibition within the Empire of Empire Films," the committee states that, as American civilization is as much foreign to the Indian viewer as European or British civilization, "if too much exhibition of American films in the country is a danger to the national interest, too much exhibition of other Western films is as much a danger."[80] Acknowledging the hold of Hollywood over the Indian viewer (the report estimated the American share of the Indian film import market at 80 percent), the committee refused to institute a "quota" system for empire films. In a rare instance of the British free-market rhetoric being returned from the other side of the colonial divide, the committee deemed British films unfit for competition: "When British Empire films can show the quality and finish and can be had for the same prices as other Western films, there will be no difficulty in those films finding such market as is available in this country."[81] If the government decided to patronize any particular cinema, it should be Indian cinema produced indigenously: "India has got her own film industry which . . . needs to be protected, guided, and encouraged."[82] As Jaikumar's book details, the shift in British official consensus away from the idea of a centralized bureaucratic control of film production coincided with the outpouring of opinions against British or empire films. That subsidizing British films in India to beat Hollywood's dominance would be counterproductive was something the government had realized soon enough.[83]

When the *Report of the Indian Cinematograph Committee* was presented to the government in 1928, none of its recommendations were ever discussed or refuted, at least officially. Despite the lack of direct impact it had on official policies, the report emerged as something significantly larger than a bureaucratic gesture or exercise; it became a tome of scholarly research, remaining to this day a significant piece of evidence of Indian cinema's unruliness, its uncanny ability to defy official control. In a way, it anticipates the postcolonial Indian government's failure to rein cinema in, starting in the 1950s. The report's interviews and analyses bring out the complex picture of a modernity broken loose from colonial control, a modernity run amuck. This was radically different from the neat colonial modernity that just brought chaos upon indigenous societies. This was the wild, wild East, where misshapen modernity mixed freely with undeveloped, uncontrolled capital, according to M. Madhava Prasad:

> The logic of the colonial social order was revealed here: Ideally, there must be no space as such—the social fabric must consist entirely of the communities each with its separate, closed social order, its moral and cultural leaders, its rules of conduct, etc. The inner life of one community must not be made public, made visible to the gaze of an individual from another community. Cinema came in the way of such a conception of colonial society. Its realistic images of private life caused such an acute sense of violation of the right of communities to privacy in a polity organized as a series of discrete, mutually exclusive units. Before the advent of cinema, it was only the native communities which sought to protect their "inner domain" from the reformist/universalist interventionist gaze of the British rulers. With the advent of cinema, the modern suddenly came loose from its presumed immanence to white society.[84]

At the time of the preparation of the report, the cultural identity of Indian cinema was entirely amorphous; there was no set of markers that could constitute a resemblance of a national cultural form. In the context of the history of cinema's relationship to the colonial government, therefore, a different response by the government to the report in 1928 could have led to the growth of empire cinema. Indian cinema did not have a singular possible future; the series of government regulations and efforts outlined above hint at various probable outcomes, ranging from a complete immersion in and imitation of American cinema to the development of an alternate modernism in the style of Baburao Painter and Dhirendra Nath Ganguly. The Indian ideological response to cinema was not homogeneous either. A significant part of the colonial Indian bourgeoisie—both liberals and traditionalists—shared the anxiety of the

British administration regarding cinema's effect on the masses. Economic and sociopolitical implications of cinema both as an artifact and as a product for consumption were unclear and therefore suspect.

The history of control and regulations is better documented than the narrative of the growth of Indian studios, the distinct contribution of each, and the evolution of pan-Indian genres that over time led to the unpredictable and exponential growing of cinema in India. However, by the time of Indian's independence from Britain in 1947, Indian cinema had established in the viewer a set of expectations that no foreign production could fulfill. This process of creation of a unique market for a unique form began shortly after the *Report of the Indian Cinematograph Committee*, with the advent of the "talkie," which enabled the Indian viewer to hear the stars speak and sing in Hindi, Bengali, Tamil, and a dozen other languages. By the end of the 1930s, the number of foreign films shown in the Indian subcontinent dropped to less than 20 percent. The end of the "silent era" therefore ushered in a new beginning for Indian cinema.

The Unruly Music and Sound of Indian Cinema

The race to produce Indian talkies became intense in 1929, which was also the year of the production of the first American, British, French, Russian, and German films with 100 percent sound. In the 1981 commemorative volume *Fifty Years of Indian Talkies: 1931–1981*, V. P. Sathe outlines the landmarks in the history of Indian talkies leading up to *Alam Ara*:

> The first sound film on an Indian subject to be shown in London at a private screening in October 1929 was *A Throw of Dice*, produced by Himansu Rai in collaboration with Bruce Wolfe of U.K. and U.F.A. Studios, Germany. The picture had no dialogue but only sound effects recorded and heard. A short film presenting in "audio and visual" excerpts from a speech delivered by Hafeesji in Bengali was made by Imperial Film Co. and shown at Chitra Cinema, Calcutta. Two short talkie films featuring popular songs by Munnibai and folk songs and dances of Bengal respectively were produced by Madan Theatres and shown at Empire Cinema, Bombay, on February 4, 1931.
>
> It was, however, on March 14, 1931, that the first Indian talkie feature film *Alam Ara* was released in Bombay at Majestic Cinema. On the same day, Madan Theatres released a programme of musical short films in Calcutta. Though Madan was the first to recognise the importance of sound and despite his pioneering efforts, Madan lost the race of making the first talking feature to Ardeshir M. Irani.[85]

Twenty-six other films with sound were released in the same year in several Indian languages. *Alam Ara*, the first officially recognized Indian talkie, directed by Ardeshir Irani, had more than a dozen songs and was based on a play from the Parsi Theatre, adapted for the screen by Joseph David. Although none of the songs of the first "talkie" were separately released on vinyl discs, the "film song" would rapidly develop into a genre with a thriving market of its own, and by 1935, a playback system would be installed in most studios. Ardeshir Irani's Imperial Studios in Bombay and J. F. Madan's studio in Calcutta were merely two of several Indian studios that were eager to usher in "sound technology" to their productions. They all had their doubts and fears: new technology in production demanded upgrading all exhibition equipment and theater spaces, and the overall cost might be prohibitive. Moreover, in the context of the Indian subcontinent—where twenty distinct languages and over a thousand dialects are spoken—speech could divide the viewership into at least a half dozen mutually exclusive groups, consequently decreasing the profit margin of exhibition on a national scale. The cost of production and exhibition turned out to be less of a problem once talkies became popular, but the linguistic issue changed the intranational dynamic of Indian cinema(s): "The hold of cinema on the Indian public was strengthened if anything by the arrival of talkies. Unlike in the time of silent films, Indian cinema producers had a built-in non-tariff barrier against Hollywood competition. Films were now made in the Indian languages and immediately appealed to the millions who flocked to movie halls. In a society where the majority was illiterate, there was no question of reading subtitles whether for silent or for foreign language films. With talkies made in local languages Indian cinema could carve out its own distinctive path."[86]

Ashish Rajadhyaksha has pointed out two important thematic mutations that came with sound. A number of "allegories of the traditional" that evolved in Indian cinema in the 1930s became permanently entrenched in the filmic narrative. These allegories were initiated in the silent era "in the form of religious/devotional icons," "mainly to overcome the technical/formal problem of finding a dialogue equivalent to Phalke's or Kanjibhai Rathod's *mythologicals*." In one thematic mutation, with the coming of sound, the visual icons were replaced with stereotypes adapted from reform literature but were equally grounded in "traditional values." Social and moral codes became the basis of a new definition of the sacred. The second and "more crucial thematic shift," according to Rajadhyaksha, was the replacement of the icon by a narrative structure. Rajadhyaksha uses Susie Tharu's words to describe the structure as signaling "a complete and interpreted action and a dominant narrative point of view . . . with which the reader [viewer] must identify to make sense of the text."[87] These mutations resonate with Rajadhyaksha's well-known formulation of "epic melodrama" as the emergent cinematic form of the sound era.[88] The significance of the elements that became intrinsic to Indian cinema—non-diegetic music, for example—is that they were the specific elements brought by the advent of sound in Indian cinema, which put an end to any possibility of anything akin to empire cinema. It is worthwhile to remember that the development of the specific narrative form of Indian cinema was coincident with bourgeois nationalism's spilling over into a mass movement. If there is something that can be described, however loosely, as an Indian national cinema, it is the dominant commercial form that has become known worldwide in the twenty-first century as Bollywood. It is equally important to make a distinction between Indian nationalism and Indian national cinema, even as they burst forth into popular imagination in the 1930s and 1940s. Indian nationalism itself was far from monolithic; there were regional variations within the pan-Indian bourgeois imagination of a future nation-state. Conflicting and contesting cultural aspirations remained a dominant artifact of popular Indian cinema throughout the decades.

The advent of sound in cinema initiated a crucial transformative moment in the history of the Indian film industry. Explaining how requires examining several layers of transformation. Uncertainties in the face of American and European imports during the silent film era dissipated with the coming of sound. Films with Indian speech and music could be produced profitably only in India. The transformation of the film industry that occurred in the early 1930s was not so easily foreseeable; it entailed a complex shift in the dynamic between production and the market. The reasons behind Indian studios' slower adoption of sound are easy to comprehend. The British Indian Empire did nothing to promote Indian silent films, but the sheer expanse of the empire defined the market for all films exhibited in India. According to some estimates, that market comprised several hundred million people, including Ceylon and Burma.[89] Imperial apprehension that the single grand market for silent films might fragment along linguistic lines was reasonable. Additionally, investment in new equipment and training in a fledgling industry was risky, to say the least. Finally, it would take a complete restructuring of distribution facilities and equipment for sound technology to reach the several hundred million viewers—such a transition could take several years to complete. The first sound film exhibited in India was *Melody of Love* in 1927 at one of Madan's theaters in Calcutta. The hiatus of four years before the release of the first indigenously produced Indian film, *Alam Ara,* can be attributed to the reasonable apprehension of the Indian producers.

While the success of *Alam Ara* (and several peer films in Hindi and other languages) proved that the industry was capable of meeting the new challenges, three unforeseeable developments compounded the difficulties in doing so: (1) limits put on location of production, (2) a shift in the demography of actors and directors, and (3) the rise of the music recording industry, which had its own star-centric system. In 1926–27, only 15 percent of the films shown in India were local productions. The government had rejected the Indian film producers' appeals for limiting foreign film imports. With the advent of sound, Indian producers who had previously struggled to compete with a steady flow of foreign films found themselves in an advantageous position: the indigenous audience preferred talkies in a language close to their own speech. Films made in Indian languages with Indian actors had to be produced in India.

At the same time, however, sound had begun to render a particular linguistic pattern to the Indian film industry. Film industry scholar Tejaswini Ganti explains:

> Filmmakers finally settled on a type of Hindi known as Hindustani—a mixture of Hindi and Urdu—a language associated with bazaars and trading that served as a lingua franca across northern and central India. This led to a peculiarity—Bombay became the only city where the language of the film industry was not congruent with the language of the region, Gujarati and Marathi being the dominant languages of the region. The fact that cinema in the Hindi language developed in multi-lingual Bombay, rather than in the Hindi-speaking north, dissociated Hindi films from any regional identification, imbuing them with a more "national" character.[90]

Eight decades after the advent of film sound in India, the fact that Bollywood and Hindi cinema have become synonymous in popular parlance and that either is often used as a synecdoche for the Indian film industry as a whole is in itself an interesting cultural anomaly with a complex history. The politics, position, and market of Hindi/Hindustani have had an interesting trajectory within the general ebb and flow of Indian cinema, particularly in comparison to non-Hindi languages, notably the southern linguistic cluster comprising Tamil, Telugu, Kannada, and Malayalam. The designation of Hindi as the national language was a highly contentious issue in the 1930s, and there is no clear correspondence between the various Hindi language movements and any assumption of the Bombay film industry of spreading the knowledge of Hindi throughout India. Indian languages during the colonial period had widely varying statures not only in official spheres but also in the academic and cultural realms. The Hindustani language simply emerged as having the broadest coverage in terms of geographical area, albeit spread thin. With the passing of British India, Hindustani thus held two discrete, politicized positions: Hindi as supplementary to

English in official usage in India, and Urdu as the state language of Pakistan. In 1950, significant pockets of population in India resisted the imposition of Hindi. Various Tamil groups, for instance, agitated against what they interpreted as the tyranny of the north. India's linguistic problem would stretch beyond the status of Hindi, as Jawaharlal Nehru, India's first prime minister, would redraw the map of states within India along linguistic lines.[91] Riots blazed through Bombay as it was divided into two states: the Gujarati-speaking state of Gujarat and the Marathi- and Konkani-speaking state of Maharashtra, with the prize city of Bombay falling in Maharashtra's share.

Other languages aside, what constituted "Hindi" was by itself a highly contentious issue throughout modern Indian history. Even the matter of choosing the version of Hindi to be used in the programs on All India Radio was far from straightforward. Sardar Vallabhbhai Patel, nationalist leader and the information and broadcasting minister for the interim government in 1946, had advocated "the point of view of the common listener," as the use of "Sanskritized words in place of commonly understood phrases would make the bulletins unintelligible," and therefore the news bulletins were "to be in Hindustani and not in Hindi."[92]

On the one hand, Hindustani, Hindi, and Urdu were different names for the same language that grew during the Mughal Empire and shared a common syntax and grammar. Hindi was Hindustani written in Devanagari script, while Urdu was Hindustani written in a derivative of the Persian Nastaliq script. On the other hand, the growing politicization from the 1930s onward of the Hindu/Muslim opposition made assertion of a common linguistic thread impossible at any stage of policy making. The 1947 partition of India and the creation of the nation-state of Pakistan reinforced the Hindi/Urdu dichotomy, especially given Urdu's privileged position in Pakistan. In India, Urdu and Hindi were forever separated, with the Constitution of India formulating a complex hegemonic status for Hindi in Article 351: "It shall be the duty of the Union to promote the spread of the Hindi language, to develop it so that it may serve as a medium of expression for all the elements of the composite culture of India and to secure its enrichment by assimilating without interfering with its genius, the forms, style and expressions used in Hindustani and in other languages of India specified in the Eighth Schedule, and by drawing, wherever necessary and desirable, for its vocabulary, primarily on Sanskrit and secondarily on other languages."[93]

Ajanta Sircar has marked three important moments in the Hindi language in the twentieth century. The first moment, according to Sircar, was the emergence of the United Provinces, or the Hindi heartland, as hegemonic in the nationalist construction of Indianness. That construction was based on Orientalist equations of the Indian nation with a specifically North Indian, upper-caste

Hindu identity. Far from being ultimately delimited by this hegemony, Hindi as a language became the vehicle for forging alliances across social boundaries during Gandhi's leadership of the Indian National Congress. Coming out of this Gandhian intervention, the second moment, according to Sircar, was the point when "these alliances would be given official endorsement in the form of the reorganization of the nation into linguistic states/regions in 1956, ostensibly as a gesture towards federalism." However, Sircar finds the "troubled status of Hindi as 'official language' of the Indian democracy" as "an indicator of the fact that such federalism was never properly implemented." The third and final moment would come in the 1980s, when "the interaction of global capital with the internal contradictions of the post-Nehruvian era of Indian political life" saw Hindi "move in to share with English the status of the national modern."[94]

Irrespective of the political debates surrounding the Hindi language, film songs in Hindi have been catalytic in the spread of both the language and its cinema, something that would not have been possible without the preponderance of non-diegetic songs. The first Indian talkie, *Alam Ara*, had a dozen songs. "De De Khuda Ka Naam Par Pyaare," sung by W. M. Khan, is considered the first ever "film song" in Indian cinema. *Alam Ara* was modeled on productions coming from the Parsi Theater, thus initiating the non-diegetic song sequence as a permanent fixture in Indian talkies. The theater's use of songs could be transplanted easily, almost seamlessly, into the early talkies. In the beginning, such talkies were produced using the system that allowed the simultaneous recording of the sound on the film. Moreover, many early narrative talkies were largely cinematographic versions of stage plays, and the recording of sound was used indiscriminately.

The history of the production and sale of film music is an engrossing narrative by itself. The use of playback arrived in Indian cinema as early as 1935, but the songs were sung by the actors and then dubbed. The singer-actor Kundan Lal Saigal is a prime example; he remained a much sought-after candidate in the profession until specialized playback singers rose in number and stature. Within a decade of the transition from silent films to talkies, the singing actor became as dated as the silent actor. An account of the early career of A. V. Meiyappan, the founder of AVM Studios in Madras, illustrates the precarious stature of the singer-actor and prefigures the rise of the playback artist:

Meiyappan's success in the gramophone industry led him to compete with HMV and Columbia for releasing the songs from films on records. In the mid-30s, songs were recorded live for films with orchestra—placed out of frame, by the side of the camera—lending support to the performing singer-actor. However, these songs would be recorded again, using the same singers and orchestra in acoustically better equipped sound studios, for their circulation through gramophone records. When the singer-actor M. K. Thyagaraja Bagavathar (a.k.a. MKT) became a superstar with the success of his film *Chintamani* (Dir: Y. V. Rao, 1937), his fees, apart from his remuneration as an actor, for later singing for the recording companies was a phenomenal 10,000 Rupees per song. Meiyappan refused to part with such an amount and instead hired Thuraiyur Rajagopala Sharma, who had a similar voice to MKT's[,] to sing for his Odeon records. As the labels on the records just carried the logo of "Odeon" since it was not mandatory to reveal the name of the singers, the sales escalated and it led to other songs of MKT from his earlier films similarly being released by Odeon successfully. MKT, who initially refused to reduce his remuneration, finally caved in, and signed the contract on Meiyappan's terms and sang for the Odeon label.[95]

This was how film songs were produced, a fact that helps explain the king's breaking his journey to sing a song in the film recalled by Damle earlier in this chapter. The non-diegetic song was a formal absurdity only to the outsider. The indigenous viewer, trained in the tradition of songs within performances, had a familiarity with it that trumped any new aesthetic code, including cinematic conventions. And while songs were "disruptive" in scenes such as the one described by Damle, there are instances where songs smoothed over linguistic difficulties in an era where filmmakers and artistes alike straddled multiple languages. One of the best examples of the integrative function of songs is found in *Kalidas*, the film widely billed as the first Tamil talkie that had dialogue in three languages—Tamil, Telugu, and Hindustani—and fifty songs in Tamil and Telugu. In his work on the early Madras studios, Swarnavel Eswaran Pillai repeats an argument made by Stephen Putnam Hughes that the appeal of early Tamil talkies "lay in the universality of music rather than in the specificity of the Tamil language" and notes the widespread practice in Tamil productions of using tunes from popular Hindi films.[96] However, *Kalidas* owed its musical success to extra-cinematic factors. As Pillai explains, T. P. Rajalakshmi, the heroine of the film, was a "well known star in Tamil dramas, and sang some of her already popular numbers for the film on stage. She had two 'nationalistic songs' unconnected with the main plot: one on the need to unite, and the other praising the charka (wheel), the symbol of Gandhian nationalism. . . . She sang the Carnatic compositions of Thyagaraja as well. Apart from these compositions in Telugu, she spoke and sang in Tamil throughout the film, whereas the hero spoke in Telugu."[97]

Over a period of four or five pre-global decades—before the advent of MTV in India in the 1990s—Indian film song developed as a popular art form that, as Peter Manuel explains, "unlike most commercial popular musics worldwide, did not emerge from an extensive base of amateur and professional live performance."[98] Manuel described the film music production as under the same "star-stranglehold" and "media control" that characterized Indian cinema in general. From the 1940s through the 1980s, "the vast majority of film scores have been produced by seven or eight music directors, who [were] each generally involved in several pictures at any given time. . . . Even more notable than the oligopoly of music producers [was] the almost exclusive reliance on only five or six playback singers . . . Mukesh, Talat Mahmud, Mohammad Rafi, Kishore Kumar, and above all, Lata Mangeshkar and her sister Asha Bhosle."[99]

A synchronous evolution of genres and techniques took place in the different Indian studios across languages and regions. Multiple realms of print, art, and live performances existed concurrently with film production. They vied with the same political forces as cinema did, and it is worthwhile to recall the concordances between cinema and the other arts. The question most relevant to our account of Indian cinema would concern the origin of the various styles, genres, and themes that defined Indian cinema as distinctive from the American/European imports. The substantial influence that Hollywood exerted over films across India aside, it is easy to identify three broad indigenous sources from which the filmmakers derived inspiration. First, folk traditions influenced mythologicals more than any other genre. These traditions went by many names: *lavani, yakshagana, jatra*. The various versions of myths, the comedic interludes, and music for the songs flowed out of the folk traditions. Second, the proscenium theater was in vogue in the four metropolises and the various wealthy towns in the empire. It was known variously as the Parsi Theatre in Bombay, simply "Theatre" in Calcutta, and "Company Drama" in the south. Finally, filmmakers also drew on modern narrative genres that grew out of the colonial encounter, such as novels, short stories, and plays written for the stage.

Of the above three influences, it was the proscenium theater that had the most enduring impact on Indian cinema, shaping both the silent and the early talkie eras. The growth of commercial proscenium-style theater as a private enterprise in the nineteenth century was remarkably similar to the growth of cinema in the next century. Stage drama in colonial India, as a vestige of the pre-colonial forms, suffered mainly from decay of a patronage-based system and gradual tapering out of the precapitalist economy. Professional traveling theater groups were formed in the mid-nineteenth century in the Bombay, Calcutta, and Madras Presidencies, in that order, when wealthy businessmen established "these companies, borrowing from the British theatre tradition the format of proscenium stage, drop-curtain, flats, painted backdrops and other trappings that went with modern stage," as S. Theodore Baskaran describes in his book *History through the Lens*.[100] The pioneers in the commercial enterprise of Indian theatre were Parsi businessmen, and therefore "Parsi Theatre" became a phrase used to describe commercial theater in various parts of India.

There is little agreement among historians regarding the influence of theater on commercial cinema or on the ways in which influence has flowed back and forth between the two mediums. The historiographies of literature, cinema, and other arts in India have remained separate, both on the national and regional levels. The separation seems justified in the following passage by Chidananda Dasgupta, one of India's pioneering film scholars:

> Indian cinema never succeeded in emerging into the area of national resurgence in the way painting, dance, drama, or music did. Although in terms of subject matter, films like K. Subramanyam's *Balyogini* or Himanshu Rai's *Achhut Kanya* were against superstition, the language of cinema had not, in their time, become articulate enough to be effective. . . . It failed to develop a valid artistic form, a cultural contact-point with tradition or with reality; it subsisted on an imitation of the West, mainly Hollywood, without producing the fusion of art and box office that Hollywood often represented. Except with Phalke and later Himanshu Rai, contact with world cinema was almost nonexistent. The cinema lived in partly enforced isolation in British India, enclosed comfortably within its own standards. The search for identity which brought a new life to literature and the other arts in India had not begun in the cinema.[101]

Dasgupta's indictment of the unevolved social-realist form of commercial Indian cinema is tinged with a high modernist contempt for populist entertainment. The above passage is an excerpt from his book on Satyajit Ray, in which he establishes Ray's pioneering modernism in Indian cinema. "Modernism" and "modernity" have remained contested issues in the history of Indian cinemas, especially with the coming of sound. The deployment of sound and music in films, along with the concentration of dialogue, varied greatly between regional cinemas, especially in the first decade. Differentiation of modernism only in the sense of "high" and "low," quite irrelevant to the first two decades of talkies, became useful only with the advent of art cinema via Ray's *Pather Panchali* in 1955.

From Studios to Stars

The single most significant event in the history of the Indian talkie is the rise of star-centric production. This model owes its development to the economic upheavals of the World War II years. Recounting this event from the various points of view it demands creates nothing less than a Rashomon effect. In what follows, we will hear the story from the vantage points of an actor, a director, the government, and a film historian respectively.

Actor Balraj Sahni recalled his bewilderment at the changed atmosphere of production and consumption of films after his return from England, where he worked for BBC Hindi Service for four years. Chetan Anand, Sahni's friend from college, had begun his career in movies in Bombay, and it was from him that Sahni got an insider's perspective on the changed scenario:

> Chetan was full of news about the radical changes the war had brought about in the world of films. Besides producing films themselves, the owners of film studios were also now letting out their studios to other producers and thereby earning more money. The demand of films had increased so much that the studios were working round the clock, with eight to ten films being shot simultaneously. The star system had come to stay, whereby the producers could hope to get money from the financiers, only if their films had "marquee names." The system worked greatly to the advantage of popular stars. Indeed, [Kundan Lal] Saigal was then earning more than forty thousand rupees a month, which was about ten times more than what he did as a New Theatres' artiste.[102]

Balraj Sahni and his wife, Damayanti, had tried, as aspiring actors, to get a break at studios such as New Theatres in Calcutta without success. The number of films made in India per year had taken a leap from 43 to 210 in the four years the Sahnis were in England; the "market" had literally exploded. It is important to recognize the complex consequences of the breakdown of the older studio system. Though the increased market mobility of the stars is the most notice-able consequence of the changes, it is possible to think of the shift in terms of the subversive implosion and mobilization of capital within an increasingly tightening political system. B. R. Chopra, a journalist who began making films during the transition period, provides a nuanced view of the changes. "During the war years," he writes,

> there was shortage of raw stock and rationing was introduced. There were, however, certain adventurers who managed to get hold of raw stock and

made their unwelcome appearance as producers. For the first time in the history of Indian motion pictures, we saw the emergence of the so-called independent producers who had no studios nor any organization to back them up, and who, in a short while, brought about or encouraged free-lancing for the first time in the industry. This movement of the independents gained momentum when the Partitioned [*sic*] ripped our country into two and hordes of refugees crossed over from the North in search of livelihood. . . . For the refugee producers an organizational set-up was not possible. Nor had they the resources of the old production concerns.[103]

The influx of new money helped producers such as B. R. Chopra to make films without having ownership of the expensive infrastructure that the studios had. For a few brief years the breaking away from the rigorous and bureaucratic structure of the established studios seemed fashionable, pragmatic, and commercially more viable. But the short-term gains were quickly absorbed by the burgeoning system of star-centric production. According to film journalist Devendra Pratap Lahoti,

> The stars prospered. Their prices rose by leaps and bounds and their tempers, attitudes and life styles underwent an undreamt-of metamorphosis. While their fellow stars of yesteryear were content to be servants—and on the payroll of a producing company, bound to work for it and only for it, these johnnies-come-lately began to pocket enormous amounts of money from working simultaneously for a number of producers—two hours here, half a shift there, a dubbing session here, a close-up there. They divided the normal working day into unimaginably remunerative bits and wallowed in their newly acquired affluence.[104]

The phenomenon of "free-lancing actors" that was born in the 1940s entered into an interestingly reciprocal relationship with the formula film, which persisted until a particular star image ran its due course and was exhausted. At some point in the 1960s, the stars "began to dictate terms to writers, producers and directors, assuming the role of supremo in every film production with which they were concerned." Gradually, "the film industry learned to live with the star tantrums and star hauteur."[105]

The pamphlet for the first National Film Festival in 1954 provided a restrained account of the combination of the fall of the studios and the rise of stars, glossing over any reference to illegality: "World War II was a boom period for the industry. While the number of films produced increased, their quality suffered and good films were few and far between. The number of feature films continued to increase till they reached the peak figure of 289 in 1949. Thereafter there was a slight recession, and the number fell to 221 in 1951. The number of films produced subsequently has shown an increase, the figure reaching 260 in 1953."[106] The S. K. Patil Committee report (submitted in 1951) had pointed out the shift that the black market had caused in the film industry, but the government was not ready to have an open discussion about financial illegality. It was only scholars who offered lucid accounts of the shift accompanied with a clear depiction of the illegal transactions that prompted it:

> The war brought sudden wealth to speculators and black marketeers. This was not legal money that could openly be reinvested, and the black marketeers began to look for ways of putting their money to use.
>
> Film was an industry that could not and did not show concrete proofs of investment. But there was money in it. So they began to speculate with film. They enticed away stars from the studio to act in independent production[s]. Stars were offered huge amounts, half of it in "black," undeclared, nontaxable income. Star fees shot up from Rs 20,000 to Rs 200,000 per film. From a pre-war average of Rs 90,000 the cost of production escalated to a post-war average of Rs 500,000, wrote the *Journal of Film and Industry* in April 1950. Offers of exorbitant fees were soon extended to another key figure in film—the music director. Fly-by-night producers sprang out of nowhere, made their money on one film, and disappeared. . . . More and more films began to be made on this basis. But there was no corresponding increase in the number of theatres, as wartime shortages extended to building materials as well. Power passed from the studios into the hands of the distributors and exhibitors who could now choose the kind of film they wished to handle. Their aim was easy money and quick returns, and they laid down the criterion for what they thought would be a surefire hit at the box office: *a star, six songs, three dances. The formula film was born.*[107]

The above quotes show how it is nearly impossible to understand the perception of the tumultuous shift without multiple points view. Gautam Kaul, in his study on cinema and the Indian freedom struggle, has offered some interesting insight into a possible beginning of the shift. Kaul credits a single producer, Chimanlal Trivedi, with the idea of using a star as the primary building block for a production. Trivedi left his job as a writer for Sagar Movietone and established his own production company, Circo Production, in Bombay and Ahmedabad. Departing from the usual practice of hiring an entire crew, he would choose a project and then hire the most popular actor available. Trivedi would employ actors above and beyond their existing contracts with studios, paying them amounts higher than their salaries. Numerous actors accepted Trivedi's offer, the practice caught on, and the end for the studios was initiated.

Some histories of Indian cinema trace the roots of the star system to the ad-hoc way films were made in the 1930s, even under the aegis of the studio system. Apparently, the system, which was based "on the principle that all technicians and actors were employed by the studio and the whole cost of the film was borne by the studio," was not entirely true of all studios.[108] A special publication by the Directorate of Film Festivals in 1981 quoted Wilford Deming, an American sound technician who worked on *Alam Ara*, on the un-Hollywood mode of operation of Bombay studios: "Financially the Indian film industry is rather strangely aligned. There are few individual companies adequately financed. Rather there will exist a company foundation, and after a script, if prepared, finances for this particular production will be obtained, and the picture and company property pledged as security. Often individual directors will obtain financial assistances, and by renting the use of some studio property and equipment, produce a picture."[109] Our attention, therefore, must remain trained on the material conditions of cinematic production in our pursuit of a coherent historical narrative on cinema in colonial India. From the burst of early experimentation through the era of the studios to the indigenous musical's capturing the market, Indian cinema remained notoriously disorganized and unruly. It remained so not by choice or principle but by virtue of its thrust against the political, economic, and ideological forces that formed its field of play. If India was governable, Indian cinema was less so. The natural death of "empire cinema," the stillbirth of British cinema's profitable market in India, and the triumph of the messy formal absurdity of the indigenous musical in the Indian subcontinent vouch for the power of Indian cinema's unruliness, which would enter a new playing field—that of the postcolonial nation-state with its own ambitions, ideology, and apparatuses. We will explore that new playing field in the next chapter.

CHAPTER 2

Shadow Nationalism

Cinema and the Nehruvian
State of Culture

On February 27, 1955, Jawaharlal Nehru, the first prime minister of India, formally inaugurated a weeklong seminar in New Delhi on Indian cinema. Once welcomed to the podium, he was addressed by Dr. P. V. Rajamannar, a chief justice and the president of the Sangeet Natak Akademi (Academy of Music and Drama), as "the supreme director" of "one of the greatest films in history—the film of New India's destiny."[1] The tone of Nehru's own brief remarks alternated between chiding and dry appreciation of Indian cinema so far. He called it a "huge" industry that had been built from scratch without much official assistance and admitted that it had "undoubtedly produced from time to time some very notable films."[2] Addressing the two most pressing points for Indian filmmakers—taxation and censorship—he bluntly dismissed the possibility of relief or reform in the foreseeable future. Referring to a letter on these issues sent to him ahead of the seminar by director S. S. Vasan, Nehru said that he simply did not understand "why entertainment should not be taxed" and that it was "absurd for anyone to talk about unrestricted liberty in important matters affecting the public."[3]

The seminar was a semiofficial event of the Sangeet Natak Akademi under the Ministry of Information and Broadcasting, and it was convened by actress-producer Devika Rani Roerich and actor Prithviraj Kapoor. Attendees included forty actors, directors, music-composers, and technicians handpicked by Roerich and Kapoor. These participants were to present prepared arguments and engage in discussions moderated by B. N. Sircar, the founder of New Theatres Studios in Calcutta. It was a limited gathering of the post-studio star-centric milieu that Indian cinema had become.[4]

The year 1955 was for Nehru an especially busy one, with an intense travel schedule. He had already visited Ceylon and Indonesia and had just returned from England. Lying ahead were the Asian–African Conference at Bandung and a no-less-significant visit to the USSR and several countries of the Eastern Bloc. Since India's independence in 1947, Nehru had emerged as an influential statesman; he effectively steered India's position away from the Cold War binary and championed a postcolonial global model centered on the United Nations. In India, his stature in politics was uncontested, and he played an active role in molding cultural polices as well, which explains why he would be invited to inaugurate a film seminar. However, Nehru's apathy for both the art and the business of cinema was a matter of public record. He had spoken on the inadequacies of Indian cinema at the Motion Pictures Congress in 1939 and again at the first International Film Festival in India in 1952. Accompanied by Indira, his daughter and political protégée, he admitted to coming to the seminar only at the insistence of Devika Rani Roerich, who had sent him a personal invitation, along with a hastily written report on the history of Indian cinema. Nehru's opening words had the same directness that marked most of his speeches as prime minister but lacked the enthusiasm of some of the more memorable ones, such as a July 1954 speech marking the building of the first of a series of massive dams at Bhakra-Nangal, in which he described modern India's dams as no less sacred than temples or mosques.[5]

Nehru's sanctimonious rebuke did little to alter the general tenor of the seminar. The two regimes—Indian cinema and the Nehruvian state—each had influence locked away in close-knit, self-selected groups at the top with little transparency, and each had its own preconceived notions about public taste, public morals, and the public good. Official interfaces such as this seminar only appeared civil and normalized. On the surface, cinema and the state seemed to have something akin to a gentleman's agreement vis-à-vis the Indian public. But underneath that surface of polite exchanges and supplications, battles were waged and fought furiously over every aspect of cinema, including production, licensing, and distribution. Hovering in the backdrop of all exchanges was an insurmountable and yet unspoken anxiety about the "public." The Indian government's anxiety echoed the British colonial administration's fear of the masses' capacity to (mis)interpret, internalize, and subvert any message from cinema.

The independent nation-state had inherited its colonial predecessor's anxiety, but it had also sublimated it with a sense of its own purported moral duty to educate and protect the masses. The Constitution of India, drafted in 1949, had reserved the licensing of cinematograph films for the union government under Schedule VII, thus not risking variations in censorship among different regions of the country.[6] Both government and the film industry claimed to know what the public needed. The government wanted to align the imagined national community's aspirations to the state's vision of development and progress.[7] Cinema, on the other hand, had been instrumental in creating that imagined community in India; it had performed the role of an unofficial ideological apparatus.[8] Now that the nation had been legitimized as a state, cinema merely wanted recognition and legitimation for itself, or at least to be left alone to grow as a private enterprise. But as the seminar continued through eleven grueling sessions over five days, the two prongs of state control over cinema—censorship and taxation—remained outside the limits of discussion, precluding any real change in the status quo. Presentations by actors, technicians, directors, producers, and musicians were punctuated by discussions on the state of the art, which in the state's view was not an art, and the development of an industry, which was not (yet) an industry. In the end, there was no real dialogue between state and cinema, not even the semblance of an equal relationship, and no real détente.

I have chosen the film seminar as well as the year 1955 to introduce the politics of cinema in early postcolonial India, in medias res, as this seminar was characteristic of the interstitial space where cinema met the state's paternalistic yet dismissive gaze. This chapter examines that space through almost two decades, from the start of India's independent nationhood in 1947 until Nehru's death in 1964. Although postcolonial Indian cinemas saw sprawling growth during these years across languages and locations, Hindi cinema's conflicts with the state continued to escalate. All reconciliatory steps taken by the government, such as plans for an official film archive and the establishment of annual film awards (both geared toward all-Indian cinemas), failed to assuage the Hindi film industry's feeling of marginalization and its general apprehension about state intentions.

While resisting the state's normalizing attempts, the Hindi film industry managed to create its own postcolonial nationalist narrative through the popular genre that was closest to the modern sensibility: the social genre. In this chapter, I will underscore one subgenre in particular, the "nationalist social," epitomized by Raj Kapoor's *Awaara* cycle of films (*Awaara*, *Shree 420*, and *Anari* [Naive], 1951–59), which, with the serendipitous Soviet discovery of Indian melodrama, helped create the dominant language for cinematic nationalism. The social subgenres complementary to the nationalist social form were twofold: first, the "melancholic social," exemplified by *Devdas* (1955) and *Pyaasa* (The Thirsty One,

1957), which foregrounded individual angst and dissent unassimilable into the nationalist narrative, and second, the "social noir," exemplified by *Jaal* (Net, 1952), which delivered sanitized and stylized narratives of the middle-class hero's brush with the criminal underbelly of society.

An Unruly Inheritance: Post-Studio
Indian Cinema, 1947–1952

The film industry that the postcolonial Indian nation-state inherited was an unorganized behemoth, prolific in output and spread over three major cities—Bombay, Calcutta, and Madras. Some 200 films were released in India in 1946, and 283 in 1947. Import regulations on raw stock—placed as a wartime measure—ended in 1945, and the steep rise in the number of films (from 100 in 1945) gave proof of the industry's potential for growth. This was particularly significant in the context of the many disruptions to national life in the 1940s, apart from World War II: a Bengal famine that killed 2 million in 1943–44; the Naval Mutiny of 1946; the partition of Britain's Indian empire into India and Pakistan, which killed 1 million and displaced 12 million in 1946 and 1947; and the general heightening of police brutalities against nationalist activists. Most of the films in 1946 and 1947 were produced not by the studios but by independent groups, under the new freelance system that grew during World War II. During the transition of India from empire to an independent nation-state in August 1947, most studios in and around Bombay and Calcutta had ceased operation and become service providers to independent film producers. Films were financed independently, with money that came from untraceable sources. As outlined in the closing section of the previous chapter, a single extrinsic factor—the unregulated flow of money into the film industry from the wartime black market—caused the simultaneous breakdown of the studios and the rise of a new star-centric system of production funded and managed by private individuals. From the vantage point of first-generation postcolonial filmmakers, these freelancing producers and stars thus rescued film production from the economic crisis that the studios faced. While freelancing helped Indian cinema survive the war years, the process also created an insurmountable problem from the point of view of governability: it birthed a permanently unstructured cinema, one lacking the previously controllable infrastructure of studios and their financing. The net outcome was that Indian cinema clearly emerged as a survivor.[9] Indians continued watching films in record numbers as their status shifted from British imperial subjects to citizens of independent India. Eighty percent of the films released in 1947–48 were Indian, produced by a disorganized industry that for decades had faced government apathy, censorship, and regulations.

As Jawaharlal Nehru was sworn into office as India's first prime minister on August 15, 1947, plans for decolonizing both economy and polity began. But the confluence of the various 1940s crises mentioned earlier presented a political predicament. Complete changes and sharp turns would be impossible. The birth of postcolonial India was fraught with "paradoxes, of continuities as much as change," as Sumit Sarkar wrote in his seminal *Modern India: 1885–1947*. According to Sarkar, the paradoxes were already taking shape through the final phase of India's anticolonial struggle:

> The Congress fought against the Raj, but it was also progressively becoming the Raj, eventually taking over without major change the entire bureaucratic and army structure, the "heaven-born" civil service and all, merely substituting the brown for the white. Independence Day was replete with contradictions: unforgettable scenes of mass rejoicing, the swearing in as Prime Minister of [Nehru,] a flaming radical of the 1930s by Lord Mountbatten amidst all the pageantry of Empire, and a "Father of the Nation" [Gandhi] who said that he had run dry of messages and who was to spend the last months of his life in a lonely and desperate struggle against communal violence. Riots and Partition represented the most obvious of the failures from the point of view of the ideals of the Indian national movement.[10]

With the old administrative infrastructure—including the civil services and the police—in place, Nehru trained his efforts on two tasks: national integration and rigorous planning and development. The first task began with the drafting of a new constitution, under the leadership of Dr. B. R. Ambedkar, and continued until internal state boundaries were redrawn along linguistic lines in 1956. Nehru's second task entailed organizing natural resources for rapid industrialization, a task he began with "Five-Year Plans" in 1950. Founded though it may be on nationalist principles and struggles, the nation-state once realized rewrites nationalism in its own terms, and Nehruvian India was no exception. In his fight against colonialism, Jawaharlal Nehru was guided by two philosophies: "national and political freedom as represented by the Congress and social freedom as represented by Socialism." Combining these two into what he called "an organic whole," however, remained a problem.[11] Once political freedom was achieved in 1947, Nehru as the architect of postcolonial India advocated a top-down developmental approach with his policy of national planning and regulatory governance for the greater common good.

In the course of such reorganization, the power of the moving image was understood by the postcolonial developmental state with as much urgent concern as it had been by British colonial predecessors. In 1948, a plan to use cinema to popularize state programs and reinforce national integration was deployed, resurrecting the colonial government's documentary production units as Films Division of India, under the aegis of the Ministry of Information and Broadcasting.[12] Commercial Indian cinema, however, still looked unruly and ungovernable, given the studios' breakdown. The state had inherited powers over certification and taxation from the British imperial structure left behind. Four censor boards, located in Bombay, Madras, Calcutta, and New Delhi, were in charge of film certification for release in their respective regions, but their operations would be centralized in December 1949. Entertainment tax, collected at the point of sale in each theater, was as high as 50 percent in some regions. In the absence of a realistic expectation of stopping or regulating the undocumented profits that were channeling through the film industry, the nascent state could at best control only the final product: the film, after it was made. Censorship and taxation were all the government could control, but it did so with impunity.

The disorganized film industry gave the government the benefit of the doubt. At the first postindependence Annual General Meeting of the Western Theatres Ltd. within a month of India's independence, the chairman of the association expressed hopes for government's recognition of the industry, which needed "all the possible backing and protection in the shape of adequate facilities for more and better cinema houses, facilities for imported cinema equipments which would set high standard of reproduction . . . and raise the production value of Indian pictures."[13] Western Theatres Ltd. represented one of the organized sectors from the studio era, which had suffered inexorably from the advent of freelancing and illegal funding. Its only hope lay in the government's recognizing legitimate enterprise and cracking down on illegal funding. As it turned out, no such government actions were forthcoming. Instead, the government packaged cinema as a whole as inessential entertainment. Several state governments adopted policies banning "nonessential" structures until such time when building material and resources would be abundant. Bridges, hospitals, and schools were deemed essential; cinema theaters were not. In western India, the "Building Ordinance" stopped work on "unnecessary luxury buildings, such as cinemas and palatial homes."[14] Entertainment taxes continued to rise. On June 30, 1949, a countrywide strike primarily protesting excess taxation caused all theaters to close for a day. The unprecedented "token strike," as it was called by the *Times of India*, was an unforeseeable triumph, given the unstructured state of cinema at the time. Within two months, on August 29, a commission was appointed, chaired by S. K. Patil, to objectively assess the status, needs, and problems of Indian cinema. The *Report of the Film Enquiry Committee* (also called the Patil Committee), published in 1951, presented to the newly independent government an updated version of what the Cinematograph Committee report had presented to the British imperial government in 1928. Both reports offered a complex picture of Indian cinema as an indomitable force for mechanical cultural production, unfathomable in its reach and popularity, messy in its financial dealings, and with a seemingly endless potential for growth. For all the differences in ideology, method, and goal, both British imperialist and postcolonial nationalist governments faced the same insurmountable cultural force when it came to the cinema. It would bend to the will of no government.

As mentioned earlier, the 1955 seminar was symptomatic of the state's paternalistic yet dismissive attitude toward Indian cinema as a whole. By the time of the 1955 seminar, cinema and the state were already in the middle of a political game, the attacks and defenses on the board matched with a media campaign, mainly via newspapers. Within a single decade, two behemoths—cinema, as the fastest growing private sector, and India's federal government, with its enormous bureaucracy—had stared each other down, settling into a stalemate that seemed to serve both sides well for the next four decades. Scrutiny of how this unfolded, however, will show how the game was neither structured nor well thought out. The government's steps to discipline the unruly industry were either diffused by a bureaucratic fog or thrown off course by the idiosyncrasies of individual ministers.

The government had to accept the reality of a disorganized post-studio film industry tied to illegal funding. The 1949 Enquiry Committee had provided a candid and accurate assessment of the entente between the film industry and wartime profiteering. But this assessment was also notably concordant with Nehruvian skepticism toward capitalism, and thus it served partially to validate that skepticism in the context of cinematic art specifically. Beyond that validation, however, the report had little effect on policy, since it was largely ignored by the government, much like its 1928 predecessor. Published in 1951, the new report recommended a rational application of the principles of censorship and suggested concrete methods for consolidating the relationship between government and the industry. None of these constructive suggestions made their way into official policy when the Cinematograph Act was passed in March 1952.[15] It was the first comprehensive legal act on cinema in postcolonial India, replacing the Cinematograph Act of 1918. Three of the act's four sections applied to the whole of India; the other applied only to the Union Territories (certain regions in India that were governed directly by the union government in lieu of state governments and assemblies). The two objects of the act, reflecting those of its 1918 predecessor, were, first, the censorship and certification of films for public exhibition and, second, the licensing of cinema houses to exhibit those films once certified. In a small irony, India followed the British example in renaming the censor boards collectively as the Board of Film Certification. The 1952 act therefore was quite clearly the resurrection of the paradox of colonial film policy in its postcolonial avatar.

The Board of Film Certification became the line across which the two competing behemoths stood their own ground and waged their battles. From the state's regulatory point of view, cinema was a wild-grown phenomenon that could not be subsumed or managed under the rapidly expanding public sector. The constitution that had been implemented on January 26, 1950, contained reference to cinema twice, only in the context of the division of legislative power between the union and the states regarding the sanction of exhibition of films. Within a decade of India's independence, the various arts—literary, performance, visual, and musical—were legitimized by state encouragement and patronage. Academies (Hindi-ized as *akademi*) were formed between 1952 and 1954: Sangeet Natak Akademi for music, dance, and drama; Sahitya Akademi for literature; and Lalit Kala Akademi for fine arts. Cinema, however, went unclaimed by these *akademis* (though the Sangeet Natak Akademi would be mentioned in the brochures of the National Film Awards ceremonies). Nor was cinema recognized officially as an "industry," either. None of the rights or regulations associated with the production sector applied to films. In the resentful eyes of the film industry, the only concrete exchange between cinema and the government of India was in the form of censorship and taxation. The government of India effectively maintained authority over a business that it refused to legitimize.

It is possible to think of the Cinematograph Act of 1952 as a necessary step toward legitimizing cinema by consolidating and streamlining licensing and taxation under a central authority. But the makeup of the Board of Film Certification showed it to be, from the very beginning, a political body—the federal government of India appointed the chairman and other members of the board. This was a manifestation of the legacy of the colonial administrative system. Civil servants and judges were the guardians of society, polity, and culture, called in to scrutinize art and culture and to offer policy ideas. While the prospective civil servants and judges had a broad training in the humanities, it was largely a matter of chance that Diwan Bahadur T. Rangachariar and S. K. Patil, chairpersons of the 1927 Cinematograph Committee and the 1949 Enquiry Commission respectively, were capable of producing consequential studies of the Indian film industry. The regular operation of the censorship system, organized under the Board of Film Certification, could not possibly depend on such serendipitous pairing.

On the surface, the business of issuing a license for each film was trivial. The banality of certification was perhaps only amplified by the sheer volume of films that passed through the board.[16] But the board had the right to refuse certification to a film or direct the applicant to excise or modify the film before it could be certified, which could easily channel the government's apprehensions toward the film industry in general. Moreover, the board's right to censorship vis-à-vis the freedom of speech guaranteed under Article 9 of the constitution was justified by that same article's allowance of reasonable restrictions imposed for the greater common good. Part II, section 5B of the 1952 act defined the principles guiding certification of films as follows:

5B. Principles for guidance in certifying films:

1. A film shall not be certified for public exhibition if, in the opinion of the authority competent to grant the certificate[,] the film or any part of it is against the interests of the sovereignty and integrity of India, the security of the State, friendly relations with foreign States, public order, decency or morality, or involves defamation or contempt of court or is likely to incite the commission of any offence.

2. Subject to the provisions contained in sub-section (1), Central government may issue such directions as it may think fit setting out the principles which shall guide the authority competent to grant certificates under this Act in sanctioning films for public exhibition.[17]

These were the guiding principles for censorship of cinematic content; they were, for all practical purposes, too vague to follow. The vagueness of "prohibition" in the social context became the subject of one of the pioneering scholarly articles on Indian cinema by M. Madhava Prasad, who pointed out that on-screen "kissing" was allowed by the Board of Film Certification in foreign films but not in Indian films, though it was not expressly prohibited in the 1952 act.[18] Beginning in 1958, a series of amendments and supplemental rules were drawn to expand on section 5B in order to provide the Board of Film Certification a clearer guiding principle. The guidelines were revised several times before the following notice was released in January 1978:

1. The objectives of film censorship will be to ensure that:—The medium of film remains responsible and sensitive to the values and standards of society;

a. Artistic expression and creative freedom are not unduly curbed; and
b. Censorship is responsive to social change.
2. In pursuance of the above objectives, the Board of Film Censors shall ensure that:—Anti-social activities such as violence are not glorified or justified;
   a. The modus operandi of criminals or other visuals or words likely to incite the commission of any offence . . . are not depicted;
   b. Pointless or avoidable scenes of violence, cruelty, and horror are not shown; (ii-a) Scenes which have the effect of justifying or glorifying drinking are not shown; . . .
   c. Human sensibilities are not offended by vulgarity, obscenity and depravity;
   d. Visuals or words contemptuous of racial, religious or other groups are not presented;
   e. The sovereignty and integrity of India is not called in question;
   f. The security of the State is not jeopardized or endangered;
   g. Friendly relations with foreign States are not strained;
   h. Public order is not endangered;
   i. Visuals or words involving defamation or contempt of court are not presented.[19]

It is significant that new ideas were appearing here now—artistic expression, creative freedom—and the censor was being responsive to social change. It was the 1970s, and parallel or "new" cinema had the government's proactive support. It is therefore unclear whether the presence of these ideas in policy actually represented a laxation of censor policies with respect to commercial cinema. As we shall see in chapter 3, a gradual bifurcation between parallel and popular cinema would continue to evolve through the 1960s and 1970s, leading to a final confrontation between the two when the government eventually proposed to transform the National Film Development Corporation into an apex body in 1980. If we consider the government documents as archives of film history, the more consequential yet problematic clauses, listed under guideline 2, can be read as validation of Hindi cinema's ahistorical or synthetic Indian modern society that was carefully crafted to avoid any conflicts or controversies with the political realities of the nation-state. Social inequities based on class, caste, and gender were carefully dissociated from the films' central conflicts. With a few exceptions, the ostentatious rich were either unambiguously criminal (like the black marketer Seth Sonachand Dharmanand in *Shree 420*) or benevolent (Ramnath in *Anari* [1959]), thus drawing the narrative's focus away from class differences to moral choices. Regional differences were largely ignored, albeit nonintuitively. Family names, the near-transparent marker of regional and caste identities for Hindus, were picked carefully to avoid specificities. The ethnic group that came to be represented in the most unambiguous manner were the Hindu Punjabis; surnames such as Khanna, Kapoor, Malhotra, Chopra, and Arora are ubiquitous in Bombay films.

Tejaswini Ganti has noted how choice of language was a crucial factor in the formulation of Bombay cinema's identity.[20] Hindi or Hindustani, the lingua franca for India, was not the native language for Bombay. Gujarati and Marathi were the city's two main regional languages, and following the 1956 States Reorganisation Act, the city of Bombay became part of the state of Maharashtra, which had Marathi as its state language. The native Hindi-speaking population was divided among the states Uttar Pradesh, Madhya Pradesh, and Bihar, with regional variations and dialects. While the state-run All India Radio developed a refined yet wooden Sanskritized version of Hindi, the Hindi language that Bombay films adhered to steered clear of both the state's standardized version and the regional dialects. During the first four postcolonial decades, it went on to develop its own metropolitan, urbane, and more democratic form of Hindi, which entered into a feedback loop with the Hindi that was spoken in the streets of Bombay and has since influenced the Hindi spoken by nonnative speakers. This form of Hindi underwent additional urbanization when, in the aftermath of globalization, Bollywood cinema began incorporating English vocabulary into its dialogues. In the first postcolonial decades, Hindi cinema, the only cinema with a national reach, remained an ethnic and linguistic anomaly.

Nehruvian Expectations and Indian Cinema

Leaving aside the finer points of the censorship system, most of the government's policies toward the postcolonial cinema industry were shaped by an a priori cultural standard. This standard was largely and vaguely Nehruvian. Jawaharlal Nehru, the political successor of M. K. Gandhi and the architect of India's postcolonial national identity, had an ambivalent attitude toward cinema as an art form. While we have already seen his paternalistic attitude toward Indian cinema, he was openly appreciative of performance artists. In 1931 he went so far as to visit the office of the Tamil Nadu Actors Association in Madurai to convey his appreciation for the association's political activism, especially for their portrayal of anticolonial resistance and Gandhian satyagraha.[21] But although he viewed a few films while studying in England, he was largely disappointed by Indian cinema and said so, having watched Bombay Talkies' *Achhut Kanya* at the behest of fellow activist Sarojini Naidu. His message to the Indian Motion

Picture Congress held in Bombay in 1939—published in the July 1939 issue of *Filmindia*—sums up Nehru's view on Indian cinema in general:

> I am far from satisfied at the quality of the work that has been done. Motion pictures have become an essential part of modern life and they can be used with great advantage for educational purposes. So far greater stress has been laid on a type of film which presumably is supposed to be entertaining, but the standard or quality of which is not high. I hope that the industry will consider now in terms of meeting the standards and of aiming at producing high class films which have educational and social values. Such films should receive the help and cooperation of not only the public, but also of the State.[22]

Having characterized nation-building as the only redemptive feature of the otherwise trivial business of cinema as early as in 1939, Nehru would continue imposing a national role on cinema after India's independence, during his tenure as the prime minister. But Nehru's model of nation-building—even if sensibly progressive compared with those adopted by his successors—required a Soviet-style fashioning of uniform vision and the continuous production of public consent. The premodern past of the Indian subcontinent, in Nehru's nationalist historiography presented in his book *Discovery of India* (1946), contained disparate elements of integration that could serve as the building blocks of the modern political edifice of the nation. An essence existed, but the edifice of the nation-state had to be built using modern tools to make manifest that essence. While dams, industries, and others modern infrastructures needed to be assembled, a preservation of the nation's cultural past and a cultivation of current artistic media were necessary. Within this framework, cinema as a cultural-artistic medium was destined to be part of the nation-building project. It is in this context that Sumita S. Chakravarty, in her study of nationalism and Indian cinema, called Indian cinema the "mistress" to the "master narrative" of Indian nationalism.[23]

The mistress-master relationship between cinema and Indian nationalism is complicated by the entry of a third factor: the nation-state proper. Commercial films, the kind of cinema that offered the most powerful emotive support to the master narrative of nationalism, came to be abhorred, harassed, and criticized by the state. The government's official focus of the performance arts in the 1950s was on reviving and preserving classical and folk forms; cinema simply did not make the cut. In an intriguing irony, Hindi films and film music from the Nehruvian era—*not* state-sponsored programming—would form the core of nationalist cultural memory in later decades. Cinema was nurtured in popular memory as an emotive expression of cultural nationalism with a wide range of narratives, all within the sphere of commercial production.[24] From optimistic and developmental activism to nostalgic melancholia, the private lives of the male protagonists of the dominant genre, played by actors such as Raj Kapoor, Guru Dutt, and Dev Anand, became the stock of social history. Even Bollywood, since its emergence in the 1990s, has successfully incorporated the filmic archive of national memory in its portrayals of diasporic nationalism.

The most common embodiment of Bollywood nostalgia is aural. Old Hindi film songs embody Indianness to both expatriates and resident Indians and affirm their Indian cultural core. Apart from the obvious informality and ease that films of the Nehruvian era offer to a popular cultural reconstruction of history, they also represent a nationalist aura that has shed the struggles, contradictions, and complexities of that history. The lyrics of "Mera Joota Hai Japani" from *Shree 420*—the most requested song of 1955 on Radio Ceylon's popular weekly program *Binaca Geet Mala*—were composed by Shailendra, who died in 1966 at the age of forty-three as a poor and depressed alcoholic. The song was never aired on All India Radio because the industry had withdrawn film music from radio in reaction to restrictions imposed by the Ministry of Information and Broadcasting in 1952. While "Mera Joota Hai Japani" celebrated Indianness, another song from *Shree 420*, "Dil Ka Haal Sune Dilwala" (You Need a Heart to Hear My Story), gave a somber account of the protagonist's childhood, spent in poverty, hunger, and destitution: "Bhukh ne hai badi pyaar se pala" (I have been lovingly nurtured by hunger). Sahir Ludhianvi's song "Jinhe Naaz Hai Hind Par Woh Kahaan Hai" (Where Are They, Who Are Proud of India?) for *Pyaasa*, sung by the male protagonist in the midst of squalor in the city's redlight district, was a direct reference to a speech by Nehru where he spoke of his pride in India. The nationalist social genre that dominated postcolonial Indian cinema (more on which below) may have smoothed out the discontents within the nation, but subtexts were aurally embedded through dialogue and lyrics, which made visible those discontents to the perceptive observer or listener.

Hindi cinema, therefore, had an uneven affiliation with the Indian nation-building project and was only partially enthusiastic of the nation-state's developmental philosophy and claims. It would be wrong to read this lack of enthusiasm as a mark of rebellion, as its deviations from the nation-state did not always produce critical or intellectual results. An example of this cinema's regressive tendencies is the film *Mr. and Mrs. 55* (1955), which mocks and demonizes the 1955 Hindu Marriage Bill, an act that gave Hindu women the equal right to divorce, through a romantic comedy in which the heroine's feminist aunt is the villain. For this cinema, the question of the state's social ideology was less of a problem than the continuous wrangling over economic pressures and the lack of support for infrastructure. In the absence of an official media policy and an organized or quantifiable industry, the entanglement became a protracted stalemate between disaffected opponents: cinema and the state. Though a wide range of political discourses have looked back from the era of globalization on the devolution of Nehru's developmental nation-state into the increasingly inept and corrupt bureaucracy of the 1970s and 1980s, the state's interface with cinema offers a particularly nuanced sense of the dysfunction that was endemic throughout the postcolonial years.[25] A large dysfunctional bureaucracy that resented but could not ignore cinema's reach and resilience continued to negotiate its own cultural authority over cinema's. I will return to this aspect of the state's co-optation of cinema later in this chapter. In the section that follows, I will elucidate how cinema resisted the state's authority and yet developed a parallel ideological sphere in which the nation-state's supremacy was undiminished and naturalized.

The Nationalist Social Genre: Cinematic Heroism in Nehruvian India

The films that were being shot, edited, and submitted for censor certificates at the time of the 1955 New Delhi seminar had narratives with logic bounded by the laws of the nation-state that had already come to fruition, thus making questions of reform or revolution moot. The cinematic genre that had already replaced the primacy of the mythological in British India was the social. In the first postcolonial decade, a further modification upended any academic discourse that Nehru and his state apparatuses favored. In the nationalist social genre, as I would call it, the nation-state becomes the invisible force that surrounds the protagonists, society, and personal destiny without ever intervening. Moral, social, and emotional crises must be resolved by human agency and fortuitous turns of events. The law of the nation-state is evoked ceremoniously—through nationalist iconography such as images of Gandhi and Nehru in the court-rooms—only to remind the characters and the viewers of its omnipresence. The tweaking of the social melodrama into the "nationalist social" form could be as simple as the protagonist's family acting as a stand-in for the nation. This could be accomplished easily because of the role of the family in the political embedding of the social, as Ravi Vasudevan explains in *The Melodramatic Public*:

> The family is the remarkable symbolic, if not literal, locus of the narrative's organization of both conflict and resolution. At its centre lies the iconic

presence of the mother, stable in her virtue and her place, a moral orientation for her son but also a figuration of the past; for the space of the mother
must give way to the changes introduced by the shift of authority from
father to son. The family binds the son back into its space, securing him
from the perils of the social void and restoring his name, his right to an inheritance and his social place. But it is a transformed family, one over which
he must now exercise authority. The nucleated space of this new formation
often emerges under the benign agency of the law, suggesting a complicity between state and personality in the development of a new society.[26]

The complicity between the state and the family—however transformed—
resonated well in the 1950s as this was the decade in which the postcolonial
Indian state established its secular, democratic, nonaligned identity. Friends and
enemies were integrated into the body politic of the nation-state. Poverty and
wealth, rural backwardness and urban modernity were all justifiable, coexisting guilelessly within the nation. In the case of a confrontation between the
village and the city, between honesty and greed, the resolution lay in returning
to the place of purity from where the protagonist emerged. Class, caste, and
religion were normalized under the umbrella of the nation, with the secular
state claiming to be home to all. "Unity in diversity," the Indian state's motto
fashioned after the American *E pluribus unum*, was sung more powerfully by
the nationalist social form than by the politicians' endless repetition of it.

It is in the context of this crystallization of the nationalist social genre during
the Nehruvian era that the rise of actor-director Raj Kapoor must be narrated.
Raj Kapoor's induction in the film industry as a "clapper boy" and an "extra"
in the 1940s had coincided with the tumultuous change caused by an influx of
black money into the industry. While studios collapsed, Kapoor became one
of the numerous independent producer-directors who established their own
studios on a smaller scale. Once his 1951 film *Awaara* earned him fame via its
record run in the USSR in 1954, he became a powerful broker of influence in
the industry. His father, Prithviraj Kapoor, had picked him to be one of the
attendees of the 1955 seminar organized by the Sangeet Natak Akademi, and
Raj in turn established one of the most powerful film dynasties in Bombay,
with brothers, sons, and grandchildren as popular stars.[27] In the 1950s, he was
the most recognizable Indian actor-director in the USSR, Eastern Europe, and
Asia. Sultan Khan, Pakistan's consul in Turkey in 1954, reminisced about the
popularity of *Awaara* in Turkey:

What a rage the film was in that country that year! Practically every week,
one theatre or another in the city would advertise the showing of the film's

most popular scenes. There were open-air shows of just the "awara hoon" song sequence—a few public announcements, and thousands would show up. Anyone wearing a sari would be followed down the street by a horde of urchins singing "awara hoon" gleefully. In fact, when the word got around that we had a record of that song, a strange phenomenon began. Young boot polish boys would show up at our place offering to polish every shoe in the house free—if we would just play that song for them![28]

The account provides further anecdotal evidence on the Turkish success of *Awaara*. When a print of the film first arrived in that country, it lay unclaimed at the airport for several months. A man not in the film business finally decided to pick it up. He paid a duty of about 700–800 liras (approximately $1,000) and, to everyone's surprise, made a small fortune. From the profits he even built an apartment building, appropriately called "Awara Apartments."[29]

Between 1950 and 1959, RK Films produced seven films that featured Raj Kapoor as the hero. Of the seven, Kapoor directed only two, but the other films followed Kapoor's or RK Films' signature style in narrative, cinematography, and use of music. The focus was always on the hero, and beginning with *Awaara* and continuing through *Anari* in 1959, Raj Kapoor created a lasting scene image with several variations of his "Charlie Chaplin" act, giving shape and form to the urban hero whose vaguely North Indian origin faded in each film into an equally vague yet resolute identity that claimed to be Indian. This is the bourgeois upper-caste Hindu male who has just enough of the rogue about him to be discounted as elite. Raj Kapoor's representation of Indianness was based more on cinematic convention than on verisimilitude; this particular cinematic convention was also largely his creation in the context of postcolonial Indian cinema. Of all the filmmakers of his time, Raj Kapoor was the most fluent in the creation of the complex spatial reality that, with the support of a melodramatic plot and playback music, could effectively stand in for the nation. *Shree 420* and *Anari* do not have any significant use of rural space; *Awaara* does to a limited extent. The synecdochal use of the "city" was perhaps an element of necessity, as the early postcolonial popular Indian film "had to construct its nation myth out of the elements it had at hand—the urban populace of the big cities."[30] The hero—who wears Western clothes almost without exception and can impersonate anyone irrespective of socioeconomic class—is the most mobile and indeterminate among all the characters, the star element being the most constant factor. Named Raj or Raju in several films and faced with problems familiar to the educated middle class, such as unemployment, he could easily be the embodiment of the Indian middle class. However, the indeterminacy in his character prevents total identification with any particular class, caste, or even region. He is picaresque enough to be considered a pan-Indian, pan-cinematic, or universal type. The universal/national type could be given free agency within the newly defined limits of a "secular source of authority," the nation-state, which did not and could never completely replace the other lived communities: family, class, and caste. Chakravarty's characterization of "judicial law" as the all-purpose surrogate is particularly relevant to Raj Kapoor's films:

> Mass audiences for Hindi films also constituted the new citizens of India and as such faced the problems of developing some notions of social responsibility, of building community and solidarity that went beyond the "traditional" loyalties to family and caste groups. In a new "impersonal" context, they had to find ways of seeing in the harsh conditions of their existence the promise of change and renewal, with the old certitudes brought back via the new agencies of state power and authority. Since no institution better symbolizes state power, particularly in the popular consciousness, than judicial law, it becomes a means whereby questions regarding a person's role *vis-à-vis* the state can be explored and suitably dramatized.[31]

In *Awaara*, the father quite literally embodies the "law of the state": he is a judge. Justice Raghunath, played by Raj Kapoor's father, Prithviraj Kapoor, is a formidable patriarch confident in every judgment he makes, private or professional. Jagga, a petty thief wrongfully sentenced by Raghunath, finds the law of the state oppressive and unjust and resorts to his own brand of justice by abducting Leela, Raghunath's wife. Jagga releases her when he discovers her to be pregnant, but Raghunath, though happy at Leela's return, is plagued with doubts about the paternity of Leela's child and abandons her. Raj grows up in his mother's care in a shanty. Struggling to take care of his ailing mother, he drops out of school against Leela's wishes. Jagga, still vengeful toward Raghunath, resurfaces and recruits Raj in his gang of miscreants. Raj and Raghunath cross paths when Raj befriends and later falls in love with Raghunath's foster daughter Rita, a lawyer's daughter and a lawyer herself. Raj tries to escape his life of crime and ends up killing Jagga in a scuffle. During the trial featuring Raghunath as the judge and Rita as Raj's defense counsel, Raj discovers his connection with Raghunath and, in yet another twist, attempts to kill him. In the end Raj receives a three-year prison sentence and Rita promises to wait for him. If in *Awaara* the law of the father and law of the state fuse together, the synthesis does not make the citizen's predicament bearable. Raj's destitution is caused by Raghunath's heartlessness and the state's failure to protect the vulnerable. While Raj will presumably get a chance to redeem himself once he is out of prison, there are two characters in the narrative who suffer injustices at the hands of Raghunath the patriarch and Raghunath the judge respectively: Leela and Jagga. Jagga's claim of innocence and Leela's abandonment by her husband are loose ends that are never tied up. Leela's misery, caused by Jagga's war against the state and then Raghunath's cruelty, stays concomitant to Raj's destitution.

Raghunath, *Awaara*'s oppressive authority-figure father, also recalls Kapoor's first directorial venture, *Aag* (Fire, 1949). In that film, Kewal, an aspiring actor and theater producer, has a lawyer father who wants him to choose the same profession and disinherits him when Kewal refuses. Kewal leaves home, stumbles upon Rajan, a wealthy patron of theater, and forms his own theater group. He finds his dream heroine in a young beautiful woman (played by Nargis Dutt) who, by her own account, has emerged out of "the hell that is post-Partition Punjab"; all her family members had perished in the riots. Kewal decides to call her Nimmi, after an estranged childhood friend who shared his passion for the theater. The heroine's past trauma, however, is quickly glossed over; the focus shifts to the rivalry between Kewal and Rajan over Nimmi. In the end, Kewal attempts to eject himself out of the triangle by self-destruction: he sets himself on fire. Although he survives, he is disfigured and has to leave the theater. The entire narrative is recounted in flashback, with Kewal narrating the story to his bride on their wedding night. Both *Aag* and *Awaara* have an anxiety-driven complexity that is missing from any of Kapoor's later films. The intricate plots and deft manipulation of melodramatic elements that characterize *Aag* and *Awaara* remain, but the vulnerability of the characters, especially of women victims of violence or trauma that is never redressed, disappears in the later films. In *Shree 420* and *Anari*, individual suffering becomes embedded in the grand narrative of the nationalist social, and one solution emerges in the end to redress both the individual and the collective problem.

Shree 420 is more grounded in Bombay than any other film by Kapoor. Bombay is both the financial nerve center of the nation-state and the ultimate colonial-modern metropolis where identities melt and merge.[32] In *Shree 420*, Bombay's urban landscape enters the diegetic space through a highly selective process, even as the visual narrative unfolds in diverse locations, ranging from pavements occupied by the homeless poor to hotels, offices, and mansions where dishonest oligarchs live their privileged lives and carry out their questionable businesses. Raj Kapoor's performance as the hero Raj shows him at his most Chaplinesque. Optimistic, hardworking, honest, and educated, Raj is an outsider who arrives in Bombay in search of employment. He discovers soon enough that his university diploma and a gold medal attesting to his honesty have little worth. He takes up the first menial job that comes around and befriends Vidya (played by Nargis Dutt), who lives with her disabled father and runs a school for poor children. Even as he is willing to build a modest life with Vidya, he is drawn into the world of gambling and fraud. He loses Vidya's affection, and his moral spiral downward is interrupted when he learns that he has unwittingly become part of a scheme that has defrauded the poor and homeless, some of whom had befriended him when he first came to Bombay. He takes responsibility for his actions, and after a short prison term he is united with Vidya, who persuades him to stay in Bombay.

The last shot pays homage to Chaplin's *Modern Times*, as Raj and Vidya walk away from the camera toward the skyline of Bombay. Raj in *Shree 420* is unfettered as a subject, unlike his namesake in *Awaara*. And since he grew up in an orphanage, he is literally a ward of the state, without familial complications—a young, educated, hard-working citizen of a free country. With a persona free of narrow cultural moorings, endowed with transparent, universal mobility, he becomes a cinematic everyman (tinged with local color) when he sings,

My shoes are Japanese
My trousers are English
My red hat is Russian
Still, my heart is Indian.

The supernationalist mélange spelled out in this song is not unique to this film; it just makes it explicit and verbalizes it. In 1955, this mélange was an easily recognizable signature of most heroes (at least the urban ones). They are allowed a much freer-floating signification than their women counterparts. *Shree 420* is memorable for verbalizing this "free-floating" state through the oft-quoted song and for creating the perfect crossover between the personal and the national, the private and the public aspirations, within the structure of melodrama. This film is heavier in symbolic and melodramatic elements than both *Awaara* and *Anari* and subsequently has a narrative structure that is directly controlled by the above elements. The two young women whom Raj meets in Bombay are transparent symbols of good and evil: the teacher with middle-class Hindu values and attire who instills in Raj the desire to stay honest is named Vidya ("learning"), and the woman who initiates him into the world of gambling bears the name Maya ("illusion"). Vidya has long hair, her body demurely wrapped in a sari in public and in private, while Maya wears a gown that reveals her shoulders, has short "Western-styled" hair, and appears with a cigarette in a holder, blowing smoke. In the only scene of the film in which Maya and Vidya come face to face, Maya cruelly mocks Vidya, blows smoke in her face, and flicks off the loose end of a cowering Vidya's sari. As Vidya hastily leaves in shame and disgust, Seth Dharmanand, Raj's black marketer boss, keeps Raj from joining her by offering him an exciting night of gambling ahead, and Maya begins a seductive dance, reining Raj in. A drunken Raj shows up at Vidya's door later in the night, waving a thick wad of currency, but a disgusted Vidya drives him away, promising only to take him back if he returns as the honest pauper he was when she first met him. Raj chooses money over Vidya and comes to his senses only when his partners in crime defraud his homeless acquaintances and are found preparing to flee with the ill-gotten money, leaving Raj to take the blame. Raj's change of heart does not disturb the formulaic good/evil pattern of melodrama, as he emerges as a victim as well. He parts ways with Seth Dharmanand and takes the side of the homeless poor, and by the time he gets out of prison and is reunited with Vidya, his transgressions are forgotten and forgiven by any viewer's standard of judgment. Here is exemplified the informal law of limited change in popular cinema that will persist well into the era of Bollywood.

Anari concludes the "*Awaara* cycle." Raj, called *anari* (naive) by his landlady Mrs. D'Sa and later by his love-interest, Aarti, is a painter who struggles to find a job. He is naturally honest and compassionate, lacking the street-smart manners of the hero in *Shree 420*. When he falls in love with Aarti, he is ignorant of the fact that she is an incredibly wealthy young woman. Aarti had on a previous occasion introduced herself as Asha, Aarti's maid, and Raj had in turn introduced her as his prospective wife to Mrs. D'Sa. Raj feels betrayed when Aarti's white lie is exposed, and the relationship is further complicated by the involvement of Ramnath—Aarti's uncle and Raj's employer—in a drug contamination scandal. In the familiar bridging of the public/private, Raj administers a contaminated pill to Mrs. D'Sa and inadvertently causes her death. Raj is arrested, brought to trial for murder, and is acquitted after Ramnath admits the complicity of his drug manufacturing company in the contamination of the drug that caused Mrs. D'Sa's death. As Ashish Rajadhyaksha and Paul Willemen note, the film, despite being directed by Hrishikesh Mukherjee, had Raj Kapoor's authorial signature: the underscoring of the evils of capital accumulation and private wealth.[33]

What I choose to call the "*Awaara* cycle" exhibits several distinctive features: a solid mooring in certain set elements of melodrama, an indictment of capitalism, and an emphasis on the dubious nature of the new citizen's inheritance, including patriarchy, nation, tradition, and the compulsion to become "modern." The *Awaara* cycle forms the core of the nationalist social genre. In *Awaara*, both the public and the private—the nation-state and the familial—are burdened with an oppressive, punitive patriarchy that demands obedience and obeisance at any cost. The biological father whose overbearing presence pervades both *Aag* and *Awaara* is noticeably absent from the later films. In *Shree 420* and *Anari*, Raj has only a surrogate parent in the form of a kindhearted mother figure, played by Lalita Pawar in both films. The systemic power of the state—endemic in *Awaara*—becomes diffuse in *Shree 420* and *Anari*. The police drop in intermittently and trials run in courts seamlessly, offering logistic support to the narrative. The burden of history, whether private or public, is likewise diffused in *Shree 420* and *Anari* compared with *Aag* and *Awaara*. Nothing wrong is perceived in the workings of the state in *Shree 420*. In the end, the hero goes so far as to proclaim his faith in the state when he suggests to the homeless victims of Dharmanand's elaborate fraud that they take their meager savings to the government and ask the government to build cooperative houses for them. The insurmountable challenges that the system posed for individuals in *Aag* and *Awaara* is phased out smoothly in *Shree 420* and *Anari*. Profit within ethical and moral limits is justified. It is only the illegal and immoral profiteering of predator capitalism that poses danger in *Anari*. Ramnath is a "capitalist with a conscience" who sells life-saving drugs. Moreover, he values honesty and hard work in his employees, a quality that was noticeably absent from the black marketer Seth Dharmanand in *Shree 420*. *Anari* validates Ramnath's position by rendering realistic depth to his wealth: he owns a company that manufactures medicine. Also, the fact that he was once poor and remembers it makes him a more human character than Dharmanand.

There is more than populist fondness and nostalgia in the *Awaara* cycle's enduring popularity in India and abroad (it was particularly so in the USSR, where *Awaara* held a twenty-year box-office record). To this day, Indian commercial cinema recurrently harkens back to the themes and motifs from these films. In a way, Raj Kapoor had stumbled onto the perfect formula for a mainstream postcolonial art form. It could pit the private against the public without any serious subversion or reversal. As the creative force behind every RK Films release, Kapoor used the star-centrism of the 1950s to build his production house amid the demise and dispersal of studio-centric production. The fact that he could keep on playing the lead male character in the dominant Hindi film industry put him in an advantageous position. In Hindi cinema, the Anand brothers, notably Dev and Vijay, who worked under the Navketan banner, and Guru Dutt, who directed and played the lead in several successful films in the 1950s, had comparable careers. The nationwide distribution of Hindi films was the primary factor behind their iconic status and Kapoor's. For example, someone like V. Shantaram, the maker of meaningful and successful films in Marathi and Hindi such as the nationalist social *Do Aankhen Barah Haath* (Two Eyes, Twelve Hands, 1957), had little clout beyond the educated middle class. Similarly, the popular stars in the Bengali, Tamil, and other film industries were virtually unknown beyond their home states and the linguistic diasporas. The unapologetic liberal nationalistic spectacle that Raj Kapoor's *Awaara* cycle embodied had concurrent resonances in regional cinemas, though Kapoor himself could not replicate and reproduce the formation beyond the 1950s. The lone film that follows the *Awaara* cycle—*Jis Desh Mein Ganga Behti Hai* (The Land through Which Ganga Flows, 1960)—is replete with familiar character types and motifs from Kapoor's earlier films: bandits, an orphan, the almost religious belief in the greatness of the nation. It remains Kapoor's last nationalist social film until he attempted a return to the form in 1985, with *Ram Teri Ganga Maili* (Ram, Your Ganga Has Become Impure).[34] Separated by twenty-five years, both *Jis Desh Mein* and *Ram Teri Ganga Maili* do little more than repeat and mirror the *Awaara* cycle.

The success and singularity of the *Awaara* cycle is reaffirmed by Bollywood's continued recapitulation of Kapoor's iconic gestures (which in turn imitated Chaplin's) and songs, such as Shah Rukh Khan's fantasy dance performance in *Rab Ne Bana Di Jodi* (A Match Made by God, 2008), which begins by compressing in its first verse the entire *Awaara* cycle along with Kapoor's *Sangam* (Confluence, 1964). However, it is crucial to remember that Kapoor's particular variations and other films from the 1950s spoke to each other through a common body of symbolism, consisting of prototypes, plots, and aurality by way of playback songs. In films starring Dev Anand and Guru Dutt, for example, the law, the state, family, the city, and sexuality concatenate in ways that were both 1950s stock and specific of subgenres, such as in the Bombay variant of noir in *Kala Bazaar* (The Black Market, 1960) or in a melancholy romantic form in *Devdas* or *Pyaasa*. The common thread running, we should remember, is that of melodrama, notwithstanding the carefully constructed urban realism. For example, the city that Raj Kapoor uses so effectively in *Shree 420* and to a considerable extent in *Awaara* becomes a persistent motif in the 1950s. Ravi Vasudevan explains how the bustling urban scene encodes meaning in the language of melodrama:

> Whatever the degree of fabrication, the street scene of the 1940s and 1950s is animated by the activity of newspaper hawkers, vegetable peddlers, construction workers, mechanics, urchins and shoe-shine boys, petty thieves, pedestrians going about their business. Vehicles—cycles, trucks, cars, trolleys, buses, and significant places—railway stations, cafes, the red light area, are also deployed in the semantics of the street and of night and therefore of a physical, social, and sexual drive.
>
> But the melodramatic narrative's invocation of the "real" is merely one level of its work. . . . Things cease to be merely tokens of social intercourse

whose meaning is assigned by a social code; they become the vehicles of metaphors whose tenor suggests another kind of reality.[35]

Different levels of reality could be layered in through the presentation of the city and the street scenes in different subgenres. The Indian metropolis (Bombay, in most Hindi films) could be used effectively to interject a variety of formal and thematic elements, both in visual and narrative domains. Unpredictable characters, scenarios, and situations could be introduced, extra-diegetic songs could be added with ease, and masquerades and pastiche could be naturalized. The metropolis could also provide a physical platform for the exteriority of the "public" sphere that—with the irreversible rise of the star system and melodrama—was systematically drained of any sociopolitical depth. And it is the male star's body that becomes the display board for the urbanization and standardization of the public sphere. A mélange of clothing (ranging from the two-piece suit and tie to the open-button shirt and a bandanna) and mannerisms gleaned from nonindigenous visual sources, mostly Hollywood, could be used in conjunction with the city streets as a way both to situate the male body in the narrative and to dislocate it from realist specificities of region, community, and period: "It is the hero's very mobility between spaces, spaces of virtue (the 'mother's' domain), villainy, and respectability (the 'father's' domain) which problematizes social identity," Vasudevan points out. "Often the street, the space of physical and social mobility, is also the space of the dissolution of social identity, or the marking out of an identity which is unstable."[36]

Not much has been written on the evolution of male attire in Indian cinema over the last six decades, let alone with a specific focus on the 1950s. However, as post-Bollywood cinema continues to draw more critical attention, there have been some recent studies on the increased cosmopolitanism of the Bollywood stars. Bhaskar Sarkar, for example, has observed how the appearance of Shah Rukh Khan—the archetypal Bollywood star—has morphed over a period of fifteen years (1995 to 2010) into a carefully synthesized, global metropolitan "look."[37] It is not hard to see prefigurations of these recent Bollywood syntheses in an earlier pan-Indian morphing of the hero's body in 1950s Hindi cinema. Independent of then-ongoing standardization of Indian attire in the urban public sphere, 1950s Hindi cinema plotted a more metropolitan and international dress code onto the male body. The difference between male and female dress codes in films of the era is especially glaring in the urban setting, where, ironically, social identity was often dissolved. In *Awaara*, *Shree 420*, *Kala Bazaar*, *Pyaasa*, *Baazi* (Gamble, 1951), and *Aar Paar* (This or That, 1954), the heroes wear mostly a coat-and-jacket ensemble, often standing in stark contrast to the lighter shirt and trousers or Indian-style cotton ensembles worn by the other characters. The male leads' attire and mannerisms remained heavily influenced by Hollywood and were thus almost devoid of innovation. Women's attire, by contrast, evolved in tandem with the Indian fashion world. Once used in a successful film, a new sari print, blouse cut, or hairstyle could generate a new trend in urban and semi-urban middle-class fashion. The immutability of the hero's attire (coat/jacket and trousers even in the hot, stifling humidity of Bombay) is one of the cornerstones of the era's star-centric system. The "fronting" of the hero with distinct attire and mannerisms makes the actor recognizable and plays a role in the creation of the star-text, allowing for a continuity of personal style and form across films.

Even as we speak of the Bombay variant of noir, attention must be drawn to the basic incompatibility between the star system as it evolved in the 1950s and the social noir form. One of the corollaries of the entrenched form of stardom was typecasting, whereby the good/evil and the hero/villain dichotomies could never be upset for the sake of narrative or form. Because the male star could not be the dark antagonist, the Hindi noir became an inverted or somewhat twisted version of the social/moral cinema. As Vasudevan writes, "This is a drama of downward social mobility. Most of the characters . . . originate in respectable middle-class families. But the upheaval in the hero's circumstances is never so irreversible as to prevent the recovery of his virtue and of the possibilities of social renewal."[38] The pockets of symbolic import that reside in the space of the city barely vary from the nationalist social films such as *Awaara* and *Shree 420* to nationalist social noir such as *CID* (Central Intelligence Agency, 1956) or *Kala Bazaar*.

In *Kala Bazaar*, Dev Anand plays a member of the fallen middle-class, a blue-collar worker who becomes an expert scalper of movie tickets. A particularly ingenious thematic prop that recurs in several films of the urban, noir-inspired genre is the act of gambling. In a script that refuses much depth to characters, gambling could help sketch moral value or social mobility in quick, broad strokes. Most of the noir-inspired films remained remarkably guileless in their treatment of the dark side, a feature noted even in casual histories of Indian cinema. Nikhat Kazmi shows how Dev Anand played the hero in a series of films that simply postured as noir, watering their content down with romance and a moral message. This is true of both Mangal in *Taxi Driver* (1954) and Raghuvir in *Kala Bazaar*. Mangal "cruised through the lower parts of town as the prototypal proletarian," but his "daring, street-bred adventurism" was not related to any class identity or moral revolt and lacks the generic characteristics of the typical noir character as well.[39] Likewise, in Vijay Anand's *Kala Bazaar*, the hero Raghuvir, the city's top black marketer, is quickly transformed by love and becomes a legitimate businessman.[40]

A variation darker than nationalist social noir—close to departing the nationalist social convention entirely—came in the form of melancholia. The literary lineage of that mood is readily traceable, as is the character type it favored: a brooding, melancholic, often alcohol-prone hero who turns his disappointments inward, refusing to accept the norms of citizenship. He was an invention of colonial bourgeois modernism and of the early twentieth century. The type surfaced in several novels by the popular Bengali novelist Saratchandra Chatterjee, such as *Srikanta* (volumes 1–4, 1917–33), *Charitraheen* (Immoral, 1917), and most memorably *Devdas* (1917). In *Devdas*, Chatterjee had created a sensitive yet sociopathic protagonist driven to melancholia and alcoholism.

Devdas, the novel's eponymous hero, is in love with his childhood friend Parvati, a woman of his caste but of lower socioeconomic status. He drinks himself to liver disease and death, however, after Parvati is married off to a much older widower landlord. In his journey through alcoholism and debauchery, he befriends Chandramukhi, a prostitute in Calcutta (a character that becomes the blueprint for self-sacrificing fallen women in later novels and films). In the context of early twentieth-century Bengal and India, Devdas was much more than a melancholic outsider. He was the first "outsider" hero in Indian literature, a uniquely colonial Indian concoction. He combined upper-caste elitism and entitlement with the brooding, sensitive soul of European romanticism and the apathetic aloofness of modernism.

It is important to understand fully the sociopolitical moorings of such a character before venturing out to study the subsequent variants and metamorphoses. Devdas is the son of a rural landowner family in Bengal, his family being a beneficiary of the colonial economic system that evolved out of the East India Company's policies. The two key historical markers in the immediate context of Bengal were (1) the creation of a landholding bourgeoisie following Lord Cornwallis's Permanent Settlement Act of 1793 and (2) the further enfranchisement of that class and its offshoots through an educational system of limited access validated by Thomas Babington Macaulay's 1835 "Minute on Indian Education." Colonial policy combined with colonial modernity played a pivotal role in the consolidation of a new subjectivity for the modern individual and colored every literary and cultural movement in modern Bengal and India, including the growth of the Indian novel. Devdas belonged to the Bengali bourgeoisie, the *bhadralok* (literally "gentle folk"), a class whose identity was marked by its privileged position within the colonial economy, its enfranchised and privileged status over the rural and urban poor, and a sense of entitlement that it derived from that status.

The character Devdas evolved out of its textual origins as a "type" in the 1950s. As it developed, the sociopolitical context wore increasingly thin. When in 1955 *Devdas* was remade with Dilip Kumar playing the lead role, the "type" evolved out of its Bengali *bhadralok* origins to become a pan-Indian cinematic phenomenon, the role persisting for a decade through several films featuring Kumar:

> Dilip Kumar played this [type] character in *Milan, Devdas, Shikast,* and, to some extent though without an explicit Bengali story, in *Jogan*. This person is gentle, romantic, shy and deliberately non-assertive. He is always elegantly dressed in a dhoti and kurta, both spotlessly white. Invariably he falls in love. In *Milan* he is trapped in an unfortunate situation with the wrong woman who does not know he is not her husband. In *Devdas* he loves the poor girl from the village but his timidity and her pride manage to thwart their union. So he dissipates himself in alcohol with a prostitute. The key image is of a man being ensnared by circumstances in which, despite his worldly wealth, he is helpless. It has to be conveyed by the actor that his failure is perhaps his own fault but done in a way that wins sympathy. It calls for subdued acting with passages of silence.[41]

This excerpt from Dilip Kumar's biography offers a perfect example of audience response to a star text. But it also points to the uses of melancholia in melodrama. If Devdas provided Indian cinema with the perfect melodramatic type, the reverse was also true: melodrama was the perfect vehicle for Devdas as well. Male angst in 1950s and 1960s Hindi melodramas drew extensively from the narrative of *Devdas*, moving away from any historicity whatsoever to create the perfect vehicle for the postcolonial, post-partition sense of loss and vulnerability without any substantive social critique. Guru Dutt's *Pyaasa*, in which the chief protagonist fails both as a poet and as a lover, reverberates with the same vulnerability and loss, despite the lack of any more overt narrative similarity. This melancholic social form was complementary to the nationalist social genre in its projection of the normative. The tableau of modernity and law, of society and the state, was presented exactly as it was in other variants of the social genre. Both the melancholic and the nationalist social forms, moreover, were symptomatic of the decline and fall of the reformist social film in the face of melodrama. The 1936 Hindi film based on *Devdas*, starring the singer-actor Kundanlal Saigal, had incited V. Shantaram to make *Aadmi* (Man, 1939), a love story between Moti, a policeman, and Kesar, a prostitute, that in spite of the despair and pathos in the plot was created as an anti-melodrama. Shantaram himself had pointed out the social politics of his film:

> *Aadmi* was my own reaction to the theme of frustration and tragedy of *Devdas* in which the lover, failing to get his beloved, starts drinking and visiting a prostitute and ultimately dies. As a result, hundreds of college Romeos whenever jilted in love resorted to drink. . . . The reaction of the audience was so strong that I felt the necessity of making a film stressing the fact that a woman's love is not everything in life. And I had the satisfaction that I had fulfilled my responsibility when I got a letter from a young man saying that after seeing *Aadmi* he decided not to end his life as a result of disappointment in love. This letter, which credited me with having saved one life[,] gave me far more satisfaction than anything else.[42]

Shantaram's anti-*Devdas* was more than anything a rally for the reformist social genre, in the vein of his 1937 film *Duniya Na Mane* (The Unexpected, released as *Kunku* in Marathi), based on a progressive Marathi novel by Narayan Apte, in which a young woman forced into marriage refuses to consummate the relationship with the much older husband.[43] Both *Duniya Na Mane* and *Aadmi* train the camera and the discourse on the empowerment of female protagonists in a grossly unequal society and in so doing promote a cinema radically different from the (male-)star-centric melodrama of the post–World War II years. In the 1950s, when *Devdas* was remade in Hindi, the battle against star-centric melodrama had already been fought and lost.

Would the Nehruvian state have been kinder to reformist social films (in the vein of *Duniya Na Mane* and *Aadmi*) if the studio system had persisted? What did the government want from cinema? These questions generate complicated and obtuse answers throughout the postcolonial decades. With the contending discourses on cinema and Indianness in the foreground, the material aspects of film production and distribution—including business, aesthetics, and influence—continued to evolve and crystallize after the 1955 seminar on Indian cinema ended. The image of the state that emerged from the seminar—arrogant, paternalistic, and ultimately unsupportive in its passivity—never surfaced in its material form in commercial cinema either before or after the seminar, until the late 1980s, unless we count the aural subtexts, as in the song from *Pyaasa* discussed earlier.

Speaking for Cinema: National Awards, All India Radio, and Indian Cinema

The unofficial and popular discourses on nation, tradition, and society that Indian cinema produced and perpetuated in the 1950s were inconsequential to the official decision-makers, who pressed on with their reformist agenda, forever trying to simulate a teaching moment. The first International Film Festival in India coincided with the ratification of the Cinematograph Act of 1952. Endorsed and inaugurated by Nehru, the festival was organized by the Films Division, the government's documentary-producing unit. The somber idea behind the event was to provide Indian filmmakers with exposure to international standards of filmmaking so that they could produce cinema with inherent artistic merit, beyond mere entertainment value. The eventual effect, however, was remarkably different. Since the advent of cinema in India, Indian viewers had had little choice regarding their access to imported films; they had been captive consumers of Hollywood and British cinema. The only exception was a trickle of other films into a few film societies, whose reach and resources were limited almost to the point of insignificance. The cinematic idiom of the social genre, which overshadowed the mythological and the fantasy genres with the advent of talkies, was largely modeled after Hollywood. The only divergence apparent lay in the use of non-diegetic music. That music was the most perplexing and embarrassing feature of Indian cinema to a vocal minority, including policy makers and film society members. It was at the heart not only of the dominant genre of film criticism but also of a prevalent category of film journalism that Neepa Majumdar has named the "What's Wrong with Indian Cinema?" genre.[44] The International Film Festival in India was, by extension, the government's way of contributing to the "What's Wrong with Indian Cinema?" dialogue, by asking and answering the question. The wayward pupil, however, was highly selective in picking the lesson. According to an official history, "The Festival had films like *Rashomon* but the films which created the greatest sensation were the Japanese *Yukiwarisoo* and De Sica's *Bicycle Thieves*. While *Yukiwarisoo* led to *Munna* and other films that centered on abandoned children, the neo-realistic approach of *Bicycle Thieves* opened up new horizons for Indian film-makers faced with similar problems of poverty and destitution."[45]

Ladri di Biciclette (1948) made De Sica a favorite particularly among the directors in Bombay. Raj Kapoor's *Shree 420* and Hrishikesh Mukherjee's *Anari*, both starring Raj Kapoor in the role of a Chaplinesque tramp with a golden heart, bear the mark of De Sica's influence. It is of no small significance that 1950s Hindi social melodrama drew inspiration from Italian neorealism of all places. As Hindi cinema was incorporating that influence into its own melo-dramatic form, Satyajit Ray and later Ritwik Ghatak, Mrinal Sen, and other directors of the "art cinema" movement were developing a different relationship with the same influences.[46] Satyajit Ray, who was then still working as a commercial artist for an advertisement agency in Calcutta (D. J. Keymer), belonged to a minority viewer group. With Chidananda Dasgupta, he had cofounded the first film society in 1947. The kind of "normalizing" effect that the government hoped the International Film Festival in India to have on the dominant quotient of cinema viewers and producers did not quite happen. But Italian neorealism did nonetheless leave its indelible mark on the films produced in the next ten years or so. The inherent melodramatic elements in films such as *Ladri di Biciclette* not only could be replicated in the reformist-realist social genre but also could be embellished further with the obligatory musical elements inherent to Indian cinema.

The government's effort to tame and normalize cinema appeared more organized on the occasion of the National Film Awards event, put under the authority of Dr. B. V. Keskar, India's longest serving minister of information and broadcasting. The ministry announced an "Award Scheme" in March 1954, to commence at the first National Film Awards ceremony, consisting of the following items: (1) Regional Awards for the best feature films in each linguistic group, (2) an All India Award for the best feature film in India tout court, (3) an All India Award for the best documentary film, and (4) an All India Award for the best children's film.[47] The structure and organization of the annual film festival, especially in its first year, reflected a combination of the official worldview on cinema and the sincerity of the government's efforts to open up to cinema. However, in order to communicate, it had to first acknowledge the legitimacy and importance of the object, and the Ministry of Information and Broadcasting took a paternalistic yet uninformed approach to legitimizing cinema as a new national art form. The inside title page of the festival pamphlet contained a quote in Sanskrit from Bharata's *Natyashastra*, a fourth-century treatise on classical drama and other performance arts. Below it, an English translation of the quote read, "Dramatic performance is designed to provide recreation on all occasions. The function of drama is to instruct the masses, educate the intellect, serve the cause of righteousness, besides imparting vitality to the nation, bringing it glory and furthering the welfare of the people."[48] The translation was not literal, as the words "nation" or "masses" do not appear in the three Sanskrit lines. The entire back cover was a photo-print of a recognizable historic structure, one of the gates of the Buddhist monument Sanchi Stupa in the forefront, with parts of the Stupa visible on the right. In order to claim the national essence of Indian cinema, the National Film Festival needed to cure cinema of its identity as a foreign import, a by-product of colonialism by situating it anachronistically in a classical, Sanskritic past. By interpolating the Buddhist imagery, the cultural nationalism of the governing Indian National Congress party distinguished itself from the Hindu nationalism of right-wing parties that had partly gone underground in the aftermath of M. K. Gandhi's assassination in 1948 by a Hindu nationalist.

The passage from *Natyashastra* was followed in the festival pamphlet by the names of the members of the Central Committee for Awards. Representing the government's vision of regulating and supervising cinema, the seven-member committee consisted of four bureaucrats, one professor and renowned national-ist historian, and two poets. Of the poets, one was also a professor; the other, Kamaladevi Chattopadhyay, was the committee's only female member. The main content of the pamphlet is divided in three parts: a five-page report titled "The Film in India," a descriptive list of the award-winning films in the different cat-egories, and a one-page statistical overview of the state of the industry in 1954.

The first two paragraphs of the report are worth a close examination:

> The story of the Indian film from its humble beginnings to its present position in the national life is a record of steady growth. Ranked as one of the largest medium-scale industries in India, and as the third largest film industry in the world, it seems but yesterday when the Coronation Cinema, Bombay, packed to capacity, thrilled its audience with the first Indian film *Harishchandra* produced by D. G. Phalke in 1913.
>
> In the hushed silence of the darkened hall, the audience watched a pan-orama from mythology unrolled before them on the screen. This was not the first time that "moving pictures" were shown. As early as 1896 moving pictures had made their appearance in Bombay. But they were foreign pro-ductions. *Harishchandra* was a novel experience, not easily forgotten. Its release opened out new vistas for enterprising Indians and a new medium of mass entertainment and education was introduced, though few realised its potentialities then.[49]

This is a simple and perhaps a reasonable nationalist narration of cinema. With respect to the cinema/state dynamic in the Nehruvian era, the pamphlet offered the basic official discourse, relentlessly drawing cinema, state, and the people into an imagined happy union. In so doing, the pamphlet glossed over the lack of trust and cooperation between government and the film industry. During the time of the first film festival, the state-owned All India Radio—administered, like the festival, by the Ministry of Information and Broadcasting—was engaged in a bitter battle with the industry over the broadcast of film songs, and an indirect ban on new movie theater construction was still in place. Most histories of Indian cinema refer to the government's nonchalance at the S. K. Patil Committee report. The Film Finance Corporation and the Film Institute would be set up in 1960, almost a decade later. The festival pamphlet, however, co-opted the Enquiry Committee report of 1951 within the government's own agenda:

> The various recommendations of the Committee have been considered and it is proposed to establish a National Film Board with a Film Production Bureau, a Film Institute and the Censorship Organisation as its constituent units. The Film Production Bureau is designed to give advice and guidance in regard to the selection of themes, treatment of the subject, the scenario, settings, costumes, music, etc. In the Film Institute, provision is to be made for training in the various technical departments and for research into problems of common concern and interest to the industry. It is also proposed to make suitable grants for educational films and children's films. It is considered that the best method of handling children's films would be to form a society under the Society's Registration Act for which steps have already been taken. Such a society can arrange to produce original films and prepare suitable children's versions of available films.[50]

The stylistically awkward use of the passive in this paragraph blunts the domineering attitude, which returns with a vengeance a few lines later, in the last paragraph:

> The Indian film has travelled a long way on the road to technical progress. There are signs that the industry is making efforts to realize its responsibilities towards new India after independence. It is hoped that with the co-operation of all concerned and by common endeavor the Indian film will increasingly fulfill its true role as one of the most powerful media for the expression of all that is best in India's tradition and culture.[51]

At best, this is condescension mixed with forced optimism. The first instance of the government's honoring of Indian cinema, therefore, remained couched in paternalism and dismissal. The year 1954 was a crucial one both nationally and internationally vis-à-vis Indian cinema's public image. The difference in how it was received by authorities in the USSR versus those in India cannot be overemphasized. While the Indian Film Festival in the USSR celebrated the stars and directors from the Bombay film industry, the national event in India shifted the focus away from popular cinema. The only Hindi film that received a certificate of merit was *Do Bigha Zamin* (Two Acres of Land, 1953, dir. Bimal

Roy), a "social realist" production with a cast and crew of leftist artists. They were all members of the Indian People's Theatre Association, a cultural affiliate of the Communist Party of India. The best film and the recipient of the President's Gold Medal was *Shyamchi Aai* (Shyam's Mother), a Marathi didactic social melodrama. The two other certificates of merit for feature films were awarded to *Bhagavan Sri Krishna Chaitanya* (Lord Chaitanya, dir. Debaki Bose) and *Khela Ghar* (Toy House), both in Bengali. *Khela Ghar* was chosen in the category of children's films, but it was deliberately refused the gold medal. The pamphlet included a full-page impression of the "Prime Minister's Gold Medal for the Best Children's Film" and an announcement following the list of awards given that "None of the entries in the Children's film section was felt by the Central Committee for Awards to be of a high enough standard for the award of the Prime Minister's Gold Medal." All three documentaries—*Mahabalipuram*, the winner of the President's Gold Medal, and two other recipients of certificates of merit—were produced by the government's Films Division, with its heavily bureaucratized system of production.

In 1955, the National Film Award's Central Committee for Awards included three directors, V. Shantaram, S. S. Vasan, and Ardhendu Mukherjee, in addition to the bureaucrats and academics. The number of medals was increased to seven—two gold and five silver medals—and two Hindi films were among the recipients of medals. The overall tone of the event was less confrontational toward the industry than it had been in the previous year. The program brochure had a balanced tone, its information mostly quantitative. It listed all 274 feature films that were approved for public exhibition in that calendar year and announced India as the third nation in production of full-length feature films. It also listed all documentaries made by various branches of the Films Division. A balanced tone was also evident in a comment on the quality of India cinema: "In technical quality the Indian feature film has been considered to be as good as any produced elsewhere. As far as themes are concerned, there is a section of film producers who show awareness of the needs of a resurgent national and are trying to make the Indian film an artistic expression of human values."[52] Over the year, the belligerent and the defensive tones of the first and the second National Film Awards respectively dampened, and the event became an annual civil exchange between the industry and the government in the late 1950s, the two connected like a Möbius strip.

The nationalist framing of cinema in the 1954 National Film Festival was very much in tune with a spirit of cultural revisionism. It was not, however, representative of consistent state policy. It was but one of many manifestations of the nation-building project undertaken in the Nehruvian era. Likewise, the curious history of Hindi film music on government-controlled All India Radio was representative less of the Ministry of Information and Broadcasting in the abstract and more of the personal idiosyncrasies of the minister. Dr. B. V. Keskar, a political scientist by training and an enthusiast of Indian classical music, held the post of minister from 1950 to 1962. He was responsible for an impasse that lasted for seven years, from 1952 to 1957, between All India Radio and the Indian film industry. In the same year that his office paid officious tribute to the industry by organizing the first National Film Festival, it failed to arrive at an amicable agreement with the Film Producers Guild of India over music rights. All historical accounts of the All India Radio impasse reflect on the contempt for film music that Keskar clearly expressed. By the 1950s, it had become established practice for film producers to send their discs to radio stations before the films were released. In 1952, Keskar's office issued instructions to radio stations "to screen both the text of the lyrics and the music and to approve for broadcast only such records which were in conformity with good taste."[53] As members of the Film Producers Guild withdrew their music from All India Radio, Radio Ceylon, the broadcasting body of India's neighboring country, inaugurated a weekly program of Hindi film music moderated by Ameen Sayani. Sayani's show, titled *Binaca Geet Mala*, began as a half-hour jackpot show, playing "winning" songs picked from a pool of letters. The first show received as many as nine thousand letters, making insurmountable work for the scant team. The format of the show was changed in December 1954 into an hour-long "hit parade":[54]

Each week's show, recorded in Bombay, would be flown to Colombo and broadcast from 8:00–9:00 p.m. on Wednesday and as Sayani reminisced, "the streets would be empty on Wednesday nights . . . in fact, Wednesday nights came to be known as *Geet Mala day.*" . . . The overwhelming popularity of *Geet Mala* led to complaints from music directors when their songs did not feature in the weekly countdown. Sayani suggested appointing "an ombudsman from the film industry" who would check the countdown list. With established figures like G. P. Sippy and B. R. Chopra assuming this role, producers and music directors seemed satisfied with the process and according to Sayani, information regarding record sales and popularity among audiences in different parts of the country began circulating in the film industry. But the mid-1950s, directors and stars from the film industry were participating in weekly sponsored shows on Radio Ceylon and film publicity quickly became a central aspect of Radio Ceylon's programs. As Sayani recalled, no film was ever released without a huge publicity campaign over Radio Ceylon and later, [the channel] Vividh Bharati. Radio, in other words, provided film stars, directors, music directors, and playback singers with the opportunity to listen, speak to, and imagine an audience.[55]

Binaca Geet Mala's popularity, spread through Radio Ceylon's powerful transmitters over all of Asia, compelled All India Radio to resume the broadcast of film songs, albeit on a separate channel created for "light music" and programming. Even in capitulating to the demands for film music, however, Keskar's office would not name its enemy. How are we to understand the cultural logic of Keskar's pathological view of culture? Since he was a self-proclaimed connoisseur of Indian classical music, the most reasonable place to start would be Keskar's lectures and articles on Indian music. Available in a slim volume titled *Indian Music: Problems and Prospects*, his writing reveals an intense, somewhat irrational dedication to the subject. His conjectures on the origin and development of music are premised on a Hindu nationalist historiography. He uses the Indo-Aryan hypothesis (Indians and Europeans having a common, proto-Aryan ancestry) to establish a link between the roots of Western and Indian classical music, citing the heptatonic scale as evidence. In Keskar's view, Indian classical music grew rich in ancient Hindu India and declined during the Muslim rule; it was therefore a sacred duty of the government to educate itself and the public in the history and practice of an art that was worthy of national attention and priority.

> Just as there are different languages in the world, there are different musics. Though it would not be correct to say that every country has its own music, every region certainly has its own. Of course, there are regions whose music is very much undeveloped, or still in a primitive form. India is a country, greater in extent and musical development[,] and it has a classical or higher music which is inter-provincial. Western classical music is also international and current in Europe and America though there are different trends in different countries. There is a Japanese music, Chinese music, Arabic music, etc. Some of these musics are purely national and some international. For example, Arabic music is generally similar in most Arabic countries. There is similarity between the Japanese and Chinese though they are not the same.[56]

Keskar's paragraph, though not explicitly about Indian film music, is indicative of the lack of substance in the cultural logic that drove his policies. Never one to mince his words and always eager to pass his personal preferences as educated opinion, Keskar had predicted in 1946 the disappearance of the game of cricket from India, showing his arrogance and erroneousness were not limited to music: "Cricket can only thrive in the atmosphere of English culture, English language and English rule. It will never be able to survive the shock of disappearance of British rule from our country. With the fall of British power, it is bound to lose its place of honour and slowly grow out of date."[57] Nevertheless, B. V. Keskar had made a difference in the cultural experience of radio listeners, beyond the realm of popular film music. In the same year film music went off All India Radio, national programs of classical music began to be broadcast—both Hindustani and Carnatic, vocal and instrumental. Among the young artists recruited to conduct and play music were Ravi Shankar and the Carnatic violinist T. K. Jairam.[58] A lasting outcome of such programming was an archive of Indian classical music that became available to listeners in the 1990s when All India Radio began releasing compact discs of the recordings made in its studio. Though it is difficult to derive any coherent political line from his articulations, Keskar's policies have been understood as a conservative program, working toward "a new nationalist image, a countrywide broadcast of nationalist programmes and the promotion of Hindi as the national language."[59] Under Keskar's administration, All India Radio came to be known as Akashvani from 1957. In the absence of broadcast via television, Keskar used radio as the state's cultural arm, an antidote to the morally decrepit medium of cinema, and acted upon that instinct.[60]

Indiiskie Melodramy and the Heart of Indian Cinema

While the shadow of Nehruvian apathy hung over the 1955 seminar on Indian cinema, a handful of attendees had returned from an unprecedented felicitation in the USSR. A year before Nehru's first visit to the country as prime minister, Raj Kapoor, Nargis Dutt, and K. A. Abbas were received at the USSR's Indian Film Festival with more warmth than the organizers of the New Delhi seminar would offer. And it was the nationalist social genre, with its songs "unworthy" of All India Radio, that received recognition for the first time abroad as India's national cinematic form. Sudha Rajagopalan's 2008 volume, *Indian Films in Soviet Cinemas: The Culture of Movie-Going after Stalin*, traces Indian cinema's ties with the USSR back to the 1946, when Soveksportfil'm set up its office in Bombay. Indo-Soviet film exchange began five years later, when Vesevolod Pudovkin, legendary director who served as the head of the Soviet Society for Cultural Relations, and actor Nikolai Cherkasov visited India in early 1951.

The unexpected break came in 1954 with the Indian Film Festival in the USSR. The Indian government selected five films for the festival: *Awaara*, *Do Bigha Zamin*, *Aandhiyan* (Cruel Winds, 1952), *Baiju Bawra* (Baiju the Insane, 1952), and *Rahi* (The Wayfarer, 1952).[61] A delegation of actors, singers, directors, and producers—including Bimal Roy, Raj Kapoor, Nargis Dutt, K. A. Abbas, Dev Anand, and Nalini Jaywant—was sent to various events in Moscow and other cities. Indian films were shown in all major theaters in Moscow, including Udarnik and Metropol, for three months beginning mid-September 1954. Raj Kapoor's *Awaara* became and remained the highest grossing film in the USSR for an entire decade. The 1954 festival occurred in the shadow of the de-Stalinization under Nikita Khrushchev, and from that point onward, Indian cinema, especially popular Indian cinema—referred to frequently as *indiiskie melodramy* in the Soviet press—was embedded in post-Stalin Soviet culture. The dominance of Indian cinema in the market was so persistent that it deserved a separate category in the repertoire of films in the Soviet era, the other three categories being "Soviet," "foreign," and "films from socialist countries." Beginning in the Khrushchev era and continuing until 1991, the Soviet Union's popular film imports came, apart from India, from Hollywood, France, Italy, and Mexico. Of the foreign films that drew the most viewers between 1954 and 1989, fifty films were from India, forty-one from the United States, thirty-eight from France, and twelve from Italy. Rajagopalan's study confirms the persistent popularity of entertainment film genres: comedy, melodrama, and adventure. A letter written to *Sovetskii Ekran* that Rajagopalan quotes in her book explains the attraction of the entertainment value of those three genres and how Indian cinema could successfully straddle those popular genres and offer satisfaction: "It [the state of things] is simply offensive. My brother returned from his work shift at the factory. Weary and wishing to relax, he turned on the television, only to see his second work shift begin—a film about a factory. It makes me want to smash the television set to smithereens. Seriously, one is able to see beauty only in Indian films. Life is gloomy, dull, tedious, but in Indian films one sees so much beauty, love, music! Indian films are incomparable among the cinemas!"[62]

An explicit politics of culture and identity underlay the process of cultural identification that Soviet viewers felt with Indian cinema. India was an ambiguous category—as exemplified by its sliding back and forth between "developing" and "capitalist" in the Soviet official categorization of nations—and that played a role in the perpetuation of the mystique of Indian culture. Beyond the official ambiguity there were vague cultural preconceptions as well. An orientalist designation of India as a land existentially different from the West, steeped in Eastern wisdom and feelings, could be heartwarming or regressive. Indian socialists still faced an uphill struggle under a bourgeois nationalist regime, a detail that could have added to the ambiguity. Many of Rajagopalan's interviewees spoke of Indian films as akin to *skazkas*, or fairy tales, and how the emotional content of the films appealed to the Russian/Slavic *dusha,* or soul.[63]

In the end, however, Indian cinema's Soviet experience was more of an Indian story than a Soviet one. If the *skazka* that Raj Kapoor's nationalist social genre offered to Soviet viewers seemed to them to convey Indianness, the same was true for Indian viewers. The antidote to the gloomy, dull, and tedious life of the Soviet viewer worked exactly the same way for Indian viewers. It did not matter that the *skazka* that appealed to one-third of the world's population was an antidote. It was also the very antithesis of the life and the nation it claimed to represent.[64] If the initial formulation of this antithesis was accidental, its perpetuation was not. The nationalist social form and the broader melodramatic form had stumbled upon a code that could be used to communicate with viewers. The act of imagining the community (to invoke Benedict Anderson's definition of nation as imagined community) was performed through the act of viewing.[65] Even more, it was performed through the act of listening to the songs, which were heard, sung, and remembered in the original language all over the Indian cinema-viewing world.[66] It was this indeterminate carrying power of melodrama and film music that produced a proxy nationalism—nationalism as affect.

In view of its perpetual nonconformity with the political and ethical standards of the state, Indian cinema's aura can also be interpreted as shadow nationalism. This is especially true if one considers its questionable origins (the illegal finances that engendered it) and its equally questionable modus operandi (a star-centric system of production with arbitrary standards of recruitment), factors that make it unruly. Nehruvian government, through the reforms and organizations described in this chapter, pursued the idea of a national cinema, one that the government could call its own or align itself with. The idea that this form might be the nationalist social or the romantic melodrama or, worse still, music unworthy of All India Radio was barely tolerable. The search for a national form, therefore, continued, especially when another form of Indian cinema became ascendant. This was Indian "art cinema," also called "New Cinema" by its proponents in the 1960s. It was born with Satyajit Ray's *Pather Panchali*, which premiered at the Museum of Modern Art in May 1955, was shown in Cannes in 1956, where it received its first award, and had a record-breaking run at the Fifth Avenue Playhouse in New York in 1958. The "art cinema" that grew in the shadow of *Pather Panchali*'s success departed sharply from the melodramatic aesthetics of the star-centric system. As we shall see in chapter 3, an ideological rift slowly developed between a populist cinema that reproduced ideology as affect and a realist cinema that was high-modernist in attitude and reception.

The history of Soviet reception of Indian cinema is particularly useful in helping us understand the mechanics of shadow nationalism. Both Soviet and

Indian viewers, drawn in by nationalist affect and melodrama, were interpellated by a state that, in the case of entertainment cinema, had to depend on work produced by parties with no interest in the state's program or ideology. The state could only allow or deny access in its unsubtle attempts to moderate cultural, and therefore political, opinion. Under such conditions of arbitrarily limited access, the films that "rose to the top of the heap" were not "as a rule the artistically challenging works," dictated by a mentality of the viewers that Maya Turovskaya has called "alternative taste."[67] Turovskaya's formulation allows us to understand that even among Indian cinemas, the *indiiskie melodramy* was preferred by viewers to "art cinema." Alexander Lipkov has written from his experience as a film critic how Soviet viewers emptied the halls when films by Satyajit Ray and Mrinal Sen were screened.[68] In a similarly controlled environment, the Indian viewer in India gravitated toward the nationalist and melodramatic affect. What makes the "alternative taste" operate differently from any other variant of public taste in a capitalist economy is the resistance alternative taste offers to control from above. The critical mass of alternative taste, resisting the well-meaning paternalistic nation-state, imparts power to its object: the unofficial or shadow nation of cinema. The narrative takes a different turn when Indian art cinema mounted its own resistance. That history unfolds in the next chapter.

Postscript: The Linguistic Diversity of Indian Cinemas

The market-driven triumph of a popular culture artifact such as Hindi film songs, as exemplified by the All India Radio–Radio Ceylon saga, has become part of the lore of Indian cinema. However, the constructive role of the National Film Awards is visible in the surging linguistic diversity of Indian cinemas, from six languages in the 1930s to twelve in 1971 and over forty in 2018. Although only Bombay-based Hindi cinema was distributed nationally, the National Film Awards created and maintained a multilingual and multiregional focus from 1954 onward. Hindi cinema was considered one among many Indian cinemas, thus maintaining an equal field for the national awards. It was part of the Nehruvian federalist vision of "unity in diversity" that was echoed in the redrawing of the Indian map through the States Reorganisation Act of 1956. That act, by creating states on the basis of linguistic majority, stimulated nascent regional film industries and engendered many more. From the three port cities—Bombay, Calcutta, and Madras—producing the lion's share of Indian cinema on the eve of India's independence in 1947, the field of production grew to nine major locations in the twenty-first century. This growth was largely the result of a map redrawn along linguistic lines.

In southern India, Kannada cinema's emergence from the shadow of Tamil cinema could be related to the above-referenced geopolitics. Kannada cinema was produced in two locations, Hyderabad and Mysore, two of the many discrete kingdoms in the Indian subcontinent that were only indirectly connected with British India. The creation of the Karnataka state in 1956 with Kannada as the state language consolidated Kannada cinema as well as its collective viewership. The 1960s saw the dominance of the Kannada "superstar" Rajkumar, whose star-text differed significantly from his counterparts in Tamil and Telugu cinemas. Rajkumar's career spanned an enormous range, from mythological and historical characters in *Bedara Kannappa* (Pious Kannappa, 1954), *Bhookailasa* (The Legend of Bhookailasa, 1958), *Ranadheera Kanteerava* (King Kanteerava, 1960), and *Sant Tukaram* (Saint Tukaram, 1963) to lighter action and romantic roles in films such as *Anna Thangi* (1958), *Jedara Bale* (1968), and *Operation Diamond Racket* (1978). M. K. Raghavendra, in the first scholarly study of Kannada cinema, argues that the most important aspect of Rajkumar's stardom was the building of a "super-ethical hero in contrast to the Tamil ideological hero in M. G. Ramachandran and the Telugu religious hero N. T. Rama Rao." Raghavendra argues that in the 1960s, Rajkumar emerged as the voice of good and increasingly became a "voice of conscience" with "the message of the film articulated through him." He was "fully installed as a figure for public veneration in the 1970s—not as an individual but as an emblem of local values."[69]

Likewise, Oriya and Assamese cinema from the eastern Indian states of Orissa and Assam carved out their own regional identities through local production. Significant growth occurred in Oriya cinema in the 1960s, with the narrative sources drawn from popular works of contemporary novelists, thus facilitating the Oriya social form. Amar Ganguly directed *Abhinetri* (1965) and Basanti Patnaik's *Amada Bata* (1964), based on novels by Kanhu Mohanty and Basanti Patnaik respectively; Upendra Das's novel *Malajanha* was adapted for the screen and directed by Nitai Palit in 1965. Kalindi Charan Panigrahi's *Matira Manisha* (1966) was directed by Mrinal Sen, and Prashant Nanda, who played the lead, won the National Award for Best Actor. A series of Assamese films received various state awards through the 1950s and 1960s: Nip Barua's *Mak Aru Marom* (Mother and Love, 1957) and Anwar Hussain's *Tejimola* (1967) received the All India Certificate of Merit; Nip Barua's *Ranga Police* (1958), Prabhat Mukherjee's *Puberun* (1959), Sarbeswar Chakraborty's *Maniram Dewan* (1963), and Dr. Bhupen Hazarika's *Shakuntala* (1961) received the President's Silver Medal. Writing in 1974, Kiranmoy Raha commented on the distinctive features of Assamese cinema that secured its cultural and aesthetic identity: the films were based on local narratives and characters and were mostly shot on location. These rendered a certain authenticity to the Assamese film industry, which could turn its meager finances into an opportunity to stay apart from the style of Hindi commercial productions.[70] The regional film industries competed primarily with Hindi films within the boundaries of the respective states and with imports mostly from Hollywood in the metropolises. Beginning in the late 1960s, they would face a third competitor in the form of art house films in Hindi or in the local language, whose ticket prices were subsidized by the respective state governments. Overall, the history of the struggle, survival, and growth of the regional cinemas is varied and diffuse. Largely, it remains undocumented beyond the numbers of films produced. Extensive physical archives of film journals in every regional Indian language need to be built and then digitized for easy access, so that film scholars can explore, excavate, and analyze. Such records could be used to complicate and enrich the history of Indian cinema in a global context.

CHAPTER 3

Culture Wars and Catharses

Cinema after the NFDC, Television, and the Emergency

Nargis Dutt, an actress and an elected member of the Rajya Sabha, the upper house of the Indian parliament, was interviewed in 1980 for the magazine *Probe India*:

NARGIS: Why do you think films like *Pather Panchali* became so popular abroad?

INTERVIEWER: You tell me.

NARGIS: Because people there want to see India in an abject condition. That is the image they have of our country and a film that confirms that image seems to them authentic.

INTERVIEWER: But why should a renowned director like [Satyajit] Ray do such a thing?

NARGIS: To win awards. His films are not commercially successful. They only win awards.

INTERVIEWER: What do you expect Ray to do?

NARGIS: What I want is that if Mr. Ray projects Indian poverty abroad, he should also show "Modern India."

INTERVIEWER: What is "Modern India"?

NARGIS: Dams . . .

INTERVIEWER: Can you give one example of a film that portrays "Modern India"?

NARGIS: Well . . . I can't give you an example offhand . . . [1]

Nargis Dutt had a successful acting career in 1950s and 1960s Hindi popular cinema, playing many memorable roles such as the female lead in *Awaara* and the title role in *Mother India*. She was also the first "foreign" actress to be featured on the cover page of *Sovetskii Ekran* (Soviet Screen) in 1957. In the 1955 New Delhi seminar organized by the Ministry of Information and Broadcasting, she had represented the film industry in its defensive verbal battle with the government. Twenty-five years later, as a public and political figure, she found herself facing a second adversary: parallel cinema or "art cinema," as it was more frequently called, for which the government exhibited both respect and financial support. The conflict between government and cinema appeared triangulated with the advent of a different kind of cinema.

The focus of the *Probe India* interview was a comment that Nargis had made in July 1980 in the upper house of the parliament about Indian cinema's social and artistic obligations and about the films of Satyajit Ray in particular. Ray had been appointed as the chair of the National Film Development Corporation (NFDC), and the government was taking the final steps toward making the NFDC the ultimate authority on trade, import, and export of both films and equipment. A debate had begun a year earlier, in 1979, when the government announced the consolidation of funding and import of "good" films under the NFDC and appointed a committee to formulate a film policy.[2] The report of the Working Group on National Film Policy, chaired by Dr. K. S. Karanth, was published in May 1980. The NFDC, originally founded in 1975, was largely defunct when the Karanth report was published. Funding for parallel or art cinema from the 1960s onward came from a separate body called the Film Finance Corporation, and trade in films was controlled by the Indian Motion Picture Export Corporation. The proposed reconfiguration of the NFDC in 1980 was to make it an apex body, replacing and subsuming all government funding, export, and import, as well as the annual festivals and awards. Throughout 1979 and 1980 this plan in the making drew sharp criticism. To the producers and directors in Bombay, the plan was tantamount to "backdoor nationalization," yet another move by the government to control cinema, to fund and promote films that were incapable of turning a profit and were produced for consumption by a minority of intellectuals. As a star of Bombay-based Hindi cinema, Nargis Dutt had little need or respect for the NFDC.

Parallel filmmakers were not satisfied with the proposed changes surrounding the NFDC, either. To them, the changes were a bureaucratic power play at best and surreptitiously subversive at worst. Their objection was directed against the government's appointing influential producers and financiers from Bombay and Tamil Nadu to the Board of Film Certification, claiming those individuals knew nothing about filmmaking and good cinema. "People who had nothing to do with cinema as a medium" and those in "the powerful trade section of the film industry had found their way to the Board as a majority group," reported C. S. Lakshmi.[3] The Forum for Better Cinema, an ad hoc representative group comprising artists, journalists, and nonmainstream filmmakers, mobilized against the "takeover of the NFDC" by the industry. They were anxious of losing the support the FFC had provided parallel cinema over two decades, since it was founded in 1960.

When Nargis Dutt addressed the Rajya Sabha on July 24, 1980, it was in response to discussion about one of the Forum for Better Cinema's letters. Dutt opposed the forum's stance, as she made clear in a tirade about Indian art cinema's spectacle of poverty and deprivation. The finer points of the preceding discussion (concerning taxation, exhibition, and the government's desired role in filmmaking) were quickly forgotten once Dutt, defending popular cinema against the onslaught of intellectuals, named Satyajit Ray's films in her litany of objectionable representations of India. Ray, one of the pioneers of Indian art cinema, was among the letter's signatories, and Dutt's ad hominem attack in the Rajya Sabha transformed the fight over resources for filmmakers into a simplistic "culture war." The contention was between good cinema and good enjoyment, between a cinema that enlightened and one that entertained.

In the broader historical context covered in this book, the simplified cultural divide between two cinemas (call it the Nargis-Ray binary) reveals the radically changed dynamics between cinema and the government, shifted incrementally between 1955 and 1980. Moving beyond the mere policing and taxation of cinema covered in the 1955 New Delhi seminar (discussed in chapter 2), the government had finally adopted a media policy. Arguably built upon the momentum created by Ray's first film, *Pather Panchali*, the policy was to support directors who sought and found methods outside the star-centric mainstream production. While most Indian "art film" directors of the first generation, including Ray, were self-taught, the evolving media policy had made it possible for their work to be preserved, perpetuated, and turned into a certain form of cultural capital for a developing nation-state. The National Film Archives, the NFDC, and the Film Institute (later renamed the Film and Television Institute), established between 1960 and 1975, supported new and experimental cinema in a dozen languages other than Hindi.[4] The support for cinema in various regional languages was built into the structure of the National Film Awards from its inception as well. Every year, the major industries such as Hindi and Tamil competed on equal grounds with Marathi, Gujarati, Oriya, and Assamese cinemas. Hindi cinema produced in Bombay had no special status.[5] The result was that by the end of the 1970s, there was a reasonably established parallel Indian cinema with dedicated viewers in select urban enclaves, in India and abroad. Within India, the government's support for parallel cinema extended beyond production into distribution and exhibition. Films funded by the FFC or a similar body on the state level were not charged the various entertainment taxes, thus lowering the ticket price by 50 percent or more. Notwithstanding the lowered ticket price, "art films" were shown only in select theaters that catered to an urban, college-educated viewership mostly in metropolises, as well as through film societies that catered to an even more exclusive crowd. In January 1979, the FFC announced subsidies for construction of new theaters, in collaboration with various state film development corporations.[6]

Financial support from the FFC and the NFDC had helped cinema in Hindi and other languages. Using trained actors and location shooting and eschewing non-diegetic songs, directors such as Mrinal Sen, Adoor Gopalakrishnan, and Saeed Mirza made films that were critically acclaimed and won awards at the National Film Awards (NFA) of the Government of India and at international festivals such as Cannes, Berlin, and Karlovy Vary.[7] In a downward turn of fortune for popular Bombay films, most of the Indian films sent to the Moscow International Film Festival's competition that began in 1959 were the work of auteurs or regional directors, in contrast to the first Indian Film Festival in Moscow in 1954, when the Indian government had chosen to represent Indian cinema with five popular Hindi films produced in Bombay.[8] In 1959, Satyajit Ray's *Jalsaghar* (The Music Room, 1958) was the Indian selection for the first Moscow International Film Festival and received a Silver Medal for music. *Jalsaghar* also won two Indian national awards: for the second-best feature film produced in India and the best film in Bengali. The national first prize was won by another Bengali film, *Sagar Sangamey* (The Island, 1959), directed by Debaki Bose. In the same year, Bimal Roy's gothic melodrama *Madhumati* (1958), the highest-grossing film of 1958, was selected as the best film in the Hindi language.[9] *Madhumati* featured Dilip Kumar and Vyjayanthimala, two of the highest-paid stars from Bombay; it had songs performed by star singers Mukesh, Lata Mangeshkar, Manna Dey, and Mohammad Rafi. While it was not the top awardee at the NFA, *Madhumati* received nine Filmfare Awards out of the twelve categories in which it was nominated. Filmfare Awards were India's first private film awards instituted in 1953 by the magazine *Filmfare*, which began publication in 1952. The magazine's focal point was Bombay-based popular Hindi films. In 1970 it added a category called Critic's Choice, designed for offbeat and art house cinema in Hindi. Mani Kaul's *Uski Roti*, and Saeed Akhtar Mirza's *Arvind Desai Ki Ajeeb Dastaan* (The Strange Story of Arvind Desai, 1978) are examples of two art house films that received the Filmfare Critic's Choice award. Given that *Madhumati* was a successful mainstream melodrama, it belongs to a minority of films acknowledged by both *Filmfare* and the NFA. Ray's *Shatranj Ke Khiladi* (Chess Players, 1977) won the best Hindi feature film at the 1978 NFA and a Filmfare Critic's award. The only film starring Raj Kapoor to win a Karlovy Vary was the social-realist melodrama *Jaagte Raho* (Stay Awake, 1957), which was directed by Shambhu Mitra and Amit Mitra, both members of the progressive artists' group Indian People's Theatre Association. The film was shot in two languages, Bengali and Hindi, the latter version meant for national distribution. The Bengali version, *Ek Din Ratre* (One Night), received the Certificate of Merit at the NFA in 1957. At the Filmfare Awards in 1956, Raj Kapoor was nominated in the Best Actor category for his role as a villager experiencing the city's heartlessness and corruption but lost to Dilip Kumar, who played the title role in Bimal Roy's *Devdas*. Barring exceptions such as these, a clear rift existed between the NFA and the Filmfare Awards. Films such as Mrinal Sen's *Bhuvan Shome*, financed by the FFC (later to be integrated in the NFDC), won three prizes at the NFA, was released nationally, and unexpectedly turned a profit but still failed to pique the mainstream Bombay industry's interest. It was not even nominated in a single category for the Filmfare Awards, which allegedly followed a system of nominations and awards based on popular choice, as opposed to the committee-driven mechanism of the NFA.

The rift between the *Filmfare* world of Bombay stars and big-budget Hindi films on the one hand and the bureaucratically maintained multilingual world of the NFA on the other was mirrored in Indian cinema's global dissemination throughout the Cold War era. The foreign market for Indian cinema was split into two distinct zones. One zone, geared toward mainstream melodramas, spanned Africa, Asia, the Middle East, the USSR, and the Eastern Bloc for mainstream melodramas, while the other zone consisted of Western Europe and the United States and focused on Indian art films. While art films did circulate in the first zone via film festivals, the second zone knew virtually nothing of popular Indian cinema until the Indian diaspora's entente with Bollywood in the late 1990s transformed the global market for Indian cinema (for more on which, see the next chapter). Since art cinema shaped India's place on the map of world cinema, it was powerful enough to incite anxiety, contempt, and professional envy from the industry mainstream. India's status as postcolonial, with an economy perpetually categorized as "developing," made recognition from the West eminently desirable for any venture. So it was perhaps logical for Nargis Dutt or producer and NFDC board member G. P. Sippy to see an elitist conspiracy behind the popularity in Europe and the United States of Ray and his art cinema kin. The planned reconfiguration of the NFDC in 1980 to promote Ray's kind of cinema only exacerbated the grievances of an already resentful film industry.

There was another material reason behind Nargis and her peers' refusal or inability to see the popular melodramatic Indian cinematic extravaganza objectively and to compare it with global cinematic trends. Indian exposure to world cinema—including exposure to Hollywood—was limited by a combination of messy import and distribution laws, and it was further affected by the "cartel" policies of the Motion Pictures Export Authority of America (MPEAA).[10] Beyond Hindi films and a select number of Hollywood films hand-picked by the MPEAA, Indian citizens in every corner of the country had access to films only in a single local language (for example, Bengali, Gujarati, Oriya, or Telugu). While Hollywood films were screened only in select metropolitan theaters, Bombay-produced Hindi cinema was the closest thing India had to a "national" cinema in terms of distribution and consequent cultural reach. The myopic view of cinema that resulted, combined with the star-centric system that defined Indian cinema since the late 1940s, made stars and other beneficiaries of the film industry oblivious to the global evolution of cinema as an artistic medium, as well as to the larger sociopolitical implications of the medium. Most stars of the Bombay Hindi film industry were politically and ideologically conservative, a position that until the late 1980s meant vague allegiance to Nehruvian federalist nationalism as well as to an even vaguer idea of "national tradition."[11] When Dutt expressed her resentment toward Ray's films, she may have sincerely believed in the "Indian reality" presented by her preferred cinematic forms, or she may not have minded the misrepresentation as long as it did not tarnish India's national image in the eyes of the world. Nargis's naive reference to dams and nothing else in modern India was mocked extensively by Indian film critics. It was also recreated memorably in Salman Rushdie's novel *The Moor's Last Sigh* (1995).[12] In retrospect, it was just a manifestation of her and her peers' limited understanding of the visual medium. She shared this misunderstanding with Indian policy makers who justified their attitudes toward censorship by pointing to the limited intelligence of the Indian public. The target Indian viewer was perennially infantilized, by either the industry or the government or both. The Indian bureaucracy, following the British model that it inherited and imbibed, routinely described the Indian public as a faceless, naive, unruly mass that must only be shown images that had been handpicked by a parental authority, such as the censorship board.

Once we comprehend the context of the Ray-Nargis debate, we can see that it was already a bit of an anachronism in 1980 when it happened. It belatedly rehashed a 1950s bifurcation between Raj Kapoor and Nargis Dutt's nationalist allegories such as *Awaara* and *Shree 420*, on the one hand, and Satyajit Ray's Renoir-inspired realism in the Apu trilogy, *Jalsaghar*, and *Charulata* (1964), on the other. By 1980, reiteration of that debate was unnecessary and out of place. Nargis resurrected it to respond to the government's consolidation of the NFDC. In 1980 Bombay, a new genre of action-based melodrama was at the forefront of commercial cinema, resonating more powerfully among the viewing public than parallel cinema and the rest of the industry combined. Seven out of the ten most successful films of the 1970s were "action films" based on narratives of revenge and retribution, and four out of those seven featured Amitabh Bachchan, whose "angry young male" persona became an enduring star-text that stretched through the 1980s as well. In the 1980s, eight out of the ten highest grossing films belonged to the action genre, five featuring Bachchan in the lead role, despite repetitive narratives and ingenuous performances by a visibly aging Bachchan.[13] In due course, the genre would falter and give way to a transitional ur-Bollywood cinema (the topic of the next chapter). Of crucial importance to our current discussion, however, is the fact that it is the "action genre" that upended the possibility of "art cinema" to represent the oppressed and the voiceless masses, in the same way Raj Kapoor's "nationalist socials" upended the Nehruvian state apparatuses such as the Films Division and All India Radio. In 1980, the battle between two cinemas—the "good," culturally superior art cinema and the unruly, culturally decrepit popular cinema—was coming to a close, and the latter emerged victorious. This chapter offers a postmortem of that conflict, examining the discourses and the cinematic texts that constituted its battleground.

A Formula for "Modern India": The Object of Nargis Dutt's Defense

While Nargis Dutt failed in her 1980 interview to pinpoint the ingredient that would make for a faithful filmic representation of modern India, critics and filmmakers on the other side of the argument were reacting against the downward slide of the 1950s social genre into what they saw as regressive melodramas and action films; they felt that commercial Bombay cinema had failed to hold a mirror up to any Indian reality, modern or otherwise.[14] If we recall the government's periodic chiding and chastisement of commercial Hindi cinema, we can surmise that critics in 1980 were stepping into a long history of strained relations between commercial cinema and national film policy. Since India's independence in 1947 through the passing of the Cinematograph Act of 1952

107

and Indian cinema's growing from the third largest to the largest national cinema between 1947 and 1971, the constant element in Indian popular cinema was its secure entrenchment in the star-centric system of production.[15] By the 1970s, the star-centric system had further established itself into a dynastic system, with children, spouses, and relatives of stars performing in lead roles and occupying important positions in the chain of production. The scions of the stellar dynasties were not trained in the trade; they were groomed. Their careers were meticulously "launched" with vast crews of technicians and supporting staff made to work around them, translating their inexperience and talent into success in the first few films. Thenceforth they would be recognized as stars, almost guaranteed offers for lead roles for years to come.[16]

The star-centric system related symbiotically with the melodramatic content of commercial Hindi cinema.[17] As only Hindi films produced in Bombay had a national network of distribution, Bombay cinema emerged as a contender for the unofficial status of national cinema, heralding the future Bollywood. In India throughout the Cold War era, the dominance of Hindi cinema was threatened only in the south, with the Tamil industry fashioning its own distinct form, style, and stars, closely followed by the Telugu.[18] However, the turbulent political climate of the Tamil film industry—a radical Dravidian political ideology, for example, was popularized through films like *Parasakthi* (Goddess Parasakthi, 1952) and *Avvaiyar* (1953, based on the life of the titular poet-saint)—largely remained unknown to viewers elsewhere in India, due to the lack of a national network of distribution for regional cinemas. Similarly, popular films and stars from the Bengali cinema produced in Calcutta, including a plethora of films starring Uttam Kumar and Suchitra Sen, were screened only in the state of West Bengal. Stars from Calcutta and Madras received national attention only when they worked in a Hindi film produced in Bombay. The cream of the cultural crop of pan-Indian popular cinema was the nationalist social genre, ranging from *Awaara* and *Shree 420* to *Naya Daur* (New Era, 1957) and *Kala Bazaar*, interspersed with melancholic melodramas such as *Pyaasa* and *Devdas* (1955). The nationalist social form, buoyed possibly by an initial postcolonial enthusiasm for dialogue with the nation-state, had exhausted itself by the early 1960s, necessitating a redefinition of film aesthetics and appearance.[19] The motifs from the nationalist social form and the older reformist social form were liminalized, leading to the dominance of romance, mystery, and narratives of private aspirations in the plots, which were couched in intensified melodrama and accentuated background and playback music.

Love stories in a traditional comic vein (in which an inherent social order is reestablished after a brief youthful rebellion) were not new to the 1960s. In the

1950s, however, they were frequently integrated into the social genre, whose narrative logic was broadly derived from the modern Indian novel.[20] In the 1960s, the traditional comic trope of mainstream cinematic narratives retained the melodramatic elements while losing the reformist or nationalist elements that gave plots their coherence and narrative logic. This resulted in the continued regressive characterization of women and the dual subjugation of the romantic couple's private life by patriarchy and the nation-state. The social order of a 1960s film, such as *An Evening in Paris* (1967), comprised "filial and fraternal ties, piety and reverence, purity of character and 'clean' love. Most extol virtues which are enshrined in tradition and preach the nobility of suffering."[21]

Kati Patang (The Torn Kite, 1970), a film that encapsulates the 1960s romance and mystery genre, is a perfect example. Madhu, a young urban middle-class woman, runs away on the day of her arranged marriage, only to discover that the lover with whom she planned to elope is a fraud who was only interested in her for her family inheritance. A desolate Madhu boards a train and meets a widowed childhood friend who, along with her young child, is on her way to meet her husband's family for the first time. An accident derails the train, killing the friend, and Madhu assumes the friend's identity and begins living in her father-in-law's house. She fortuitously meets a young man and falls in love, only to discover that he was the groom with whom her marriage was arranged. Her lover reappears in her life to blackmail her, and after several intriguing turns of plot the crisis is resolved. Madhu is united with Kamal, whom she was "destined" to marry. Apart from the simplistic reaffirmation of the idea of an "arranged" and therefore socially sanctioned marriage, the film projects the female protagonist as incapable of independence: she becomes a "torn kite" when she steps out of the marriage transaction between her family and her future husband, and she can be redeemed only by restoring that transaction. The title song sung by Lata Mangeshkar—which received the Filmfare Award for the best film song—explicates the "rightful" passage of a woman's life from her father's family to her husband's and quite literally presents the romantic core of the film through the foil of the social order. It is important to remember that there is nothing particularly Indian about the general codification of this social order. Ajanta Sircar has used Michel Foucault's argument effectively to explain how the normative modalities of pre-global Indian cinema reflected post-Enlightenment Europe's formulation of the nuclear family. As Sircar explains, not only did this formulation mean "a new ordering of sexual practices into the general currency of profit and productivity that marked the bourgeois enterprise, but it also signified a change in the nature of power itself—a new form of power that was at the same time individualizing as well as totalizing in nature. . . . While realism is ideologically geared to reproduce 'free' contracting individuals, as a narrative form, melodrama foregrounds the fact that women (as well as other subaltern groups) were not signatories to the fictive social contract."[22]

What was the production logic behind the absurd plot and regressive ideology of films such as *Kati Patang*? Not everyone in the film industry was oblivious to the tenuousness of the "social order" that melodrama repeatedly produced. K. A. Abbas, who began his career in the Indian People's Theatre Association—an avowedly leftist organization—and went on to write the screenplays of a wide range of successful films, from *Shree 420* to *Bobby* (1973), had complained, as early as 1955, about the surprising disconnect between modern Indian literature and the equivalent commercial cinema. "How many producers," he asked, "have seriously sought story material from the classical and contemporary literature of our country? . . . In our fifteen major languages, every year an aggregate of hundreds of novels and thousands of short stories are published, and at least dozens of plays are staged. Are we convinced that not even some of them would make worthwhile films?" Abbas's general remark about the state of core stories in the commercial film industry was remarkably accurate not only for the 1950s but for decades to come. Abbas went on to describe most films as devoid of "stories worth mentioning" because they were essentially one of the following: "(1) plagiarized from foreign books, if not outright from foreign films; (2) remakes of old films, transplanted from one language to another, or even re-made in the same language with just a change of cast, or (3) based on well-known legends of mythology or folk-lore. A film with an original new story has come to be regarded as an exception to the rule."[23] In claiming this, Abbas was speaking at the 1955 seminar organized by the Sangeet Natak Akademi (discussed in chapter 2), and his observations were followed by Probodh Kumar Sanyal's response that provided a slightly wider perspective on the problem. Accepting Abbas's critique and agreeable to the idea of writers collaborating and striving hard to "to take the film art out of the present 'groove' and devise methods jointly to improve production standards," Sanyal had drawn attention to the plight of "script-writers and playwrights, who work under a nerve-racking economic strain," as having "little scope to function effectively to influence the course of events in the industry, [their] activity being confined to producing 'only what is marketable.'" It was not uncommon, Sanyal pointed out, for stories to be rewritten several times to meet the producer's demands, of which the only focus was ensuring the film would be a "hit" at the box office.[24]

All criticism of Indian cinema's reliance on formula—whether of formulaic narrative, formulaic acting, formulaic expectations, or formulaic marketing—points to a lack in the other(s) and therefore results in a circular argument between the industry and the government. This is where we must incorporate into our discussion the crucial element that held together the "social order" of tenuous plots such as *Kati Patang's*: music. The formulaic narrative and characters were perfectly matched with the playback music. By 1960, a system of integrating songs into the film was firmly in place. The 1957 capitulation of All India Radio in the face of the overwhelming popularity of Hindi film music had led to the inauguration of Vividh Bharati, a separate channel for film music and other "light" music programs.[25] Production of film music (and most other music in India), in spite of the ad hoc financing practices of the film business, was under the control of the giant corporation Gramophone Company of India, which played a role in setting the tone for commercial standardization of songs, as well as in setting the limits on style, via a small group of singers—"elects" made powerful by their association with Gramophone's virtual market monopoly. In her book on Hindi film songs, Anna Morcom has offered a lucid explanation of the almost total control the film industry had for decades on popular music in India. Even though a "musical and lyric tradition can be traced in film song that is to some extent independent of cinema," the production process of film songs as well as that process's place in the overall economy of film production was crucial in determining the cultural life of such songs:

> The first thing that links the making of the music with the production of the film is the fact that the making of the songs is paid for by the film producer, who is also the producer of Hindi film songs. The film producer pays for the making of the entire film including the songs (often borrowing money from a financier), and pays all the people working in the film. . . . Next in the hierarchy is the director, who is hired by the producer to carry out and oversee the artistic side of the filmmaking. . . . The director controls the artistic side of the filmmaking, including the making of the songs: although music specialists and poets are hired to write the music and lyric of songs, they are answerable to the director and ultimately to the producer. . . . Whilst music directors may choose lyricists, lyricists rarely choose music directors, reflecting their overall lower status on the whole. It also reflects the importance given to music in Hindi films. The credits of a Hindi film present the stars' and the producer's names first and last, respectively, giving them both the highest importance. The director's name is given second to last, the music director's before the director's and the lyricist's before the music director's, giving a clear hierarchy.[26]

Until the end of the 1980s, the lyricists of Hindi cinema were Urdu or Hindi poets who were well-known to poetry readers in those two languages. Despite their low status within the filmmaking hierarchy, they found in film music the economic respite they needed to pursue poetry despite its lack of profitability. "Hindi film lyrics have drawn mostly on the Urdu poetic tradition, and also on various Hindi folk and devotional poetry," Morcom notes.[27] Even after the emergence of professional "songwriters," Hindi film lyrics continued to "draw heavily on the imagery and vocabulary of Urdu poetry for a language of emotions and love."[28] Similarly, music direction for Hindi cinema would help sustain the otherwise poorly paid original composers and innovators. Between 1952 and 1957, when Hindi film songs were broadcast regularly on Radio Ceylon's weekly program *Binaca Geet Mala*, music directors' fees started to be determined according to their placement on that show.[29] Despite the fact that music was ensconced within the tight hierarchy of film production, nowhere else did the music director and the playback singers figure so prominently in the production planning of a film as they did in Indian cinema of the 1960s. The best-known playback singers were "as much sought after by the producers as the stars," and "the stars, the music director and the playback singer account[ed] for nearly half the budget of the all-India Hindi film."[30]

The playback music that in the 1930s sealed the market for Indian cinema from foreign competition came to play an important role in the formulaic social form in postcolonial Indian cinema, especially in the 1960s. Kironmoy Raha, in Gaston Roberge's edited volume—one of the earliest texts on cinema for Indian media students—mentioned "songs" as the second constant (after "stars") in the Indian formula: "The Hindi film succeeded in evolving a kind of music which answered the pull of its broadest center. Borrowing liberally from many sources and with musical arrangements, the film song with its lilting and oversentimentalised tunes has become the new folk music of the people."[31] The name of one particular singer—Lata Mangeshkar—has been used as a synecdoche for the film music industry:

> It would appear that Lata's stylistic innovation offered a viable solution to the . . . problem of representation in the public sphere: at the same time that women's bodies became visible in public spaces via films, their presence was "thinned" through the expressive timbre granted them. The heroines for whom Lata provided the singing voice may well have been prancing around hill-sides and streets while performing a song-sequence, but this gesture[,] which otherwise threatened male dominance of these spaces, was domesticated through the timbre, tonality and stylistic stricture that marked that presence. The potentially powerful image of the heroine enjoying the freedom of the public space in equal measure to the male hero and singing

in a voice that may express an ambiguous femininity was, through Lata's voice, undermined.[32]

Lata Mangeshkar's voice offered restraint: one style delivered to perfection. That style became *heimlich* through repetition, thus also taming the *unheimlich* aspect of limitless perfection.[33] The final product was uniformity sold primarily by one recording company. No other decade fell under the spell of this uniformity more than the 1960s.

Most studies on Indian film music focus on songs. However, the use of background music began to be used broadly in all-India films in the 1960s, highlighting emotions and melodrama in broad strokes. Mainstream Indian cinema inherited the use of indiscriminate, mostly loud music from the various forms of Indian theater that had already mixed styles and instruments across traditions. According to the auteur Shyam Benegal, the arrival of sound in Indian cinema ended the "stylistic development in the silent film" and the "organic evolution of the cinema," as "cinema took its entire form from the urban theatre."[34] Benegal interpreted cinema's wholehearted adaptation of the largely melodramatic, complete entertainment packages of hybrid urban theater as the "traditionalisation of the Indian cinema." This "traditional cinema, which started with the talkies," did not merely "take the narrative alone from the theatre, it took the dialogue and its rendition, the relationships between people and their characterisations, including the concepts of good and evil."[35]

It is therefore not surprising to find a completely different philosophy of music in Indian "art cinema." Satyajit Ray maintained that his knowledge of classical Western forms gave him an advantage in his compositions, cinema being a "composition bound by time." The way Ray outlined the relationship between cinema and music is useful in understanding why a "pure" Indian cinematic form of music is difficult to create:

> Cinema is a medium which is closer to Western music than to Indian music because in Indian tradition, the concept of flexible time does not exist. Our music is improvised, one piece of music can last one hour, two hours, one-fourth of an hour. It is nothing which resembles a sonata or a symphony with a beginning and an end, irrespective of who the conductor is. There might be a minute of difference in the pace of the music, but it is the same model and it has to have a specific duration. The concept of a piece of music lasting twenty-five minutes, for example, does not exist in India. There are no "compositions"—the duration is flexible and depends on the mood of the musician.[36]

B. V. Karanth, who acknowledged the influence of Satyajit Ray on his work and would create innovative soundtracks for art house films—Girish Kasaravalli's *Ghatashraddha* (The Ritual, 1977) and Mrinal Sen's *Ek Din Pratidin* (And Quiet Rolls the Dawn, 1979) and *Parashuram* (The Man with the Ax, 1979), among others—emphasized the importance of silences and pauses. Rejecting traditional musical interpretations of moods, such as "wailing violins to underline tragic moments," Karanth would use unusual objects and reproductions of natural sounds. Karanth insisted on a "detailed sound scenario," and not just of music. "Placing the spoken words (dialogues) at the apex one should meticulously work out," he believed, the "use (or blending) of other sounds—including the music. Music, as is known generally, would form only ten per cent of the total sound scenario."[37]

Critical Discourses: Our Films, Their Films, and the "All-India Film"

Music and melodrama—the core of Hindi cinema in the 1960s—became markers for the path to avoid for makers of art house cinema such as Satyajit Ray, Shyam Benegal, Mrinal Sen, and Adoor Gopalakrishnan. However, the rift between popular and art house cinema was contingent upon a variety of other issues, which began to be explored in both official and critical discourses on Indian cinemas in the 1960s. The 1960s did not see a rift just between popular and art cinema; it also saw most Hindi genres diverge from regional cultural roots, while distinct viewerships emerged for Hindi, regional, and imported films. Outside of the industry-government binary, critics struggled to grasp the unruly implosion of melodramas that were as disconnected from any Indian reality as they were from global cinematic traditions. Other than filmmakers who wrote extensively on cinema, such as Satyajit Ray and Mrinal Sen, critics were either academics with degrees in humanities or journalists with a discerning eye trained on the interaction between cinema and the sociopolitical environment. One of the earliest analyses of Hindi cinema's national stereotyping appeared in the critical writings of Chidananda Dasgupta, who along with Satyajit Ray had founded India's first film society in 1947. Dasgupta's reading of the Hindi national cinematic form appeared in an article from 1969 called "Indian Cinema Today." Channeling an elite high-modernist attitude toward cinema, Dasgupta nevertheless offered a coherent analysis of what he called the "all-India film":

> The basic ingredients in the all-India film . . . comprise not only an operatic assembly of all possible spectacles, sentiments, melodrama, music and

dancing, but a mix of these calculated to appeal to the righteous inertia of the audience. In the absence of any other explanation of technological phenomena, it is the Hindi film which holds forth: "Look at the Twentieth Century, full of night clubs and drinking, smoking, bikini-clad women sinfully enjoying themselves in fast cars and mixed parties; how right you are in condemning them—in the end everyone must go back to the traditional patterns of devotion to God, to parents, to village life, or be damned forever." This answer does not try to explain, it merely echoes the natural fear which traditional people have of anything new, anything that they do not understand. The films thus give reassurance to the "family audience" which is the mainstay of the film industry. . . . The all-India film thus paradoxically becomes the most effective obstacle against the development of a positive attitude towards technological progress, towards a synthesis of tradition with modernity for a future pattern of living.[38]

Dasgupta's nomenclature for the film formula was inescapably reminiscent of All India Radio, the sole radio-programming body in India. All India Radio was a cultural apparatus fashioned by Nehruvian policy to impose from above a different sort of national culture. The 1969 article is clearly appreciative of the Nehruvian mode of progress and development. For it, the "all-India film" is an aberration, a grotesque parody of any "national" idea that All India Radio was based upon. The necessity to deliver a pan-Indian national stereotype justified Bombay's drive to produce the all-India film from the mid-1950s onward, when Bombay's Hindi cinema had ceased to cater to just its Hindi-speaking regional market, which by itself was of enviable size. Beyond the Hindi-speaking areas, Hindi cinema succeeded in capturing a broad base of viewers by "relentlessly working on the formula in endless permutations and combinations, pressing into service the technical improvements and innovation in the mechanics of film production."[39] In a direct reversal of the Nehruvian nation-statist dream, technical advancement in the case of cinema caused regression of ideas, not progress.

Notice the paradox: technically improved, prolific film production that was at the same time characterized by aesthetic poverty and ideological regression. That paradox was tied to the production conditions of the all-India film. In the early decades of the twentieth century, technical improvements and innovations had had a positive influence on all cinemas, and Indian cinema was no exception. The advent of sound, after all, was the catalyst for Indian cinema to emerge as a competitor against Hollywood's imports in the 1930s. But in the perhaps solitary case of the all-India film, where the limits were established by a stagnant pool of stars and producers, improvements became manifested in spectacles such as "in the form of shooting in exotic locations or in the form of extravagant costume pageantry."[40] This was particularly the case when color became the norm in the mid-1960s, as Indian filmmakers had to depend on imported Kodak color stock. As if to live up to the cost of the new medium, color became ubiquitous. The combined expense of color stock, extravagant costumes and sets, and exotic locations had a singular effect on the quality of films. Instead of the creation of different paradigms, technology intensified the "assemblage" nature of the all-India film, for the entertainment of the entire family, anywhere in India. The "family film," as this all-around assemblage came to be called, became the "safest bet" for producers.[41] All narrative and emotional elements, irrespective of the genre, had to be presented in a deliberate pageantry. The other unusual corollary of the availability of equipment was the rise of low-budget action films for the rural audience in the North Indian Hindi belt, a topic that has been discussed by Valentina Vitali in her work on action cinema.[42] Dara Singh, the wrestler, was the lead actor in such films as *King Kong* (1962), *Faulad* (Steel, 1963), and *Aaya Toofan* (Storm Arrives, 1964), which were marketed in the rural areas, often via the traveling cinemas.

The social history and the chronology of the "family film" and the selectively marketed "action film" direct us to the first-ever divisions of viewership in India. The 1960s was the first decade in which the market for cinema got compartmentalized according to viewer tastes and preferences in a consistent manner. While abstract notions such as public taste and popular demand recurred in the popular news media and political discourses about cinema, there is little or no hard data after the Patil Committee report to formulate a sound theory of film consumption. The only way to access the interface between production and consumption is via the work of contemporary critics, such as Kobita Sarkar, who offers qualitative analysis. In her collection of essays titled *Indian Cinema Today*, Sarkar describes the crystallization of the national market into four compartments, paraphrased as follows:

- Group One consists of "those who restrict themselves almost exclusively to American or foreign films (but not the Film Society type of foreign film)." They "might occasionally patronize the acknowledged classics, like the films of Satyajit Ray," but "they manage to ignore the mainstream of Indian cinema quite happily." This group is mostly urban.
- Group Two, consisting of "both urban and rural spectators," is the "largest section" of the national viewership. "It restricts itself to the Indian film—essentially the Hindi film. Once in a blue moon they might go to a regional or foreign language film."

- Group Three "restricts itself solely to the regional cinema, and may condescend to see a Hindi film very rarely." This group may be both rural and urban but consists more of older viewers than school or college students.
- Group Four is the "film society going audience which, though not numerically significant [in the 1960s], is likely to be the nucleus of the potential Art Theatre audience" (predicated upon the systematic growth of such an audience in the possible future). Those in this segment are "important" if only because of the "snobbery that prevails in them." "They would prefer to see a third-rate film with subtitles, rather than the best of their own cinema—except perhaps Satyajit Ray."[43]

Beyond the four major groups, Sarkar notes the existence of a fifth group—consisting of a small minority—"that patronises all types of films to a moderate degree, with their own special preferences and private ratings." Despite the small size of this group, Sarkar considered it possibly the most influential, assuming this group's "catholicity of taste becoming more widespread" in the future as "the only hope for the general improvement of the cinema." Supposing that Groups One, Three, and Four are more or less set in their viewing habits and expectations and are not going to be swayed en masse by a different kind of cinema outside their viewing circle, Sarkar approaches Group Two—the largest, consuming mostly the all-India film—with limited optimism, verging in tone on the sarcastic: "It is possible that they have long had a sneaking suspicion that the world presented by the Hindi cinema does not exist. But having been initiated into it, and doped consistently over a period of time with it, it has become standard 'entertainment.'"[44]

Film criticism from the 1960s and 1970s offers a rare window into the formation of the discourse of popular versus art cinema. In the aftermath of Indian cinema's induction into cinema and media studies curricula and scholarship on a global scale in the 1980s, a complementary set of theoretical formulations has emerged to form a coherent critique of and context to the mainstream Indian cinematic form. These formulations, though recognizable as ideological descendants of Chidananda Dasgupta's "all-India film," have the advantage of looking back at the classical form of Indian cinema from a radically changed, post-global perspective. Two of the most significant formulations in 1990s Indian film studies are "epic melodrama" and "feudal family romance," coined in 1993 by Ashish Rajadhyaksha and Madhava Prasad respectively. According to Rajadhyaksha, the downward slide of commercial cinema began in the World War II era with the fall of the studios and the subsequent rise of the star system.[45] Rajadhyaksha's theory of the dominant form of Indian popular cinema was premised on Indian cinema's various negotiations with the idea of realism. Realism was in itself an imported idea, in literature as it was in cinema. In Indian cinema it led to the most significant change: "the shift from the reformist social" genre into "an idiom of melodrama." "Epic melodrama," according to Rajadhyaksha, "not only provided the most propitious space for handling the realist initiative" but came to exist in perfect harmony with the star-centric system of production.[46] Epic melodrama was not an isolated phenomenon and not even the offshoot of a particular section of the industry, a fact that makes Dasgupta's formulation of "all-India film" all the more relevant. Rajadhyaksha traces the evolution of epic melodrama through the 1940s and 1950s in all regional cinemas but emphasizes the fact that once the hold of melodrama was established, Bombay-based Hindi cinema became its best medium.[47]

Madhava Prasad named the dominant melodramatic form "feudal family romance," describing it as a compromise between the progressive ideology of the nation-state and the regressive vestiges of premodern society. This is what explained the "prohibition of scenes of kissing" as an "unwritten rule" in Indian censorship. The unwritten ban on kissing, Prasad argued, had less to do with sexuality and more with a nationalist politics of culture.[48]

> The most frequent justification of this informal prohibition has been that it corresponds to the need to maintain the Indianness of Indian culture, to which kissing—described as a sign of westernness—is alien. In keeping with the logic of this justification, this principle has never been applied in the censorship of foreign films. Further, there has been the occasional Indian film (often shot abroad), in which the Indian characters have to observe the ban while "foreign" couples—usually white—who appear in the background are allowed to break the rule (Raj Kapoor's 1964 film *Sangam* is a good example).[49]

According to Prasad, a consensual ideology has always guided popular cinema as a national institution. The unofficial prohibition on kissing is directed against "representation of the private" sphere. The kiss between a couple that "inaugurates a zone of privacy, thereby dissolving all other intermediate claims to authority over the family except that of the state, is the very same kiss whose representation is prohibited on the Indian screen, between Indian citizens."[50] While the private zone presupposes the kissing couple making up a nuclear family as defined by post-Enlightenment modernity, that modernity is yet to be realized in India's postcolonial consensual ideology. The nuclear family is caught in the gravitational holds of several premodern authorities, almost all of them patriarchal. This pull of premodern regressive authorities was discussed in the 1970s by Gaston Roberge, who found them imparting to the narratives in the films a kind of entropy. This entropy, according to Roberge, was endemic to Indian commercial cinema:

> Commercial entertainment in any case is inherently entropic, opposed to change. The Indian cinema is specially so. By perpetuating a system of conditioned response to formulae the industry has developed in-built devices for resisting change. Indian cinema in consequence is obscurantist and opposed to change as few national cinemas are. The only aim seems to be to uphold values of a traditional society. However preposterous and absurd the plot, however contrived the situations, no Hindi film dares offend the social and moral codes enshrined in tradition. The characters may drive fast cars and live in gadget-loaded apartments, they may follow the latest fashion in dress and drinking etiquette but never will they question in behaviour or action the age-old tenets of Hindu society.[51]

What is this "tradition" and what are the cultural values—or social and moral codes—that are presumed enshrined in the hearts and minds of Indians in the 1960s? Drawing upon our discussion of *Kati Patang* earlier in this chapter, it is not easy to find an answer to such a question outside the ingenuous delineations of culture that commercial cinema produced and reproduced over the years. By virtue of being the medium with the furthest reach, popular cinema became an echo chamber for gender stereotypes and unspoken hegemonies of caste and class.

Financing and Archive: The Benevolent Side of the Government

The restructuring of the NFDC in 1980 appeared at a time when Indian art house cinema had established itself against the popular dominant form of Bombay cinema. This was supposed to be the government's endgame, the final indictment of Bombay cinema. Let us explore the ways in which the government had been creating a confrontation between commercial and art house cinemas. The nurture of a subversive and innovative "art cinema" by the otherwise rigidly bureaucratic and considerably oppressive government remains one of the many ironies in the complex history of Indian democracy. While the government exercised absolute control in its management of radio and television, it handled the financing of new Indian cinema unhurriedly. Almost a decade after the S. K. Patil Committee recommended government financing for filmmakers, the

Film Finance Corporation was inaugurated by the government on March 20, 1960. A government publication in 1965 described the corporation's functions vis-à-vis commercial cinema in paternalistic overtones:

> The main object of the Corporation is to assist the industry by providing finance at reasonable rates for raising the standard of the films produced. So, the Corporation follows the policy of financing the production of films portraying life in its true and nobler forms at 9 per cent rate of interest—reduced to 7 per cent in cases of prompt payment. There should be realism so that one may identify oneself with the characters, situations and problems projected in the films. The theme may be social, historical, cultural or even religious, but it must carry a message or purpose in a manner neither propagandist nor dull. There should also be healthy entertainment and humour.
>
> The Corporation is not trying to take on itself the role of a reformist movement in the Indian film world; it only aims at helping in the production of films that will progressively turn out to be works of art, laying stress on the lasting values of life.[52]

Notwithstanding its claim of not taking a reformist stance, the Film Finance Corporation clearly intended an intervention into the world of Indian cinema from the periphery. By subsidizing the growth of parallel and a "better" cinema, the Indian government wanted the commercial filmmakers to learn from examples. The dynamic that resulted from this influx of governmental funds was far from predictable. Mrinal Sen, one of India's pioneer parallel filmmakers who benefited from government funding, provided a nuanced interpretation of the dynamic in his book *Views on Cinema*. He had received funding in 1969 to make his first Hindi feature, *Bhuvan Shome*. A low-budget film shot largely on location, it received the national award for the best feature film. The significance of the fine balance that *Bhuvan Shome* managed to strike between artistic integrity and reasonable success at the box office (enough to recoup the government funding) was not lost on Sen. A persistent reproduction of such cinema on a national scale would be impossible to achieve, he understood. The promise of consistent state funding—which encouraged films such as *Bhuvan Shome*—drew inspiration from the international success of Satyajit Ray's *Pather Panchali* in 1955, as the seemingly impossible task of making films outside of the commercial circuit suddenly appeared possible. Sen recalled a short-lived enthusiasm among a section of distributors for a new kind of cinema that he presumed consisted of

1. productions of unusual type with no big star, no glamour, done mostly with the non-professionals,

2. productions budgeted very low,

3. productions which are filmed mostly outside the studios, on suitable locations,

4. productions which, structurally, mix up the creative treatment of actuality and fiction,

5. and finally productions which are run by young enthusiasts—freshers . . . who, while shooting on location, wouldn't care for princely living or for special treatment and who, throughout their uninhibited performance as members of the unit, would build wonderful rapport and collective spirit among themselves.[53]

All these were, more or less, the essential features evident in the unit that made *Pather Panchali*. All these, to take a glimpse of the world cinema, were found in large measure among the New Wave workers of the French cinema.

What Sen posits above departs from the star-centric model of production that mainstream Indian cinema was entrenched in, without returning to the studio model, either. He advocated a leftist-liberal position on filmmaking that became possible only with support from the FFC. Counting on the gradual growth of the spectatorship of noncommercial films, Sen called upon the iconoclastic directors to deliberately impose upon a "wider audience, that is, through continuous viewings, to force them to look into films which they had earlier rejected. We have to liberate the medium. We have to prove that filmmaking should no longer be an expensive proposition."[54] Sen's commitment to parallel cinema thus had an extra-cinematic politics of defiance that took aim at the big-budget, all-India film. To make low-budget films for Sen was an act against the establishment, that is, the clique of private producers and directors in Bombay.[55]

The establishment did not fail to take notice. Writing in 1981, B. R. Chopra—an influential director, producer, and member of one of the film-producing "dynasties" in Bombay—blamed the lack of integration in Indian cinema on the state's belligerent attitude toward commercial cinema. From Chopra's viewpoint, "back-breaking taxation" and promotion of art cinema were punitive toward commercial filmmakers and rewarding for the government's chosen few:

When we put this question to politicians and ministers, they have a ready answer, "you make bad pictures." With a view to teaching us how to make good pictures, the Government of India set up a financing wing, (FFC, and now NFDC) to promote talent and quality pictures. How far they have succeeded in their mission is something on which I won't comment.

Perhaps the Government feels that the only way to improve the quality of films is to load producers with taxation, so that they will either die or leave the profession, making way for those chosen by the Government to make movies at its expense.[56]

What Chopra refused to recognize was that through decades of social and political turmoil, "Indian cinema remained within remarkably narrow parameters."[57] Iqbal Masud, writing in the same year, pointed to the exhaustion of the commercial genres irrespective of government intervention into moviemaking. According to Masud, long before the establishment of the FFC or what Chopra interprets as the government's war on the industry, films such as Bimal Roy's *Do Bigha Zamin* and Satyajit Ray's *Pather Panchali* had "signalled the end of the monopoly of the Devotional-Historical-Social Syndrome."[58] Even as a revised theoretical approach to filmmaking and subsequently revised techniques were born, Masud noted, it was eventually the sociopolitical reality of a postcolonial nation-state that had outgrown its illusions that was a contributing factor in the growth of art cinema, or New Cinema, which was the name of choice for Mrinal Sen and Mani Kaul, who published a joint manifesto in 1968. In Masud's words,

> The *Pax Nehruviana*—the fairly stable holding-together structure in a subcontinent with a maze of religions and a babble of tongues—which had prevailed since 1947 was drawing to a close. Industrial growth had been fair but population increase was negating the gains. Land feudalism had not been liquidated and the income gap was widening. The Chinese invasion in 1962 was a massive jolt to the national ego. Suddenly it seemed the centre could not hold, the old certainties had gone. It was time for films "to begin an ideological debate with the cultures that bred them." It was time for the New Cinema.[59]

In 1960, the Film Institute of India was established by the Ministry of Information and Broadcasting in Pune on the premises of Prabhat Studios, which had ceased production in 1953. It was renamed the Film and Television Institute of India when it merged with the Television Training Centre, set up in 1971. The Film and Television Institute, offering courses in all aspects of filmmaking, was made into an autonomous body in 1974. An interesting dynamic existed between the institute's curriculum and the Indian film industry. When the Film Institute began admitting students in the 1960s, "entertainment came to be accepted as the prime purpose of cinema and fiction film; therefore, it got a disproportionately large amount of attention in the curriculum of the Film Institute."[60] N. K. Murthy, who was the director of the institute in 1981, has written of the students' interest in learning the technique for "picturization" of songs, as "song sequences had become an essential part of any successful film."[61] In the late 1960s and the early 1970s, students specializing in editing and direction were trained according to aesthetic standards that differed from the industry norm at that time. This was made possible through the institute's access to the National Film Archives' collection of foreign films the likes of which the students would not have been able to watch otherwise. The exposure to and training in an international model initially created a problem with immediate marketability of technical creative skills acquired at the institute. According to Murthy, while students specializing in editing and cinematography found employment, those with expertise in direction and screenplay-writing found it difficult to break through the tight-knit, informal boundaries that protected the star-centric system.[62] The trend changed only when the FFC and the various state film development corporations began facilitating art cinema, "thus allowing experimentation with techniques and application of the advanced training that the students received at the Institute."[63] It was the government's intervention, therefore, that created a favorable atmosphere for making non-mainstream films with no star actors, lighter equipment, outdoor shooting, and compact and professional crews. In a feedback loop, the institute designed its subsequent programs to cater to this parallel system of production.[64]

The FFC and the Film Institute can be read as the government's way of ensuring what it considered a worthy future for Indian cinema. The creation of the National Film Archives, inaugurated in 1964, was the complementary act of honoring the past of an industry used to the government's indifference or disavowal. The need for a "film library" was discussed in seminars and the media in the 1950s, as Indian cinema's initiation into the world of festivals and awards in India and abroad created an urgency to preserve the past of Indian cinema for posterity. With the institution of the National Film Awards in 1954, the government seemed cautiously appreciative of cinema. Inaugurating the film seminar in 1955, Jawaharlal Nehru had acknowledged the producers who "built up this huge industry" from scratch and "undoubtedly produced from time to time very notable films."[65] Between 1956 and 1964, a National Film Library grew from a small collection donated by private citizens to an official body holding copies of all films in the festival circuit.[66] The proposal to transform the National Film Library into the National Film Archives of India was approved by the Ministry of Information and Broadcasting in 1961. The archive was finally opened in 1964 under the management of the Film Institute in Pune; it became separated from the institute in 1967 and has remained such. Instituted more than three decades after the silent era ended, the archive has found it challenging to acquire copies of silent films and early talkies. An unrecoverable lacuna thus exists in the history of early Indian cinema, something that is insufficiently compensated for with writings and reports on lost films.

Government, Media, and the Emergency (1975–1977): The Dark Side

Indira Gandhi, daughter and political protégée of Jawaharlal Nehru, bypassed senior leaders of the Congress Party to become the third prime minister of India in 1966. Impatient with the democratic process, she rigged elections, promoted her son, and ruled the country with the help of a close-knit group of followers. She orchestrated the only lapse in Indian democracy, in the form of emergency rule, for the purpose of escaping deposition and a prison sentence for rigging the 1971 election. Although Indira abused the rhetoric of the "secular socialist state" during the Emergency, she had been a genuinely progressive strategist briefly in the 1960s in her capacity as minister of information. As the new minister of information and broadcasting in 1964, she introduced consultants and specialists to modernize media and programming. A committee was appointed under Asok Chanda, a former auditor-general of India, and by the time the Chanda Committee presented its report in 1966, Indira was prime minister. Couched in the polite language of bureaucracy, the Chanda Committee report was a catalog of missed opportunities and misplaced efforts. "A psychological transformation is necessary," it concluded, if radio and television were to fulfill their potential to entertain and inform the people.[67] From Indira's point of view, the old guard of the Congress and the slow-moving wheel of democratic consent were a deadly combination, something that a temporary suspension of democratic processes could cure. In the 1960s, Indira seemed to anticipate her son Rajiv Gandhi's later eagerness to change things by any means necessary in the 1980s. It is difficult to say whether Indira and Rajiv were able to recognize the irony in their power stemming from birth into political privilege, or whether they stepped into the dynastic mode as easily as the children of stars did in the world of Indian popular cinema. In any case, the Chanda Committee report did not incite any change in the rigid hierarchy. Indira failed to consider "control" as antithetical to modernization and retained the government's absolute authority over radio. When commercial advertising began in 1967 with her government's approval, a code was introduced that prohibited "advertising of tobacco, liquor and gambling, including betting on horse-racing and other sports."[68]

The government's management of All India Radio would continue to be contentious through the 1970s and 1980s. The intervention of B. V. Keskar in the broadcast of Hindi film music in the 1950s (discussed in chapter 2) may well be interpreted as one episode in a long series of political and bureaucratic conflicts over India's national radio. A parallel and similar nexus of programming would emerge in the 1960s, with the formation of India's state-run television, Doordarshan, which was placed under the government-controlled financial division that oversaw All India Radio as well. The government's oversight of this financial operation was such that no funds could be withdrawn "without an Act of Parliament."[69] Such total financial control, combined with the absolute lack of freedom that the directors-general had with respect to programming, prevented both All India Radio and Doordarshan from growing into viable entertainment media. Compared to commercial cinema, which had always found itself on the wrong side of government censure, All India Radio was devoid of any and all choices, an oppressive situation that predated Indira Gandhi's regime. During the more than decade-long tenure of B. V. Keskar, Nehru's minister for information and broadcasting, political commentaries were centrally controlled, broadcast only from the capital city of New Delhi, and relayed to all local stations. Within these constraints, a financial crunch and the regulated nature of programming significantly stunted the function of All India Radio in the 1960s: "Political comments apart, even in talks on general subjects AIR did not give expression to views critical of the government or of any part of the establishment. Government instructions on what could or could not be said over the AIR were issued confidentially to SDs. Station Directors were expected to settle matters 'tactfully' with talkers and writers should they try to transgress the bounds of what was permissible."[70]

Much starker than the censorship of cinema, the perfectly visible hand of control was felt by All India Radio, and to make matters worse, boundaries were drawn arbitrarily. "Radio came to be regarded as having all the potential of word-of-mouth rumour and street-corner rabble-rousing to incite disaffection and violence," observes Robin Jeffrey.[71] It was only in 1968 that a uniform code was adopted for both radio and television. It was oppressive but at least stated in clear terms. Revised in 1970, the code was written along the lines of the 1952 Cinematograph Act:

Broadcasts on All Indian Radio by individuals will not permit:

1. criticism of friendly countries;
2. attack on religion or communities;
3. anything obscene; or defamatory;
4. incitement to violence or anything against maintenance of law and order;
5. anything amounting to contempt of court;

6. aspersions against the integrity of the President, Governors and Judiciary;
7. attack on a political party by name;
8. hostile criticism of any State or the Centre; or
9. anything showing disrespect to the Constitution or advocating change in the Constitution by violence; but advocating changes in a constitutional way should not be debarred.

This Code applies to criticism in the nature of personal tirade, either of a friendly Government or of a political party or of the Central Government or any State Government. But it does not debar references to and/or dispassionate discussion of policies pursued by any of them.[72]

While radio could be controlled and managed, cinema could not, even in terms of sheer numbers. In 1975, with 471 feature films released, India became the world's leading producer of films. It was announced as the highest point in production since the first official feature, D. G. Phalke's *Raja Harishchandra*.[73] In 1974 the Ministry of Information and Broadcasting issued an elaborate report prepared by the Estimates Committee (1973–74) that noted the "scale and extent" of the Indian film industry. Indian cinema was declared the largest filmmaking industry in the world, with an investment of Rs 180 crore ($18 billion), over 200,000 employees, and a tax contribution of Rs 70 crore ($7 billion) annually.[74] While most of the bragging rights for this hallmark went to commercial cinema, the government's Film Finance Corporation could also claim a few achievements of its own: by the early 1970s, the FFC had already funded over 50 films, including Satyajit Ray's *Charulata*, *Nayak* (1966), and *Goopy Gyne Bagha Byne* (1968). It had also played a role in the art cinema movement, beginning with the financing of Mrinal Sen's *Bhuvan Shome* and Mani Kaul's *Uski Roti*.[75]

If the formation of the FFC is considered a watershed moment in the history of Indian cinema, the dealings of the FFC have not been noncontroversial; its investment in art cinema "spoke with a forked tongue," as Rajadhyaksha has explained. Even as the FFC gave money to directors outside the industry to pursue their bold innovative projects, the funds came "under the guise of loans to 'producers,'" forcing these filmmakers to produce their own films and commit to repay the loans. In contrast with B. R. Chopra's envious portrayal of the FFC's patronage of art cinema, "the FFC marketed these films as though they were its own, pocketed all the revenues it made on its 'loan' projects, and rarely made an account to its 'producers' who often suspected that their films were earning more money for the Corporation than it would admit."[76]

Indira Gandhi's move to nationalize banks had initiated widespread anxiety about state intervention in industries, including cinema. The fear of "nationalization of the film industry" loomed primarily because of the increasing powers of the FFC. The corporation controlled distribution and export of the films it financed. By 1973–74, it became the sole agency for the import of celluloid raw stock and replaced the MPEAA as the channel for the import of foreign films to distribute within India's borders.[77] In the history of postcolonial India, while "centralized control over the film industry" was envisaged as early as 1951 in the S. K. Patil Committee report, it was only in the 1970s under Indira Gandhi that a push was made toward that direction, only for the effort to be abandoned soon afterward. In Rajadhyaksha's words, "The FFC of the early 1970s was the Indian state's last cinematic hurrah; more to the point, it was the last state intervention in the cinema to be associated with its key supporter, Indira Gandhi. . . . By the early 1980s India would entirely abandon the New Cinema in favour of a telecommunications package assembled via the Indian National Satellite System (INSAT)."[78] Such was the impasse when India's democracy experienced a meltdown. The Allahabad High Court convicted Indira Gandhi for having indulged in corrupt campaign practices and declared her 1971 election invalid. In a preemptive strike, Indira Gandhi convinced President Fakhruddin Ali Ahmed to declare an emergency and dissolve the parliament, which was done on the morning of June 26. This left her to rule by decree and exercise authority at will, outside of the normal political processes, and introduce her "twenty-point programme." Opposition leaders and workers were arrested in the thousands, and for the next twenty-one months (until March 1977, when the Emergency was abruptly lifted and elections were announced) all press and media were virtually forced to report the worldview of Indira Gandhi and her son Sanjay Gandhi as news.

From the viewpoint of Indian cinema history, the Emergency—and the way it was propagated in popular discourse—offers a fascinating parallel to the mythmaking apparatus of all-India film or epic melodrama. Historian Stanley Wolpert writes,

"India is Indira, and Indira India" was a comment made in all seriousness by one of her sycophants. Posters with the prime minister's picture sprouted everywhere, proclaiming, "She stood between Chaos and Order." "Hard work, clear vision, iron will, and strictest discipline" was the new ethic that began now to blossom on billboards and signs throughout India. "The only magic to eradicate Poverty," Indians were assured, "is hard work." The

Ministry of Information and Broadcasting worked overtime at developing slogans and pithy messages to help a new and more unified India achieve its Twenty-Point Program. "Work more, talk less," they said, and "Rumour mongering is the worst enemy."[79]

The defeat of the Congress Party in the 1977 elections that ended Indira's illusion of control would have been unthinkable a decade earlier. Things would never be the same in parliamentary elections again. From 1977 onward, notwithstanding the rhetoric of the leaders, Indian democracy ceased to be a tame idea imposed from above. Political forces clamored from all directions instead to overturn any illusion of a federalist control. In 1976, however, Indira Gandhi communicated her personal opinion on popular cinema in a meeting with state ministers of information: "I am sorry to say that the majority of films exhibit violence and crudity. . . . They give a stereotyped interpretation of life, generally degrading women and our society as a whole, lauding superstitious beliefs and portraying goodness, if not stupidity, at least as dimness of mind. . . . It is true that in the end virtue triumphs, but that is not sufficient to wipe out the impact of two hours or more of continuous vice, crime and violence. The morality at the end is only a cloak."[80]

Directors of All India Radio were told by Indira Gandhi on September 9, 1975, that "while anybody is in government service, they are bound to obey the orders of the government. If they feel that the government policy is not right, they are unable to obey, [or] they have some other views which they want to express, nobody is stopping them from resigning and joining any organization where they will have that freedom."[81] Given that All India Radio was the only broadcasting agency in India, the choice that its employees faced was only theoretical, and thus no new code or set of rules was necessary for implementing direct orders from the government. The film magazines, operated and owned by private companies, were issued a code that instructed them to avoid reporting any news or commentary that was not for the greater good. In Aruna Vasudev's account, "For the remainder of the Emergency period journals would not comment on[,] or even mention, films that were refused certificates by the Censor Board, or make any reference to difficulties faced by individual producers or actors as a result of government orders."[82] Contradictions abound in the history of both Indian politics and Indian cinema of the 1970s. The tumultuous political events of the 1970s include the Bangladesh War (1971) between India and Pakistan, various dissenting movements in India during the early years of the decade, the dissolution of the government and the declaration of the Emergency in 1975, and through all these, the rise and fall of the autodidact Indira Gandhi (1971–77). In the middle of these political upheavals and erosion of civil liberties, there was infusion of funds into art house cinema by a proactive government, via the National Film Development Corporation. Apart from the federal government, several state governments continued to provide assistance or subsidies to filmmakers, and art cinema—as described earlier—remained well and alive through the 1970s. The somewhat inexplicable official support for a cinema that was almost always critical of the system led to the further meandering of the commercial film industry from the state's ideal of cinema. Writing on the government's largely positive though complicated engagement with art cinema or Indian New Cinema, Ashish Rajadhyaksha argues that the link between "the state support of independent cinema and the vicious disciplining of the mainstream film industry" was indicative of "a national project around media control gone badly wrong."[83]

The failure of the Indian national project(s) around media control is not necessarily peculiar to this decade, and the biggest difficulty one encounters in discussing media control in India is the fact that it has always existed in a somewhat inconsistent manner. But earlier, that kind of inconsistency was more symptomatic of big government and an apathetic bureaucracy than of malicious and repressive control from above. Indian government had never really favored the unofficial industry that Indian commercial cinema had grown into. During the twenty-one months of the Emergency, the industry came under direct attack on several different fronts and was in general constantly subjected to "a series of arbitrary orders which were issued with little or no warning, keeping producers, distributors, and exhibitors in a permanent state of suspense."[84] Censor boards were sent new instructions, the producers were temporarily made to broadcast their films on television before their release in the theaters, and film publicity materials as well as journals and fanzines were subjected to strict censorship. Given the limited reach of the television network and the paucity of television sets on a national scale, these policies were like experiments of media control with long-term results and applications rather than immediate outcomes. The control of visual media, especially the television, in the 1980s was far more organized and effective than national radio in the 1950s and 1960s. All that was tested and tried during and around the Emergency months in the 1970s came back to be implemented and applied later in the 1980s and beyond.

Cinema of the People: Anger, Amitabh Bachchan, and the Persistence of Melodrama

The political turbulence of the 1970s became the backdrop for a sea change in Bombay's Hindi cinema. The change was comparable in magnitude to both the

129

ascendance of the Indian talkies over imports in the 1930s and the rise of the star-centric system over the studios in the 1940s. The shift came in the form of normalization of anger and physical violence, the vehicle for which was the male protagonist, played in a series of films by a newcomer actor named Amitabh Bachchan. The new paradigm for the male hero resonated with an expanding market for entertainment, fueled by the rise in the urban industrial migrant population that could turn to cinema as the only mode of affordable entertainment. A shift in viewership thus corresponded with the new anti-elite heroism that came to replace the supremacy of the social genre in Hindi cinema.

The impulse for a remaking of the (male) citizen's relationship with the nation-state and its laws came from 1950s British realism that flowed into the British New Cinema of the 1960s, such as John Osborne's play *Look Back in Anger* (1956) and Lindsay Anderson's *If. . .* (1968). Anderson, who retrospectively called the term "angry young man" as one of the most successful journalistic terms in history, identified in the concept "a feeling of the New Left, of a kind of social democratic left, a kind of unifying feeling between people who wanted to change things, and who therefore by definition were 'angry' with the past, with the rigid traditionalism of the class structure."[85] A recent volume by Praseeda Gopinath has complicated the anti-hegemonic masculinity of the "angry young man" by reading in it a post-gentleman strand, since these characters "come after the Victorian/Edwardian gentleman even as they remake the traits of the gentleman that they mock and repudiate."[86]

In the Indian context, the trope of the post-gentleman was transposed on the post-Nehruvian middle-class male who was incapacitated but not angered by the circumstances. The first film featuring Amitabh Bachchan as the "angry young male" protagonist was 1973's *Zanjeer*. And in 1975, the year that Indira Gandhi dissolved the parliament and declared an emergency, the disenchanted angry hero was established as a trope in *Sholay*. *Sholay* was a tableau Western shot in 35 mm, which was then converted into 70 mm, as the producers wanted to create the kind of effect they had seen in *McKenna's Gold* (1969), which was widely popular in India. The length of the movie, three and a half hours, was an anomaly that required modification of the theaters' usual three-hour slots, but as the sales picked up after the initial few weeks, the film became an all-time blockbuster. In the same year, *Deewar* was released, with Amitabh Bachchan playing the role of a poor disenfranchised boy growing up to be a wealthy smuggler, eventually getting killed by his brother who stays on the straight and narrow path and becomes a police officer.

The mythmaking *Zanjeer* followed the story of a policeman, Vijay, who is haunted by the murder of his parents. As he becomes the victim of corruption, he turns into a vigilante. Befriending marginal characters, he avenges his parents' death. Called "a transitional movie" in the *Encyclopaedia of Indian Cinema*, *Zanjeer* appears grainy in comparison with *Sholay*.[87] Made on a much lower budget than the latter film, *Zanjeer* initiated a character unlike any other in the repertoire of the all-India film, without any indication of the direction this innovation could take. It is only through the trajectory of the star-text that a film such as *Zanjeer* gains significance. Even though *Zanjeer* is heralded as the seed film for the Bachchan star-text, the character does not come into fruition until *Deewar*, where the adult Vijay is unambiguously a criminal (and not a disenchanted police officer as in *Zanjeer*). Nikhat Kazmi in particular finds *Deewar* giving birth to a new hero, drawn not from the idealized rural poor but from the urban working class, "whose silence and suppressed rage lent a voice to the angst of the urban poor. The unprecedented migration of destitute villagers into cities and towns had manifested itself in a mushrooming of slums all over. There in the underbelly of every big city were the hundreds of haphazard bustees (slum-dwellings), spilling over with the down and outs, the unemployed, the underpaid strugglers and drifters. Chopra's protagonist [in *Deewar* and *Trishul* (Trident, 1978)] found his alter ego in the umpteen angry young men living in the shadows of the high-rise concrete jungle."[88]

The bloody and gory death of Amitabh Bachchan's character in both *Sholay* and *Deewar*—and in later films such as *Muqaddar Ka Sikandar* (Conqueror of Destiny, 1978)—became part of his star image. In the process of creating the paradigm for a new kind of hero, these films precipitated a new aesthetic of physical violence and suffering. Gashes, marks, and other visible wounds on the body, especially the male body, became a new realistic norm that would persist and intensify in the following decade. While the political sphere in India imploded and public life was scarred by unemployment, forced migration, and suppression of civil liberties, the physical action and struggle on the screen took a parallel path, with machismo triumphing over evil or dying in the attempt to do so. At the end of the decade, action, violence, and sacrifice had all been rolled into a cathartic package that left the political questions subverted and simplified. And in a strange, anomalous twist, the government, while engaged in atrocities throughout the 1970s, continued to support Indian art cinema in its usual, limited way.

The persistence and gradual intensification of long-term economic problems through the 1960s and early 1970s, the waning optimism in the remedial role of the nation-state, and the increased public awareness of communal and class violence all coincided with the rise of the action hero in the star-text of Amitabh Bachchan. According to Vijay Mishra, "masculine domination" turned Bachchan's films into "one-actor genres," thus banishing "the centrality of romance" that prevailed in the long tradition of Hindi cinema from K. L. Saigal to Rajesh Khanna.[89] Following the induction of Hindi mainstream cinema into the Anglo-American university curricula, *Sholay* has been more or less consistently associated with the genre "curry western," a seemingly logical extension of the original (Hollywood) western, via the spaghetti western of Sergio Leone and his peers. How do we define curry western beyond the obvious? What Valentina Vitali said with respect to the American- and Italian-inspired action Indian films of the 1920s applies well here: "Precise material conditions determine the circulation of films, and generic facets of cultural forms can take root 'elsewhere' because they respond to structural conditions that are economically and socially pertinent in that 'elsewhere.'" In other words, specific aspects of cultural production are borrowed and restyled because they are deemed capable of conveying important meanings about the particularities of the situation at home.[90]

In Nasreen Munni Kabir's book *Bollywood: The Indian Cinema Story*, Javed Akhtar, cowriter of *Sholay*'s screenplay, provides the industry's interpretation of the evolution of the male star figure that culminated in the Amitabh Bachchan persona in the 1970s:

> If we look back at the forties, fifties, and sixties, the hero was the paragon of positive virtues. A feudal society where the joint family dominates is a strongly patriarchal society in which obedience and acceptance are virtues. You have to obey parental authority, and you have to surrender your ego. If you see this as being submissive, you will feel like a slave. The halo over this submission is sacrifice, and sacrifice becomes a virtue in a society where exploitation is rampant. So you have a hero like Devdas in the 1930s, whose impact lasted into the 1950s.
>
> But gradually, with industrialization and a capitalist system, we emerged from feudal values—and winning became a virtue and the hero changed. So in the 1960s, we see a more positive hero, like Shammi Kapoor. We were optimistic, affluence was around the corner and better things were going to happen in the next month or the next year. But they didn't. And the dream got shattered and created a kind of cynicism and anger. This led to a lack of trust in institutions, in systems, in law and order. And the image of the angry young man was a natural, logical result.[91]

Akhtar's logic—though useful in its outlining of the shifts in the industry in broad strokes—is slightly ingenuous in its positioning of Hindi cinema as an accurate or objective mirror to society. The star-centric system of production, particularly in Bombay, had inherited from some of the studios their style of business in terms of recruitment and networking. The majority of stars in Bombay, from the 1950s to the current age of Bollywood, were cast in lead roles or were given films to direct by virtue of their being related to an influential figure in the industry. Most of them learned the trade fast and achieved independent stellar status after a few breaks; the less fortunate ones moved on to character roles or some aspect of production. Shammi Kapoor was Raj Kapoor's brother and Prithviraj Kapoor's son; his positive, flippant style was carefully crafted and marketed to distinguish his style from his brother's well-established and recognizable style. Amitabh Bachchan and Shah Rukh Khan are two rare Hindi stars whose families were not connected to the filmmaking business. Such giant leaps from modest beginnings to their phenomenal star power—Bachchan was initially given few lines because of his distinctive baritone voice, and Khan debuted on the television serial *Fauji* (The Soldier)—are rare to find in the entire history of Indian cinema.

Amitabh Bachchan was more cognizant of the marketing of a particular hero image. He dismissed his own role in the creation of the "one-man industry," as the magazine *India Today* called it in 1980, saying that he did not create the characters that he played in the films: "They were developed by the writers, the directors, the producers." Writers such as Salim-Javed, who wrote *Zanjeer*, *Deewar* and *Sholay*, seemed to conceive this character out of a certain desire and need that *they* felt was going to satisfy the everyman consumer:

> They devised this character and caught hold of an actor who could possibly deliver the goods. . . . Because this image succeeded, suddenly it was used to define the characteristics of what an angry young man should be: he must be tall, he must be lean, he must look strong, he must have an intense look in his eyes and he must have a good voice. But for argument's sake, if the same character had been 5' 2", had a thin voice and an equally thin body and had that image been successful . . . all the angry young men who followed would have been cast accordingly.[92]

The star-centric system took less than a decade to absorb this new star-text. As Bachchan's screen persona achieved iconic status, the screenplays merely became contexts for foregrounding his star image. In most films beginning with *Don* (1978), shots of him are overdramatized, with dialogue and music orchestrated to accentuate his presence. Bachchan's was "a new brand of heroism," according to Valentina Vitali, presented through a narratorial performance that points insistently and emphatically to its own qualities.[93] But the "angry young man" brand did more than usher in the age of the rebellious antihero. It also created a safety valve in the form of controlled combustion. The figure of the hero would fight and triumph over (or die fighting against) a single evil villain whose defeat would resonate with the greater common good. Incidentally, in 1975 Amitabh Bachchan himself was far from subversive in real life. Amitabh supported Indira Gandhi and the Congress during the Emergency and even campaigned for her. Noting this, Susmita Dasgupta interprets the actor's support for the "state's powers to be intensified" against the old slow-moving democratic political system strangely as "rebellious though not 'anti-incumbent.'"[94] Another recent volume on Indian cinema comments how the angst of Bachchan's characters reflected the political style of Indira Gandhi, who, in assuming ultimate control over state power, was being an iconoclast.[95] Kazmi describes the Bachchan figure as always having "preserved the status quo despite his overt rebelliousness," as his screen image was concurrent with the tumultuous politics of the 1970s and the early 1980s.[96] This could possibly explain the success of the angry young male trope that defied industry precedents.[97]

The story of the rise of Amitabh Bachchan dominates the history of Indian cinema in the 1970s and in so doing overshadows the careers of stars such as Rajesh Khanna (called the first Indian superstar), Dharmendra (who was cast as the star in *Sholay* while newcomer Bachchan was cast as his sidekick), and Shashi Kapoor (a trained stage actor whose first performances were Shakespeare's plays in England and India), as well as the handful of commercially successful films that defied the genre based on the angry young man. The trajectory of Rajesh Khanna's career is particularly relevant to the history of stars in the 1970s, as his success was concurrent with Amitabh Bachchan's, and the body of work that defined both their careers could not be more different. Between 1969 and 1972, as Rajesh Khanna rose to become Hindi cinema's first "superstar," its first "phenomenon," Bachchan struggled to find roles in films such as *Saat Hindustani* (Seven Indians, 1969), which are recalled in film histories only because of him. Khanna's first break came with the success of Shakti Samanta's *Aradhana* (Worship, 1969), in which he played the dual role of father and son, with Sharmila Tagore as the female lead. *Aradhana* is also mentioned in histories of Indian cinema as a significant milestone in playback music, as it established Kishore Kumar's prominence as the playback singer for the male leads, including Amitabh Bachchan, until Kumar's untimely death in 1987. Between 1969 and 1974, Rajesh Khanna was the lead actor in twenty-three "hit" films, with three "going on to run for over a hundred weeks."[98]

Bachchan and Khanna appeared together in two films, *Anand* (1970) and *Namak Haram* (The Traitor, 1973), both directed by Hrishikesh Mukherjee. They were unusual in their pairing of the two personalities. Though Khanna is clearly the "hero" of both narratives, it is impossible to judge the comparative "star power" they exerted, especially in the aftermath of the rise of Bachchan as the definitive star of the 1970s. There are thematic nuances in both the films that were not to be repeated in later Bachchan films; the films have continued to be popular, still drawing viewers via what Kazmi calls the "polarized allure" of the two stars. Dharmendra, who was Bachchan's costar in two films—*Chupke Chupke* (Hush-Hush, 1975, a romantic comedy) and *Sholay*—had found "his muscular frame" to be a handicap, in spite of his good looks (he appeared on *People* magazine's list of 100 most beautiful people).[99] He played mostly romantic roles up until *Sholay*, following which he would have to compete, with severely limited success, not only with the distinct acting style of Bachchan but also with the indefinable quality of Bachchan's stardom. In retrospect, the possibility of either Rajesh Khanna or Dharmendra emerging as the new star in Bachchan's stead seems somewhere between reasonable plausibility and strong probability. Shantanu Ray Chaudhuri writes about an early film in Rajesh Khanna's career, *Baharon Ke Sapne* (Dreams of Spring, 1967), that cast Khanna "as an idealistic, unemployed youth in a mould that on hindsight echoes the angry young man image that was to gain currency with Bachchan six years later."[100] Both Rajesh Khanna and Dharmendra had played characters with shades of Amitabh's disillusioned jaded hero, but as actors they were essentially more aligned with the earlier era represented by the Kumar trio: Dilip, Rajender, and Raj. The phenomenal success of *Sholay* and *Deewar* rewrote the reception histories of the earlier films, privileging Bachchan's star image. Bachchan's star power was used in diverse roles, ranging from the keeper of the law to rebel to comic buffoon. His "stardom" overshadowed the other male actors considerably.

While Amitabh Bachchan's star-text defined the action genre's sphere of influence, three outlier films proved the sheer unpredictability of popular culture: *Jai Santoshi Maa* (Victory to the Goddess Santoshi, 1975), *Pakeezah* (The Pure Woman, 1972), and *Bobby*. The first film was a mythological, the second belonged to the minor but popular genre of "courtesan films," and the third was a teenage romance. The genres are of some significance, as they are all outside the spheres of influence of both the Rajesh Khanna and the Amitabh Bachchan brand of successful formulas of the decade. *Jai Santoshi Maa* started life, according to Ashish Rajadhyaksha and Paul Willemen, "as a routine B picture" but went on to make history by becoming one of the biggest hits of the year, along with *Sholay* and *Deewar*.[101] Structured as a traditional devotional tale of the kind read ritually by women on days of Hindu *vratas* or vows, the film had a predictable core story and a series of divine miracles that perfectly fit the mythological genre. The mythological as a genre has persisted in the margins of Hindi cinema in an unchanged format since the 1930s. Significant changes in

135

appearance and editing came into vogue only with the popular televised epics in the 1980s. What makes *Jai Santoshi Maa* a B picture is not the mythological characters and storyline but the lack of aesthetic and cinematic sensibility in all aspects of the production: costumes, use of color, dialogue, and even casting. Pitted against this overall poverty of production was the use of playback songs, for which the film won multiple awards. Film music composers and lyricists have used devotional songs—*bhajan* in Hindi—variously; traditional *bhajans* could be tweaked and revised for use in a film, which then would become the popular version sung (and played on the gramophone) at religious gatherings. There is a second category of film *bhajans* that are composed for use in film and would, in a few memorable cases, add to the commercial success of a film. In the case of a film such as *Jai Santoshi Maa*, which had lyrics composed by the poet Pradeep and sung by Mahendra Kapoor, Pradeep, and Usha Mangeshkar, the songs played a significant role in the lifetime popularity of the film.

Raj Kapoor's *Bobby*, an unusual teenage romance, introduced Dimple Kapadia as well as Kapoor's son Rishi in his first adult role (he had won a special award for his role as a child artist in *Mera Naam Joker* [My Name Is Joker, 1970]). *Bobby* became the second most popular film in the 1970s after *Sholay*. It was written by the Indian People's Theatre Association veteran K. A. Abbas (who also wrote the script of *Shree 420* and was part of the delegation of Indian artists to the Soviet Union in 1954). The film's plot presented a version of class struggle that was ingenuous even by the standards of Bombay cinema. Dimple Kapadia, playing the eponymous heroine of the film, became the first in a series of actresses who emerged as stylized sex symbols in Raj Kapoor's films. Other actresses "discovered" by Kapoor would be Padmini Kolhapure in *Prem Rog* (Love Sickness, 1982), Zeenat Aman in *Satyam Shivam Sundaram* (The Truth, the God, and the Beauty, 1978), and Mandakini in *Ram Teri Ganga Maili*. Like these other films, *Bobby* was endlessly discussed ahead of its release as sexually subversive, promising a new paradigm in Hindi cinema's representation of sexuality. Irrespective of their contents and the fulfillment of viewer expectations, these films all presented strong sexual content. However, they titillated without subversion and were equally regressive in their gendered deployment of sexuality as spectacle. The uniqueness of *Bobby* thus lies not in its experiments with sexuality but in its mélange of youthful rebellion (adopting the visual elements of the "hippie" style in clothing and even in the film poster) and Raj Kapoor's earlier naive version of a Nehruvian nationalist utopia. The synthesis had its use and relevance in the Bombay industry, and the review of the film by Gaston Roberge, India's pioneer scholar-teacher of film appreciation, expands on this:

The chief quality of both the photography and the music, however, as is often the case in popular cinema, is its lack of subtlety. The director makes sure that the audience will notice a camera effect (zooms for instance), or all possible lens effects, or an intended emotional reaction emphasized by music. The décor is also superbly done. It is extremely revealing that the décor of wealth (wealthy being unreal from the point of view of the mass audience) is treated with maximum realism, whereas the décor of poverty (Bobby's home, which is something real from the point of view of the same audience) is represented in an artificial manner. In a word, wealth appears real and poverty appears unreal. . . . Thus the audience is kept in a world of dream and fantasy which has nothing to do with reality as they know it.[102]

Kamal Amrohi's *Pakeezah* remains one of the most memorable films in the "courtesan" subgenre. Amrohi wrote dialogue for a wide range of films, including *Chhalia* (1960), a rare film on the partition, and the pseudo-historical extravaganza *Mughal-e-Azam* (1960), and directed *Mahal* (1949) and *Razia Sultan* (1983). *Pakeezah* featured an aging Meena Kumari in the double role of a mother and a daughter, both courtesans. This was one of the last films to be filmed by Josef Wirsching, veteran of the German Emelka Studios and Bombay Talkies. *Pakeezah* had a haunting musical score and an unprecedented synthesis of diegetic and extra-diegetic sound, memorably in the merging of the whistle of a passing train with a song, but the extraordinary success of the film allegedly came only after the untimely death of the actress, Meena Kumari, before the release of the film. An alcoholic and prone to depression in real life, Kumari played a number of tragic-melancholic characters, and her death, from liver disease, produced the star-text that ensured, among other things, the enduring popularity of *Pakeezah*.

The other film by Raj Kapoor that resisted the "Amitabh Bachchan" influence was *Satyam Shivam Sundaram*. Advertised alternately as a sexually explicit film and a film with a "social/moral message," *Satyam Shivam Sundaram* went above and beyond *Bobby* in its dream and fantasy, anticipating his 1985 film of comparable hype, *Ram Teri Ganga Maili*. While *Bobby* was the debut film of Dimple Kapadia and *Ram Teri Ganga Maili* of Mandakini, *Satyam Shivam Sundaram* was advertised as a vehicle for presenting Zeenat Aman in a new package. Aman, Miss Asia Pacific 1970, was already an established star by 1978, frequently referred to as a "sex symbol," thus making Raj Kapoor's "presenting Zeenat Aman" rather symbolic. There are indications of Raj Kapoor's amicable relationship with the ruling Congress Party and his clout with influential journalists playing a role in the film getting the approval of the Board of Censors.[103] Monika Mehta, in her study on censorship, has described how Raj Kapoor both sold and down-played the issue of sexuality: "Kapoor's carefully engineered publicity mobilized Aman largely as sex symbol, that is, as *body*, and with less certitude promised the prospect of re-presenting her as an actress; presumably, it was as an actress that she would convey the film's soul, its 'message.' In a characteristically frank manner, Kapoor explained this decision: 'In Indian cinema, subtlety is a big gamble. So, this time I'm not repeating old mistakes [for example, the debacle of *Mera Naam Joker*, a film with a message]. I've put a lot of body into Satyam. For those who miss the soul, there's something else worth seeing.'"[104]

The cult of the action/revenge/adventure drama centered on the figure of the "angry young man" continued to be repeated in Hindi cinema, with variations appearing in other languages. The most significant figure to emerge in the Am-itabh Bachchan mold was the Tamil star Rajinikanth, who played the lead double roles in *Billa*, the Tamil remake of *Don* (1978). The most popular star after the Ganesan brothers and MGR (M. G. Ramachandran), Rajinikanth was hailed as the south's "angry young man" and rose through the 1980s to become one of the highest paid actors in India. Other South Indian male stars who followed a similar trajectory were Chiranjeevi and Nagarjuna in Telugu and Mamootty in Malayalam cinema. Amitabh Bachchan had a near-fatal accident on the set of *Coolie* in 1982 that affected his productivity. His political career from 1984 to 1987 kept him away from an active film career, which created a space for other action heroes and other subgenres.

Most of these films revisited themes from the 1960s and the 1970s, and it is possible to make a clear distinction between them and the new configura-tions of stardom, music, and narratives that would be inaugurated by *Qayamat Se Qayamat Tak* and *Maine Pyaar Kiya* (I Fell in Love, 1989), as harbingers of the ur-Bollywood moment. A pertinent example of the former would be Raj Kapoor's 1985 directorial venture *Ram Teri Ganga Maili*. There was no motif in the film that had not been explored before: an urban hero, a naive heroine nurtured by nature, the corrupting influence of cities and politics, the defiling of the essence of India and the ideal Indian woman, the conflation of Hindu sacred images with the nation—these had all been repeated in an endless loop in films by a plethora of directors, including Raj Kapoor. At some point in Ka-poor's filmmaking career, sexuality had become the only vehicle for any moral message. *Satyam Shivam Sundaram* and *Prem Rog*, for instance, carried the legacy of the heavy-handed political message from the *Awaara* cycle but depended more on the titillating exposition of the female body for the delivery of that message, the latter underscored endlessly in publicity material and director's remarks. In the instance of *Ram Teri Ganga Maili*, Kapoor spoke profusely of his discovery of the actress Mandakini—who shared the name Ganga with the river in the film—before, during, and after the shooting of the film, stressing her "Madonna-like simplicity." He imagined the character Ganga as "a very young, very beautiful mountain girl, somewhat like an unseen, unblossomed flower." There was not much room for ambiguity regarding the moral message of the film, but Kapoor felt the incessant need to explain it anyway:

> What has inspired me in making this film . . . is the rapid changing of values in our country, the changing morality, the decadence of values in our country, the loss of our spirituality. Socio-economic corruption can be understood, even explained in terms of great poverty and population explosion. Poverty itself often becomes a breeding ground for all sorts of immoral conditions . . . but what I am wondering about is what has happened to our spiritualism! The only real inherent strength of our country through our long history has been our spiritualism. This loss can be a disintegrating force, a disruptive one.[105]

In the aftermath of the 1993 terrorist attacks in Bombay, Mandakini would be widely exposed as the longtime mistress to Dawood Ibrahim, one of the "dons" of the Bombay underworld and a suspect in the attack, and the newly liberated Indian media published pictures of Mandakini and her child, feeding public imagination with pornographic insinuations, thus matching her physical exposure in Kapoor's film with her "defilement." But the film's narrative, straightforward and derivative to begin with, was sold to the public even before the film was released in 1985, on the basis of the heroine exposing her body. Kapoor was doing exactly what he did in 1978 with *Satyam Shivam Sundaram*: putting a "lot of body" in the film.[106]

To return to the debate from the opening pages of this chapter, the "big picture" of commercial cinema consisted of gratuitous "sex and violence" coupled with unsubtle symbolism, which had become the mainstay of mass entertainment. It was in the course of this evolution that the letter of protest signed by Satyajit Ray and over ninety other filmmakers and artists had incurred the wrath of Nargis Dutt. To the stalwarts of the commercial film industry such as Raj Kapoor, Nargis Dutt, and B. R. Chopra, this form of entertainment cinema was not only defensible but desirable and commendable as well. Irrespective of the divergent trajectories of the two cinemas—commercial and art—the mélange of politics and filmmaking covered in this chapter directs our attention not to paths taken but to messy eruptions that burst forth. The rise of Amitabh

Bachchan's "angry young male" persona, the astounding commercial success of the amateurish *Jai Santoshi Maa* in the same year *Sholay* was released, and the sudden and successful resurrection of the 1950s aesthetic style via *Pakeezah* in 1972 all had one thing in common: they defied rules (of the market, of aesthetics, and of systemic control). In so doing, they morphed into yet another messy, unruly layer, unknowingly waiting for a messier future called Bollywood.

CHAPTER 4

India's Long Globalization and the Rise of Bollywood

"Bollywood," a neologism circulating in Internet forums in the 1990s, was finally legitimized when in June 2001 the word was inducted into the *Oxford English Dictionary*. This induction engendered a spurt of corollary neologisms such as "Kollywood," "Sandalwood," and "Mollywood" in India and "Lollywood" and "Dhallywood" in Pakistan and Bangladesh.[1] The *OED*'s definition and etymology of "Bollywood," however, were incorrect: instead of defining the name in the context of multilingual and multilocal Indian cinemas, it defined "Bollywood" as "the" popular film industry in India and traced it to an inconsequential reference from the 1970s.[2] Notwithstanding the error, when Hindi cinema produced in Bombay acquired global reach via portable media formats and the Internet in the twenty-first century, "Bollywood" became a synecdoche for commercial Indian cinema, especially on the World Wide Web. In 2019, a Google search for the keyword "Bollywood" would yield 0.479 billion results, whereas the number of results for "Indian cinema" that represents the sum of all film industries in India would be only 7.6 million, which is clearly at odds with the relationship between the two entities. According to the official count released by the Indian government in 2017, Indian cinema's output equaled 1,986 films in forty-three languages produced in nine locations, approximately 306 of which were actually "Bollywood," that is, Hindi films produced in Mumbai, the city previously known as Bombay.[3] In spite of Bollywood's official output being a mere fraction of Indian cinema, "Bollywood" as a keyword towered over

"Indian cinema." "Bollywood" therefore is a phenomenon of a kind different from "Indian cinema," the result of digital reproduction and the consequent inflation of its projected value. While "Indian cinema" still outnumbers other national film industries in output, Bollywood's digital footprint is based not just on films but on styles, motifs, and product brand. Cookbooks, snacks, dance styles, wedding planning, and attire are some of the categories that Bollywood is now associated with. A significant number of the search results are not related to cinema.

Outside of the digital realm, the history of the use of the word "Bollywood" as a name for Hindi cinema and as a synecdoche for the Indian film industry in general is contested and complex.[4] Infrequently used—often within quotes—in Indian newspapers and film magazines until the mid-1990s, the word had limited purchase among serious scholars of Indian popular cinema. "Bollywood" began to be used without sarcasm in the titles of scholarly volumes only after its official recognition by the *OED*. The first two books to use "Bollywood" without reservation, Vijay Mishra's *Bollywood Cinema: Temples of Desire* (2002) and Tejaswini Ganti's *Bollywood: A Guidebook to Popular Hindi Cinema* (2004), were part of a new wave of scholarship on Indian popular cinema that followed in the shadow of Sumita S. Chakravarty's pioneering 1993 work, *National Identity in Indian Popular Cinema, 1947–1987*.[5] Chakravarty in her book, however, had used "Bombay cinema," "Indian commercial cinema," and "Indian popular cinema" where Mishra and Ganti would later use "Bollywood." In the twenty-first century, "Bollywood" has prominently featured in the title of books by Mishra, Ganti, Ashish Rajadhyaksha, Sangita Gopal, Rachel Dwyer, Rajinder Dudrah, Jigna Desai, Ajay Gehlawat, Rosie Thomas, Priya Joshi, and others, albeit always with reference to the name's historical dimensions and its connections with the twenty-first-century expansion of Indian cinema's global market.

The *OED*'s acknowledgment of "Bollywood" came three years after another landmark for Indian cinema. Cinema was granted "industry status" by the Indian government in 1998, a move that legitimized filmmaking as an enterprise in India for the first time. Bollywood, the celebrity offspring of popular Hindi cinema, thus gained an unprecedented national and global legitimacy, overshadowing the long, unruly past of its parent industry. By the time of Indian cinema's centenary in 2012–13, "Bollywood" was a well-circulated keyword, so much so that in Indian popular publications the distinction between Bollywood and Indian cinema frequently blurred. It is common to find both printed and online popular media in India and the Indian diaspora using the name "Bollywood" as descriptive of India's feature film industry that began with D. G. Phalke's *Raja Harishchandra* in 1913 and eventually manifested in the Hindi industry based in Bombay. The *OED*'s misinterpretation and the increasing influx of online material on the subject of cinema in India converged to create the exponentially larger search results for a Google query for "Bollywood" over "Indian cinema" in 2019.[6]

In this final part of the book, the twenty-first-century rise of Bollywood is narrated alongside the most significant shift in the official interface between cinema and the government. For the first time in the history of Indian cinema, that interface is between a pro-corporate, pro-global Indian government and India's oldest surviving modern private enterprise, newly legalized. The status of Bollywood itself remains the most indeterminate factor in this interface. The first-ever *India Film Guide*, a 260-page document distributed by the Indian Ministry of Information and Broadcasting at Festival de Cannes in 2015, contained separate chapters on filmmaking in each state. The authors took utmost care in defining Bollywood as a "category" in its chapter on Maharashtra and in drawing out a distinction between Bollywood films and all Hindi films: "A large chunk of the Hindi films produced in Mumbai constitutes what is usually described as Bollywood, a label used for a cinematic tradition built on a crowd-pleasing mix of melodrama, romance, moral conflict and music."[7] A closer look at the guide reveals a partnership between corporate and official interests in the project. It was jointly produced by the Government of India and the Federation of Indian Chambers of Commerce and Industry (FICCI). FICCI was an almost defunct body during the first six postcolonial decades but has emerged in the new millennium as a powerful and active advocate for foreign investment in India's entertainment and media industries. In his book on the transformation of the Hindi film industry from a local or national institution to a global brand, Aswin Punathambekar has mapped how FICCI, through its media and entertainment division, "has played a crucial role in mediating ties between the Indian government and the media industries and most importantly, in assembling a Media and Entertainment sector with Bollywood at the center."[8] In spite of the ascendant corporate influences, it is significant that in the global pitch to attendees at Cannes, FICCI downplayed "Bollywood" and showcased the value of each regional center for film production in India. While a world of difference separated the confrontational interface between government and the film industry at the 1955 New Delhi film seminar (see chapter 2) from the collaborative business pitch of FICCI and the government in 2015 at Cannes, the government's characterization of Indian cinema as the sum of equal regional partners has persisted.

Irrespective of the Indian government's downplaying the obvious, Bollywood was central to the meaning and presence of "Indian cinema" at Cannes in 2015, given the history of dissemination of Bombay cinema in the twenty-first century. Bollywood's global ascendance in the elite festival circuit of the West began in 2002, when Sanjay Leela Bhansali's *Devdas* became the first Indian film to premiere at Cannes. It was a film that appeared more contrived and flamboyant than most Indian melodramas in its elaborate and lavish sets, its gaudy costumes, and its indiscriminating use of music. As opposed to the screening of Satyajit Ray's *Pather Panchali* without subtitles at the 1956 festival at Cannes, the premiere of *Devdas* was powered in by the industry and its friends, with an advertisement campaign and release of merchandise to coincide with the premiere. A limited edition of Barbie and Ken dolls was even produced by Mattel, based on the characters Parvati, Chandramukhi, and Devdas. Perhaps aware of the uniqueness of the event, Sanjay Leela Bhansali, in the film's credits, paid tribute to the best-known earlier versions of *Devdas*: the 1936 version directed by P. C. Barua and the 1955 version directed by Bimal Roy. To viewers at the Cannes premiere, the credits and the ostentatiousness of the film were meant to underscore the global emergence of Indian melodrama from within its own national cinematic context.

It was also in 2002 that Ashutosh Gowarikar's *Lagaan: Once upon a Time in India* (2001)—a fictional account of Indian farmers playing cricket against British officers in colonial India—made it to the coveted final five in the foreign films category at the 74th Academy Awards. The film's star, Aamir Khan, and the director, Ashutosh Gowariker, attended the Academy Awards ceremony in Los Angeles, but the award was eventually given to a Bosnian film, *No Man's Land* (dir. Danis Tanovic). Nonetheless, it was a rare representation of Indian cinema at the Academy Awards, ten years after Satyajit Ray's Oscar for Lifetime Achievement. By the year 2015, Bollywood stars such as Shah Rukh Khan and Aishwarya Rai—the lead actors in *Devdas*—had become familiar faces both in the festival circuit and at mainstream award events. Rai served as a member of the jury at Cannes for several years between 2001 and 2015 and acted in two Hollywood films; Khan was one of the presenters at the 2009 Golden Globe Awards.[9] The confidence and zeal with which the government marketed the cause of "Indian cinema" at Cannes in 2015 thus drew clearly from the positively altered significance of Bollywood in the "West," that is, in the part of the world that was traditionally exposed to Indian art or parallel cinema during the Cold War era.

The global emergence of Bollywood as a phenomenon can thus be historically located in the early years of the twenty-first century. Beyond the symbolism and "name recognition," Bollywood came to be studied as a brand in the world of investing, finance, and prediction. Multinational consultancies, including PricewaterhouseCoopers, Deloitte, and Ernst & Young, collaborated with FICCI to produce detailed analyses of the Indian media market every year. For the first time since the opening of the Indian markets in 1991, Indian media had the American business analysts' attention as a market that has realized only a small percentage of its potential for growth and profit. While television, advertisement, and print media featured prominently in the reports, it was Bollywood as a brand and symbol that engendered international interest in the first place. Between 2007 and 2009, two major studios—Sony/Columbia and Disney—started investing in Indian film coproduction.[10] In 2008, a Hindi remake of the 2005 Tamil film *Ghajini* (dir. Murugadoss) became the first Indian film to gross more than INR 1 billion in ticket sales, inaugurating the category of the "100 Crore Club," a new "gold standard" for Bollywood films created by "a steady increase in ticket prices (an average rise of INR 10 every six months), the number of theatres and the number of prints."[11] By the summer of 2017, more than fifty films had entered the "club," signaling an unusually long and sustained financial ascendance. According to a report published in *Forbes* magazine, Indian cinema's financial rise was only just beginning, with its market share of $2 billion in 2015 only a fraction of a potential growth of $10 billion.[12]

For an unruly industry legitimized fewer than two decades ago, this narrative of promise and possibilities is arguably extraordinary, evoking the question of whether such a turn of fortune for cinema in India was inevitable in a "liberalized" economy. As we shall see in this chapter, the bursting forth of Bollywood seemed improbable in the early years of globalization. It was far from inevitable. Globalization and the subsequent opening up of the Indian market, combined with the decline of the Nehruvian socialist state, posed more challenges than opportunities. The rise of Bollywood as a popular cultural phenomenon was an unruly turn that countered those challenges and saved Bombay cinema by turning it into an archetype.

It Was *Not* Written: The Perfect Storm in Indian Cinema on the Cusp of Bollywood

Let us approach the ideas of inevitability and probability through the Indian cinematic idiom. In the British film *Slumdog Millionaire* (2008, dir. Danny Boyle), which was both a tribute to and a satire of Bombay-based Hindi cinema, the phrase "it is written" is used to condense a recurring idea in Indian imagination as well as in Hindi films: predestination. An equivalent of "it is written" is found in every Indian language, expressive of the idea of destiny or the inevitable. "It is written" is an awkward translation that is also uniquely representative of "Indian English," which routinely transposes syntax and expressions from Indian vernaculars onto English, creating an idiom that captures and communicates Indian ideas better among Indians but at the cost of diminished comprehensibility to non-Indians. The Indian idea expressed through "it is written" has run through the melodramatic film form that dominated Hindi films over decades. Chance encounters, separation and reunion under the most improbable circumstances, and the triumph of love over all socioeconomic hurdles appear throughout the specific films that Boyle used as subtexts for his film. Many of those films starred Amitabh Bachchan, Bombay's biggest star, whose star-text of the "angry young man" was the discussed in chapter 3. Played by another actor, Amitabh Bachchan appears as a character in an early sequence from *Slumdog Millionaire*. Jamal, the chief protagonist of the movie and titular "slumdog," willingly dives into a pool of human excreta in his rush to get Bachchan's autograph when the star's helicopter lands in his neighborhood. Elements from Jamal's precarious childhood and adolescence and his relationship with his brother Salim in the film are reminiscent of the Bachchan persona's narrative in *Deewar* and *Muqaddar Ka Sikandar*. The dénouement in Boyle's film—Jamal's reunion with childhood friend Latika and his winning INR 10 million in the Indian version of *Who Wants to Be a Millionaire*—could occur only through an implausible alignment of events throughout the three characters' lives that could only be attributed to destiny, as if "it was written."

If the certainty of destiny has defined the narrative drive of Hindi cinema (and Boyle's reworking of it), the Hindi film industry's own destiny of transformation from a quasi-national form to the global branding of Bollywood was significantly less certain, especially in the immediate aftermath of the Cold War era. In 1991, the government of India was compelled to change its policy on private industry, foreign investment, and imports to secure a crucial loan from the IMF and the World Bank.[13] The new economic policy or economic liberalization initiated a free flow of foreign imports into India, which among other things revolutionized the patterns of the Indian middle class's consumption of cinema and media. From two state-run and state-controlled television channels, the middle-class household's exposure expanded to over a hundred cable channels, including CNN, whose live telecast of the first Gulf War changed Indian perceptions of global polity. The onslaught of (primarily American) visual images from the hitherto inaccessible networks appears almost surreal in Arundhati Roy's description in her novel *God of Small Things*: "It wasn't something that happened gradually. It happened overnight. Blondes, wars, famines, football, sex, music, coups d'état—they all arrived on the same train. They unpacked together. They stayed at the same hotel. And in Ayemenem, where once the loudest sound had been a musical bus horn, now whole wars, famines, pictur-esque massacres and Bill Clinton could be summoned up like servants."[14]

Cinema's counterpart of this blitz arrived in 1994 in the form of dinosaurs, when the Hindi-dubbed version of Steven Spielberg's *Jurassic Park*, combined with the English version, sold 4 million tickets in the first three weeks of its run. The English version alone surpassed the record held by *Enter the Dragon* (1973) for the highest grossing foreign film in India.[15] While this unprecedented success amounted only to a small percentage of the global box office for *Jurassic Park*, the impact on the Indian film market was substantial enough to be noticed by the rest of the world and raise alarm in India. The only film hitherto dubbed in Hindi had been Richard Attenborough's *Gandhi* (1983), which was copro-duced by National Film Development Corporation, its ticket prices subsidized throughout the nation. The success of *Jurassic Park*, followed closely by that of *Speed* (1994, dir. Jan de Bont, dubbed in Hindi as *Raftaar*), was part of a new phenomenon of media globalization that liberated the Indian consumer from the regime of controlled entertainment. As much as this phenomenon could be attributed to the linear expansion of globalization—predominantly flowing out of the United States—the interface that received and absorbed the onslaught of CNN and *Jurassic Park* had a local context that unfolded between 1987 and 1993. All globalizations not being alike, the particular political and economic configuration that preceded Bollywood's formation is an important piece in the history of both Indian globalization and media history.

The regulatory, quasi-socialist Nehruvian state with its emphatic focus on federalism and secularism, damaged by Indira Gandhi in the 1970s, showed signs of clear rupture in Rajiv Gandhi's first term as prime minister (1984–89). Overall destabilization was exacerbated by the declining economy and the rise of regional and communal political formations. The late 1980s was a transitional period for Indian politics that would eventually lead to the pro-global, neoliberal state of the 1990s. But the slow dismantling of the secular nation-state was not readily accessible to interpretation by either historians or political scientists, which could account for the paucity of contemporary analyses. Between 1989 and 1991, the Indian news media paid more attention to the fall of the Soviet Union and other related events than it did to the rise of Hindutva and the de-cay of the secular state ideology. The Hindu Nationalist BJP's (Bharatiya Janata Party) electoral gains in the 1989 elections came as a surprise to both scholars and politicians, but they were proof enough that Congress and Left parties alike had misplaced confidence in old-fashioned state ideological apparatuses.

Before Hindu nationalism became a political institution to reckon with, an early third front of political parties had emerged, advocating rights and entitlements for the lower castes. The articulation of caste differences and intercaste conflicts surfaced in Hindi cinema in the late 1980s. Lower castes, the poor, women, and religious minorities ceased appearing as symbols woven into the fabric of secular nationalism. Hindi cinema had its first Muslim villain in 1988 with *Tezaab* (dir. N. Chandra). In the context of Indian political history, the vestiges of the Nehruvian state had retained enough power through most of the 1980s to maintain control over most of the natural and human resources. In 1983, India had 209 public sector undertakings with a total investment of over INR 300 billion, up from 5 undertakings at INR 290 million in 1951.[16] However, as all post-global analyses of Indian economy have asserted, the confident image of self-reliance masked numerous failures, including poor output of the public sectors, gradual depletion of foreign reserves, and the stifling effect on economic growth of the regime of bureaucracy known as the "permit-license raj."[17] Between 1984 and 1989, a combination of political and economic policies inaugurated by Rajiv Gandhi projected India's shift to a pro-global, pro-corporate future that would eventually arrive in 1991. Not only is the transitional nature of the late 1980s crucial to the immediate prehistory of Bollywood, but the slow morphing of the correspondence between media and the public sphere in this period is an important piece of groundwork for the liberalization of the market in the next decade.

Waiting for the Storm, Televised

Indira Gandhi's funeral on November 4, 1984 (following her assassination on October 31), which was broadcast live over India's only television channel, was one of several spectacles that helped create a visual political sphere independent of Indian cinema. Indira's son Rajiv Gandhi, chosen by the Congress to succeed her as the prime minister, was the focus of the camera and of the nation's sympathy. Adding to the spectacle of mourning was Rajiv's childhood friend and the most recognizable Indian: Amitabh Bachchan. Television had finally become the perfect tool to sway political opinion without claiming to do so. One of the milestones of Indira Gandhi's media policy had been the live broadcast of the 1982 Asian Games, marking the inauguration of television programming in color in India. Besides the obvious nationalistic spectacle that such an event involved, the games were also meant to highlight the leadership and managerial abilities of her son Rajiv Gandhi, who was put in charge of the planning and execution of the entire event. The telecast of the 1980 Asian Games had caused much excitement and even an unforeseen public drive to buy color television sets, but the seemingly spontaneous public spectacle of the family, nation, and the world mourning Indira Gandhi's demise two years after surpassed the feats of any athlete.

Rajiv Gandhi became the prime minister by internal vote following Indira's death and then was elected by a large margin over other parties. Under his government, the television news coverage of the prime minister increased exponentially. For the first time there were also regular late-night screenings of older classics of world cinema as well as contemporary films on the festival circuit (the first film on this slot was *Battleship Potemkin* [1925], followed by Ingmar Bergman's *Fanny and Alexander* [1983] a few weeks later), plus a prime-time slot for Indian pop music each week. Serials with young urban characters were added to the prime-time schedule on national television. Shah Rukh Khan's acting career began on such television serials before he got an opportunity to work in films. After more than a decade of Indians imbibing indigenous brands of soda following Coca-Cola's expulsion from the country in 1977, Pepsi entered the Indian market in 1991, with a new generation of film stars appearing in the television advertisements. If the above signaled a lean toward the West, the Janus-face of the nation was retained in the return to the Hindu epics that began to be serialized on television, with the Sunday morning telecast of the *Ramayana* in 1987–89. In 1988, an amendment to the constitution brought the voting age down from twenty-one to eighteen. The youngest generation eligible to vote in the general elections of 1989 had just grown up in an India on the cusp of globalization, with all the contradictions and complexities that implies. The films that they paid to watch in theaters were made with this viewership in mind, for the first time in India's postcolonial history. These films came out of Bombay's time-honored star-centric system but were synchronic with the changed conditions of production. The slight shift created by a new generation of stars and singers coincided with the decay of the state and the delicate imbalance in the market economy, and films such as *Qayamat Se Qayamat Tak*, *Tezaab*, *Maine Pyaar Kiya*, *Khiladi* (Player, 1992), and *Baazigar* (Gambler, 1993) became the precursors of Bollywood cinema.

How do we analyze paradigm shifts within a film industry that was based upon a parochial star system and undocumented finances? Where do we look? The two instances of tectonic shifts so far—detailed in chapters 2 and 3—offer little clue of any crucial transformation of the production paradigm within the industry. In both cases, the answer to the respective crises lay in Bombay cinema's reconfigurations of its dominant form, melodrama. In the 1950s, the reformist social genre was reconfigured to co-opt the nation-building rhetoric of the postcolonial state. In the 1970s, revenge and retribution narratives centered on an angry young male protagonist upended the social justice motifs of films funded by the NFDC. Both shifts were thematic rather than material; changes in cinematography, playback music, and mise-en-scène were corollaries to the thematic shifts. In the end, the combined body of Raj Kapoor's *"Awaara* cycle" and the films foregrounding Amitabh Bachchan's "angry young male" star-text were sublimated into a cinematic narration of the nation wherein differences, discords, and injustices are eventually dispelled by a fortuitous combination of chance and righteousness, propelled by the actions of a proactive hero. For example, in *Shree 420* and *Amar Akbar Anthony*—epitomes of the 1950s nationalist social form and the 1970s action melodrama respectively—the villain is a private enemy (of the chief protagonist) as well as a public enemy (of the nation). Wealth is gained only through illegal and immoral means, and it perpetuates immoral and criminal behavior in turn, thus creating a vicious cycle of violence, crime, and social injustice. In the 1970s, the melodramatic form had expanded to make space for Amitabh Bachchan's "angry young man" within a pan-Indian narrative. The star's screen persona, mobilized effectively, could neutralize intercommunity differences. According to Ravi Vasudevan, "Bachchan carried something of what [Raj] Kapoor did for the post-independence period on into the 1970s." In *Amar Akbar Anthony*, for instance, "a characteristic melodramatic narrative ensures the dispersal of the children of a Hindu family into a set of multi-community foster families, Hindu, Muslim, and Christian."[18] The incredulous set of coincidences that go into the dispersion and reunification of the "national" family in *Amar Akbar Anthony* aside, the spirit of the film could only be interpreted as secular and egalitarian, with utopian shades—a minor variation of the form popularized by Raj Kapoor in the 1950s.

The 1970s action-based cinema's eventual dilution and reabsorption into the mainstream was merely a matter of time. Notwithstanding the overarching nationalist ideology, the angry young male who bent the rules to facilitate justice in *Zanjeer* and *Sholay* was different from the heroes of the nationalist social films and romantic melodramas of the 1950s and 1960s. The hero's brooding expressions, the subject of frequent close-ups, marked his alienation from the normalcy of citizenship under the nation-state, as did his stoicism and palpable anger. By the early 1980s, that anger and alienation had dissipated. In films such as *Namak Halal* (Loyal Servant, 1982) and *Coolie*, the Bachchan persona revels in poverty and subordination as a porter and a servant respectively, and both films offer a performative and perfunctory display of his "action hero" facade through repetitive and poorly shot fight sequences. Even when Bachchan returns as an avenger and a seeker of justice in films such as *Shahenshah* and *Agneepath* (The Path of Fire, 1990), he is one among numerous male actors—including Mithun Chakravarty and Jeetendra—who played similar roles in a wide contiguous spectrum. Every film needed to have a few short and choreographed fight sequences to appease the post-1970s viewer. Relevant examples are *Zamane Ko Dikhana Hai* (For the World to See, 1981), *Disco Dancer* (1982), and *Himmatwala* (Brave Man, 1983), films with long dance sequences in which the chief protagonists—played by Rishi Kapoor, Mithun Chakravarty, and Jeetendra respectively—face their enemies in physical combat, while the primary spectacle is based on "song and dance." Without significant shifts within the industry's mode of production, "action" was easily co-opted by a star-centric production of melodrama, where heroes settling scores through physical violence reflected the "new normal" for Bombay cinema. The coterie of actors, directors, and producers involved in the perpetuation of this "normal" remained small.

The playback singers' clique that was held together by the market dominance of a single recording body—His Master's Voice or HMV, an imprint of EMI— was even smaller. An overwhelming majority of Hindi film songs from the 1960s onward were performed by four male singers—Mohammad Rafi, Kishore Kumar, Mukesh, and Manna Dey—and two female singers, Lata Mangeshkar and Asha Bhosle. The absence of competition in the recording industry—a by-product of the Indian government's regulatory policies—made it nearly impossible for new singers to enter the profession. The dynastic star-centric system of cinema extended over the world of film music as well. Asha Bhosle was married to the composer R. D. Burman; Mukesh's son Nitin Mukesh and Kishore Kumar's son Amit Kumar became playback singers.

Of Star-Crossed Lovers, Killers, and Audiocassettes: The Ur-Bollywood Moment

The transition from this stagnated "normal" to Bollywood unfolded over half a decade. The ur-Bollywood period began with the 1988 release of *Qayamat Se Qayamat Tak* (henceforth *QSQT*)—the film that "launched" Aamir Khan and made him a star almost overnight—to *Deewana* (Crazy, 1992), which was Shah Rukh Khan's first significant appearance in a film, and *Darr: A Violent Love Story* and *Baazigar*, both films released in 1993 that featured Khan in psychotic antagonistic roles, unusual for leading actors in Bombay. This ur-Bollywood collection also included *Tezaab*, with Madhuri Dixit playing a salacious dancer forced to perform by her oppressive father; *Maine Pyaar Kiya*, the film that "launched" Salman Khan's career; and *Khiladi*, a crime thriller that became Akshay Kumar's first successful film as the male lead. In retrospect, each of these films broke new ground ever so slightly. It was the combined momentum that was significant with respect to Bombay's star-centric system of production. The male and female stars were all in their early twenties, the plots were orchestrated carefully enough to make the protagonists appear vulnerable and turns of events more realistic, and most of these films had music directed and sung by new younger singers, such as Udit Narayan, Alka Yagnik, and Kavita Krishnamurthy. More significantly, the music of most of these films was released on audiocassettes marketed by new companies, led by Super Cassette Industries.

Let us unpack *QSQT* as the prototypical ur-Bollywood film. Based on *Romeo and Juliet*, *QSQT* participated in, perhaps even inaugurated, a new idiom by carving out space for a new set of stars grounded in the contemporary. One side of that "contemporary" was the new indigenism that was slowly coming in vogue in the 1980s, corresponding with the caste-ist and anti-Muslim politics that would eventually be normalized through the rise of Hindu nationalism. The other side was the carefully crafted authenticity in the characters themselves. Raj and Rashmi, played by Aamir Khan and Juhi Chawla, were Rajputs, not of a vague North Indian origin like most lead characters in Hindi films were. The theme of "family feud" (from *Romeo and Juliet*) is therefore grounded in a set of regional and not national stereotypes in *QSQT*. The outdated martial and patriarchal values of the Rajput clans are packaged in pithy expressions, a technique that would be perfected in the foregrounding of Punjabi-ness in *Dilwale Dulhaniya Le Jayenge*. In addition to that, both Aamir Khan and Juhi Chawla were visibly young and believable as college students in their looks, attire, and mannerism. To understand why this was a breakthrough to the college-going viewers who thronged the theaters, one needs to browse through the visual images of college campuses and students in the films from the 1960s, 1970s, and even 1980s, where heroes and heroines in their thirties and forties played teenagers and college students, thus seriously stretching the viewers' imagination. According to Ajanta Sircar, Aamir Khan's run as "the boy next door" continued through *Jo Jeeta Wohi Sikandar* (He Who Wins Is the King, 1992), which was also directed by Mansoor Khan, the director of *QSQT* and Aamir Khan's cousin. Nikhat Kazmi concurs with Sircar in his assessment of *Jo Jeeta Wohi Sikandar*: "Here was a pack of school kids, who throng the public schools in and around the hills. They chewed gum, romped in shorts, poured over *Playboy*, bunked school, dreamed of svelte chicks and yuppie guys. Yet, they never lost their middle-class values and old-fashioned ethics. This was the new generation that was being showcased."[19] Kazmi further observes the aura of "innocence" that Mansoor Khan's characters exuded, which he thinks was almost tailor-made for an "Aamir Khan series."[20] Special care was taken to draw out the female characters to find the perfect balance between the almost patented, time-honored trope of ideal Indian woman and women's roles in a changing society.

QSQT inaugurated an altered paradigm within Ashish Rajadhyaksha's "epic melodrama," tailored for the youth of a nation on the cusp of globalization, and the film was advertised as such. Its use of debutants and television actors, unknown playback singers, and relatively realistic and rustic action sequences was interpreted in the magazines and newspapers as a new trend that made the old star-centric system of production obsolete. Emphasis was placed on the "newness" of Aamir Khan rather than on the fact that the film was produced and directed by his close relatives. Similarly, Salman Khan, who achieved instant stardom in his debut role in *Maine Pyaar Kiya*, was the son of the well-known screenwriter who cowrote *Sholay*. The dynastic, star-centric system was thus very much at work. The most problematic aspect of the new 1980s were the "new women" characters, such as Rashmi, the character played by Juhi Chawla in *QSQT*, who lacked self-expression and any awareness of the fact that women in India had always participated in social and political processes or that India had a vibrant feminist movement with many regional variations. This developed into Bollywood's encoding of the paradox of free will and women within the Indian context of a pro-capitalist liberal modernity. The time-honored "rural belle" of the 1940s through the 1970s could not "be sustained as a viable narrative possibility" and so was "replaced by her cosmopolitan, upper middle-class counterpart—the new Indian Woman who lives in Levi's jeans but could don her ethnicity on demand."[21] Following M. Madhava Prasad and others, Ajanta Sircar has mapped the construction of this "New Indian Woman" in a field of ideology that is fed by cinema as well as by women's magazines such as *Femina* and *Savvy*:

> As a member of the global middle class, the New Indian Woman of the 1980s was constructed as even further removed from any caste-region-religion markers than her 1950s' counterpart. She was defined primarily by her "innocent" upper-middle-class status and was, above all, an individual with an agency to be publicly visible and to "fall in love." . . . The earlier opposition between Westernization and Indianness was now reinflected onto a *generational conflict*. . . . A range of 1980s' romance films show lovers as consummating unfulfilled desires of the past. When generational conflict is not literal, it takes the form of an opposition between the 1950s' parental generation (coded as backward) and the 1980s' young generation (set up as modern). Thus, while *Ek Duje Ke Liye* (Made for Each Other, 1981) portrays the parental generation as clinging onto backward regional chauvinism, *Prem Rog* (The Mania of Love, 1982) sets up the parental generation as clinging onto outmoded and conservative codes of Hindu widowhood.[22]

The diminishing of the onscreen significance of the lead female figure that began in the 1970s had continued through the 1980s. In the wake of action/revenge-oriented dramas, the female partner of the angry young male had become little more than embellishment, a fact that explains the number of B-list actresses who played heroines in most of Amitabh Bachchan's films. But the partner of the sensitive new Indian man—Rashmi in *QSQT* and Suman of *Maine Pyaar Kiya*—was a demure modern woman who remained a mere foil for her male counterpart. The breakthrough female persona of the new generation came to be embodied in Madhuri Dixit, who, in the words of popular film historian Nikhat Kazmi, "somehow managed to achieve that elusive equilibrium between the somewhat anaesthetised woman of substance and the brainless sex kitten. In short, the greatest oxymoron of the turning century."[23] Apart from asserting her own style of dialogue, Dixit established her onscreen presence through provocative dance numbers. The dance numbers from her immensely popular hits had the quality of the "item songs" that would become ubiquitous in the first part of the twenty-first century. She was the only heroine who was performing in such a style in the 1990s. "Whether the genre was action or family melodrama, Dixit's screen presence easily overshadowed her male costars. . . . Dixit brought an enticing combination of innocence, comedy, and sensuality to her performances," Monika Mehta notes.[24] Dance numbers such as "Ek Do Teen" in *Tezaab*, "Choli Ke Pichhe Kya Hai" in *Khalnayak* (Villain, 1993), and "Dhak Dhak Karne Laga" in *Beta* (Son, 1992) remain the only memorable episodes from her films that claimed success at the box office but have otherwise become unwatchable in the twenty-first century, disappearing from mainstream discourses on enduring images from Indian films. Mehta, in her study of censorship and sexuality in Hindi cinema, has clarified how Madhuri Dixit's dance performances were arguably more sensual than those of her predecessors such as Zeenat Aman. Dixit's star-text was born out of a combination of her sexualized persona and screen dominance on the one hand and her "conservative public persona" on the other. "Articles in film magazines and newspapers emphasized her classical dance training as well as her middle-class, Maharashtrian background, duly noting that her mother managed her love life," writes Mehta. "In interviews Dixit confirmed her image as a 'good, middle-class Indian daughter' who would follow her parents' guidance and willingly accept an arranged marriage (which she eventually did). . . . This public identity effectively mediated her relationship with her middle-class female fans."[25]

If conjugating the new Indian man and woman was the preoccupation of ur-Bollywood, as outlined above, the vestiges of the 1970s action genre were recast in an action-intensive pseudo-realism that was engendered by 1980s politics of caste and religion.[26] There was a slow building up of acceptability for "naming" the low-caste and the Muslim other, a process that was completed in the 1990s: while *Tezaab* had Hindi film's first Muslim villain, *Roja* built the first associative relation between Islam and terrorism. Valentina Vitali and Ravi Vasudevan have both pointed out one actor in particular, Nana Patekar, as an integral part of the gritty, pseudo-realist development. Patekar's early films such as *Ankush* (The Goad, 1986), *Krantiveer* (The Brave Revolutionary, 1994), and *Prahaar* (Assault, 1994) clearly reflected a Hindu right-wing machismo, but his roles shifted toward a certain social realism in *Salaam Bombay* (1988) and *Disha* (Direction, 1990). If Raj Kapoor's naive secular hero of the 1950s and the title characters in the 1977 film *Amar Akbar Anthony* were following the simple logic of Nehruvian nationalism, Nana Patekar's brand of heroism was more diffused and complex, according to Ravi Vasudevan. Vasudevan describes characters essayed by Patekar as a "tapestry of types," including "the psychotic gangster," a "narrator-character retailing scathing social critique for the 'small man' of an earlier socialist imagination," and a "Muslim gangster who sends up Hindu middle-class mores" in films such as *Parinda* (Flight of Pigeons, 1989), *Raju Ban Gaya Gentleman* (And So Raju Became a Gent, 1992), and *Ghulam e Mustafa* (Mustafa, the Loyal Slave, 1998).[27] Even in the early gritty action films that coincided with the Hindu right-wing party Shiv Sena's reemergence in Bombay and Maharashtra, there was a distinct rendering of the variations of space within the city itself. Vitali has observed, for example, how in *Krantiveer* "the idea of physical impact is primarily signaled by the protagonist's look and his movement across urban space," thus emphasizing the implications of his class identity.[28]

While, to the Indian viewer, Patekar's roles were reminiscent of Amitabh Bachchan as a worker in *Deewar* and *Kaala Patthar* (Black Stone, 1979), the changed political context of the ur-Bollywood films created a different set of dynamics between the urban space and the male protagonist's body. The pan-Indian discourse inherited from the 1950s and the 1970s was expanded to incorporate new class, caste, and urban/rural dichotomies in the form of "pan-indigenism." This was not an isolated phenomenon happening in Bombay films; "pan-indigenism" became the way in which the regional industries spoke to and through Hindi. Writing on "urbanity" in Bhojpuri cinema in the post-global era, Ratnakar Verma and Jitendra Tripathy note that Hindi cinema in the 1980s "had begun to habitually equate village life with slums, choosing to deal with rural themes indirectly through the mediation of the slum, which could be conveniently seen as part of the urban culture, but could also be used to emphasise social polarities of all kinds."[29] Paradoxically, this was a small piece within an emergent neo-nationalist vision—expressed through what Sircar calls a Hindi-English modernity—that was linked to multinational capital's rapid replacement of the "regional markets with a national market." Sircar reads the "pan-indigenism'" of the 1980s as a force that "displace[d] the earlier specificity of regional identities in India and, relatedly, the emergence of a changed equation between Hindi and various regional languages. As opposed to the anti-Hindi sentiments expressed by several of the regional movements of the 1950s, the chauvinism of 1980s' regionalism now feeds into the logic of a resurgent Hindu fundamentalism, one that actively advocates Hindi as national language. It was this emergence of Hindi as the new lingua franca that provides the conditions of possibility for the 'new' Bombay commercial cinema of the 1980s."[30]

The Sound of Audiocassettes

The final defining element of ur-Bollywood films concerns film music. Irrespective of their ties with the old world of star-centric production and melodramatic form, the new films that became vehicles for the careers of Aamir Khan, Madhuri Dixit, Shah Rukh Khan, and other stars of the 1990s benefited from a tectonic shift in the production of film music. While in 1980 most of the playback music was recorded by HMV and sung by its fewer than half-dozen contracted singers, by the end of the decade, HMV was struggling to regain a part of the market. A plethora of young artists had emerged, recording for nascent music production companies. The change was brought about by the introduction of audiocassettes, which were significantly cheaper than vinyl records. As cassette players and recorders, manufactured in Japan, flooded the Indian market, ownership of film songs became much more affordable. All that was needed was a set of experimentations in recording and sales, which inaugurated a new line of entrepreneurship. The change affected not just film music but the entire music industry, as detailed by Peter Manuel:

> The advent of cassette technology effectively restructured the music industry in India. By the mid-1980s, cassettes had come to account for 95 per cent of the recorded music market, with records being purchased only by wealthy audiophiles, radio stations and cassette pirates who prefer using them as masters. The recording industry monopoly formerly enjoyed by HMV (now Gramophone Co. of India, or "GramCo") dwindled to less than 15 per cent of the market as over 300 competitors entered the recording field. While sales of film music remained strong, the market expanded so exponentially—from $1.2 million in 1980 to over $12 million in 1986—the film music came to constitute only about half of the market, the remainder consisting of regional folk and devotional music, and other forms of "non-film," or in industry parlance, "basic" pop music.[31]

The execution of independent music production was a difficult task up until the 1980s, because competing with the gargantuan HMV meant both manufacturing vinyl records and cutting into a market where only a minority owned record players. The enormous amount of control that the Indian government exercised on manufacturing industries, combined with its sluggish and corrupt bureaucracy, made it almost impossible to initiate new enterprises. The result was the seemingly natural invincibility of a company such as HMV and the few artists it employed. The astonishing numbers associated with a handful of singers such as Lata Mangeshkar and Mohammad Rafi owe more to the closed loop that characterized the film music market. Film producers had to hire from the tiny pool of music directors who worked with HMV and its league of singers. Apart from the prohibitively expensive vinyl records, the only outlets for film songs were the state-controlled radio and television. With the limited field of exposure, GramCo (the parent company of HMV in India) was not making significant profit. In fact, it could continue as a powerful corporation only because it was catering to a captive and severely limited market. Once cassette players flooded the market, the possibility of selling music on cassettes and making substantial profit became a reality. Cassettes could be produced at a mere fraction of the cost of vinyl records and, even after keeping a profit margin unthinkable to vinyl producers, could be sold at hugely affordable prices. HMV's last vinyl release of a Hindi film was in 1997. In 2011, vinyl production of film music resumed as an experiment for niche markets consisting of wealthy patrons; its eventual destiny remains to be determined.

The transition from vinyl to cassettes in the 1980s echoed the 1940s shift from studio-based production to the star-centric system. Both changes significantly reconfigured the content and form of Indian popular cinema, and both were initiated by individual interventions that could not be controlled by the state. The Indian copyright law that dated back to 1957 did not have provisions for the protection of a recorded performance by a particular artist. The first disruption in the market for film music was created by "clones" of popular songs—a song originally sung by Kishore Kumar or Lata Mangeshkar, for example, would be recorded by Kumar Sanu or Anuradha Paudwal—which would be sold on non-HMV labels at a fraction of the price of the original HMV cassettes. Most of the singers who would emerge as established by the end of the 1980s—Kavita Krishnamurthy, Udit Narayan, Alka Yagnik, Sadhana Sargam, Abhijeet, Kumar Sanu, Sudesh Bhosle, and Mohammed Aziz—imitated the singing style of the HMV greats, such as Mukesh, Kishore Kumar, Mohammad Rafi, Lata Mangeshkar, and Asha Bhosle. Rafi and Kumar died in 1980 and 1987 respectively, and Mukesh had died in 1976. These losses created a space for male lead singers to emerge in the late 1980s. The female playback was still dominated by

Mangeshkar and her sister Bhosle, but the rise of the clones engineered by the non-HMV companies managed to diversify the market.

The unlikely agent of the audiocassette revolution to finally break through HMV's monopoly was Gulshan Kumar, a bootlegger, who began selling pre-recorded audiocassettes with illegal copies of soundtracks out of his fruit juice stall in Delhi. He slowly began a low-cost recording company that produced cassettes under the "T-Series" label. His company, Super Cassette Industries, rose steadily through the mid-1980s. But the defining break came with the overwhelming success of *QSQT*.[32] The soundtrack of *QSQT* featured Udit Narayan and Alka Yagnik, who began their careers as copycat performers and would not have been able to showcase their talents had Super Cassette Industries not come along. The rise of Gulshan Kumar invoked both admiration and disgust. He was the "small man" who defeated the giant corporation HMV, but he was also viewed as a petty shopkeeper who verged on the criminal. The narrative of his success was extraordinary, nonetheless, and the final twist in it was more unpredictable even than his achievements: Gulshan Kumar was shot dead in broad daylight in Bombay in 1997. The investigations that followed confirmed the Bombay industry's clandestine relationship with the underworld. Super Cassette Industries has since continued to dominate the film music market, having served as the platform for the rise of most of the leading playback singers since the late 1980s. Venus and Tips were Indian labels that rose in the shadow of Super Cassette's success. In 1998, they were joined by Sony Entertainment, when the global giant entered the market in 1998. HMV has since been able to absorb the initial shock and remains one of the major producers, though most of its sales come from the recordings made in the pre–T-Series era. The government has since closed the loophole in copyright laws that had enabled Gulshan Kumar and his peers to produce clone recordings. The concurrence of the audiocassette movement and the cluster of ur-Bollywood films offered the perfect degree of instability to break the regulated market's hold over both films and film music once and for all.

Bollywood's Nationalist Trifecta: Nation, Diaspora, and Enemies

The ur-Bollywood moment coincided with concrete changes within India's film and media world, including the rise of a new generation of stars and the end of HMV's monopoly over film music. The transitional political climate was conducive to those changes. But for ur-Bollywood to morph into the brand "Bollywood," a much closer alignment to the emergence of a new, pro-global

India was necessary. It was in the era of globalization that both India and its commercial film industry underwent a radical change in their respective global images. Ostentatious in self-expression, both entities organized their identities and loyalties around three myths. The first was the idea of a reemergent India, which was on its way to acquiring immense material wealth to complement its alleged spiritual and cultural strengths. The second was that there was an innate Indian culture that was self-evident and ran through every Indian, binding him or her with the global Indian family. This blind belief and propaganda in "Indian culture" helped secure a neo-conservative hold on society and build an emotional bridge with the affluent diaspora. The third, as corollary to the "culture" theory, was in the definition of enemies of nation and national culture and well-being: Muslims, Pakistanis, the poor and disenfranchised, the lower castes, the feminists, and the communists could all be marked as detrimental to the extended body politic of global India.

An emergent India became the focus of popular and critical publications in the first decade of the millennium, and there exists a relatively clear narrative of its evolution.[33] It begins with the end of the Cold War, which did not directly affect India since India was part of the third front represented by the Non-Aligned Movement inaugurated in 1955. India's post–Cold War transformation was thus far subtler than that which happened in the "second world." Five-Year Plans, the nationalized banks, and the state-controlled radio and television would continue, but the tenor of official discourse on the nation-state and its relationship with the people was transformed radically. The downward slide of the socialist world in the last two years of the 1980s had coincided with the Indian economy reaching a tipping point. With foreign currency reserves depleted and the potential for a severe shortage of resources for its burgeoning population, the Indian government opened its markets to foreign investments and privatization in 1991. As India, with its billion-strong population, was seen as the new land of opportunity for developed capitalist countries, India's cultural life was reimagined and recast in a global mold. For the first time, the same new Indian national image was being marketed in both India and the world outside. The myth of a "shining India"—a phrase used frequently in national and international media—was premised on some facts mixed delicately with dreams and layers of collective desire from a suddenly visible Indian middle class. This was the largest growing consumer sector that global companies entering the Indian market targeted—from cosmetics to soft drinks and fashion labels. The newfound freedom to choose and purchase global brand names gave this class a confidence that it readily poured into a neoliberal nationalist image of itself.

Around the same time, along with other South Asian nations, India learned to utilize the economic success of its diaspora. Susan Koshy and R. Radhakrishnan have written on the material effect of the Indian diaspora, as labor exported out of South Asia became "a strategy for economic development and poverty reduction" and India became "the world's leading recipient of remittances with inflows totaling $23.7 billion." And these were simply the official numbers.[34] In 2003, the Indian government institutionalized its celebration and acceptance of the diaspora by marking January 9, the day of Mahatma Gandhi's return from South Africa, as Pravasi Bharatiya Divas, or Overseas Indian Day: "The choice of Gandhi as the quintessential expatriate patriot was an inspired one; both overseas Indian and nationalist leader, he embodies the reconciliation of multiple loyalties that the commemoration promotes as possible and necessary. Gandhi offers an idealistic figure for the economic, political, and cultural patriotism that the Indian government solicits from its diasporic subjects."[35]

The Indian nation-state had moved away from the Gandhian ideal of self-reliance and small economies even during the Nehruvian era; globalization only pushed it further. But just as the Nehruvian postcolonial state had created a ritual out of remembering Gandhi, the post-global state reinvented the ritual, using him as a stand-in for whatever was the need of the moment. In classical Hindi cinema as well as in other regional cinemas from the 1950s through the 1980s, Gandhi appeared as the silent giver of laws. He was, after all, called the "father of the nation"; his photograph loomed ubiquitous in the courtroom in every film produced in India. In new India, Gandhi is reinvented, and so is khadi, the handspun cloth that he popularized, in the wake of India's liberalization of cotton export policies. In Bollywood films, he is various things: a positive political figure in *Hey Ram* (Oh God, 2000), an egotistical stubborn politician in *The Legend of Bhagat Singh* (2002), and a "management-guru"-style deviser of universally applicable strategies in *Lage Raho Munna Bhai* (Carry On, Munna Bhai, 2006). The changing globalization-era Indian iconography of Gandhi holds a mirror up to the reorientation of India's national imagination.

The rise in visibility of the Indian middle class—and India's few billionaires—in the eyes of the world gave India the shining image that its ideologues desperately wanted. The world had much to gain from India's "shine"; India was, after all, a safe ally to global capital and a tame frontier, radically different from the secretive and stubborn "red China." But India's record national growth—reported to be between 5 and 8 percent since 1990 and repeated in every pro-globalization account—provided a severely restricted view of the national reality. The first aspect distorted by this view is the nonlinearity of national growth. According to Stanley Wolpert,

For India's impoverished 300 million landless peasants and urban slum-dwellers bogged down in mud and squalor, at the mercy of monsoon rains bringing famine and flood, however, Manmohan's [Prime Minister Manmohan Singh] reforms brought little relief and less comfort. The daily drudgery of village India's bullock-cart economy remained as precarious as it had always been, while the wretched crowding of megalopolis slums in Bombay, Calcutta, and Delhi became more painful to those who labored to erect palaces of urban prosperity without earning enough to feed their families. Globalization increased disparities between the very rich and most poor, making those differences more disconcertingly glaring and harsh.[36]

At this juncture in history, Bollywood stepped in on the side of the nation-state, providing the template for a neo-nationalist imaginary and thus further complicating a political scenario caught between religious nationalism and global capitalism. While the contradictions within the Indian economy made "shining India" an impossible ideal to sustain in material terms, what the shine lacked in substance was made up for with an aggressive nationalism reared in the shadow of Hindutva, a political ideology based on a selective interpretation of Hinduism.

The ideology of Indian popular cinema vis-à-vis the nation-state in the first four postcolonial decades had been nonlinear and complex, caught as it always was between disorganized market forces and state control. The nation in Indian cinema has more than often been presented as an embodiment of a glorious cultural past on the one hand and an austere Nehruvian (with some shades of the Gandhian embedded in it) present on the other. The 1990s saw a radical shift in its imagination of the national community. The idea of India as secular nation was gradually clothed in a rhetoric of neoliberalism that equated a catholic Hinduism with secular India and Bharat (one of the Sanskrit mythological names for the Indian peninsula) with the modern Indian nation-state. Incorporating the right-wing, Euro-American critiques of Islam as incapable of coexisting with post-Enlightenment modernity (or with secularism), the Hindu nationalist idea championed India's Hindu identity as the authentic modern identity for India. "Akhand Bharatiya Parivar," a politicized phrase meaning the "undivided Indian family," entered popular political usage, used first by the extremist religious leaders and then adopted by Hindu nationalists at large. The organizing of the Pravasi Bharatiya Divas fit very well into the overall vision of the undivided Indian family. Within the realm of nationalist politics, the seemingly innocuous nationalist phrase contained a jingoist vision of the Indian subcontinent as one nation, evoking pre-partition (or literally nonpartitioned or *akhand*) India as a rallying point. India or Bharat was the eternal nation, Hinduism was the eternal religion (*sanatana dharma*), and Indian expatriates (particularly wealthy expatriates who were potential investors in India's pro-globalization private sector) were beloved members of the same extended family. Interestingly, it did not require the invention of a totally new political idiom to make this idea popular. There had been enough variations of Hindu and Indian identities in the nineteenth and twentieth centuries to deploy in new formulations. M. K. Gandhi's political rhetoric was steeped in religious ideology, and Nehru did nothing less than "discover" a nation in India's hoary past in his seminal work *The Discovery of India*. The idea of a Hindu nationalist India that could also lay claims on secularism, democracy, and modernity was thus within the limits of possibility in an era of unprecedented changes.

Home and nation, in the neoliberal imaginary, are nothing if not defined by walls or boundaries to keep the outsiders at bay. This was one of the prongs of the new Indian nationalism, which was manifested in Bollywood as a departure from the Hindi cinema's time-honored trope of avoiding maligning particular ethnic or religious communities. In 1992, Mani Ratnam's *Roja* became the first Hindi film to conflate Islamic terrorism and Pakistan (although originally shot in Tamil, the film was also dubbed in Hindi) and to name these as India's unequivocal enemy. A young couple from Tamil Nadu travels to Kashmir, and the husband, Rishi, a computer scientist working for the Indian government, is kidnapped by Kashmiri secessionists, the ransom demanded being the release of their imprisoned leader. The wife, Roja, appeals unsuccessfully to the state for help. After a few twists in the narrative, the film ends with the couple reunited. The villains in the narrative—especially Wasim Khan, the imprisoned leader, and Liaqat, who orchestrates Rishi's kidnapping—are portrayed in shades that were quite rare in the pre-9/11 era. The timing of the film was extremely crucial: in 1992, through the events leading up to the fateful demolition of the Babri mosque by Hindu extremists on December 6, Hindu ultranationalists had been extremely provocative toward Kashmir and Indian Muslims, and their anti-Muslim rhetoric had maintained a high pitch. Kidnapping for ransom of government officials and businessmen in secessionist areas—in Kashmir as well as the northeastern state of Assam—had happened several times in the late 1980s and the early 1990s, with most incidents ending in the death of the abducted individuals. The threat that Roja's husband, Rishi, faced to his life in the film was therefore more real than anything the heroes of the all-India film ever encountered, making *Roja* a new kind of film and bringing realism from the realm of the "art film" into the world of melodrama. In Rustom Bharucha's view, the fact that the film carries its politics lightly and seems innocent on the surface made the message even more dangerous. The private life together of the ideal woman (who is naive, reasonably educated, and devoted to her husband, the gods, and country) and the ideal man (a Brahmin boy with enough technological know-how to be a cryptographer who, guided by tradition and nostalgia, lets his mother help him find a bride from a village) is seen as flowering under the nurturing guidance of the state (Roja's village, as it is shown, could be a model village in any propaganda film), until the misguided politics of the enemies of the nation collides with their happiness. Compared with villains in past Hindi films who were corrupt or dishonest or "evil" in a general manner, *Roja's* "terrorists" were, in Bharucha's analysis, "specifically marked as Kashmiri and Muslim. Far from being flamboyant or even caricatured, they are played realistically."[37] Incidentally, *Roja* was not a single cinematic text with a particular politics; it was the breakthrough film into Bombay cinema for a celebrated South Indian director.

Mani Ratnam's next film, with an equally profitable soundtrack by A. R. Rahman (*Roja's* Hindi soundtrack was Rahman's breakthrough album), was *Bombay* (1994), which was based upon the riots that occurred in Bombay around the demolition of the Babri mosque. Bharucha describes the clandestine conditions under which *Bombay* could be released: "The film needed nothing less than the extra-constitutional clearance of Bal Thackeray, the leader of the extremist Hindu party, the Shiv Sena, which had masterminded the riots. . . . Thackeray had the film edited according to his dictates before it could be released commercially."[38]

Mani Ratnam's oeuvre was distinguished as much for its form as for its content. As Manjunath Pendakur has described, "Mani Ratnam in the 1990s was perhaps the most adept at combining elements of visual and aural style from the West with those from India to tell his stories," using creative music composition by A. R. Rahman and Ilaiyaraaja and methods such as the "jump cut" in picturization of songs, as opposed to the "earlier traditions of continuity."[39] In retrospect, an updated and sophisticated form that could distinguish Ratnam's work from his contemporaries and could leave an overall enduring influence has clearly superseded the enormity of ideological problems in his representation of the nation and its enemies. Ratnam's influence has cascaded in various directions. Once *Roja* had crossed the threshold of naming the enemy, a film such as *Border* (1997) could use the popular format to cover the subject of the 1971 Bangladesh war, and *Gadar: Ek Prem Katha* (Revolt: A Love Story, 2001) could revisit the violence of the 1947 partition. *Border* was directed by J. P. Dutta, whose next two films, *Refugee* (2000) and *LOC Kargil* (2003), would not match up to *Border's* success. Neither *Border* nor *Gadar* had the technical sophistication of Ratnam's *Roja* or *Bombay*, but they were nevertheless part of the milieu of ultranationalist cinema that Mani Ratnam made popular.

Bollywood's incarnation was completed in 1995 when *Dilwale Dulhaniya Le Jayenge* (hereafter *DDLJ*) marked the advent of the Non-Resident Indian (NRI) as the protagonist in Indian mainstream cinema. An entire subgenre of big-budget films followed the success of *DDLJ*; the trend also coincided with the stellar rise of Shah Rukh Khan as a global Indian star. Anupama Chopra notes that "in 2003, a Nielsen EDI survey reported that seven of the top ten Hindi films in the UK from 1989 onward starred Shah Rukh."[40] My 2010 essay on Bollywood and globalization discussed the concept of the NRI in the film:

> In *DDLJ*, the Non-Resident Indian (the NRI), hitherto portrayed in Hindi films as the marginal outsider with affected speech and behavior, was redeemed and validated as not just a possible Indian national subject, but possibly one of the best. . . . The film broke several established Bollywood models; the men rather than the women were projected as guardians of "tradition" and "honor" (albeit Simran—the woman—was still locus of the struggle as well as the prize to be won), and it was the male hero who had to atone and toil to make up for his brief youthful misgivings. Covering two continents, the drama as it unfolded was visually and verbally "Indian"; it was openly vocal about Indian values and customs, in spite of the fact that the major protagonists lived their lives in England. Moreover, the NRI was not required to return to India and stay there—and this was the twist that made it for *DDLJ*—the NRI could remain NR and be the "I," that is, Indian.[41]

That *DDLJ* was not an isolated text glorifying the Indianness of expatriates was made clear by the cultural leanings of films that followed it, such as *Kuch Kuch Hota Hai* (Something Happens, 1998), a film that predicated itself on the reprisal of *DDLJ*'s romantic pair, Shah Rukh Khan and Kajol. In a particularly overstated show of expatriate Indianness, the character Pooja (played by Rani Mukherjee), a student transfer from Oxford to an Indian college, stuns the overtly Westernized students who had gathered to harass her by singing the Hindu devotional song "Om Jai Jagdish Hare," popularized immensely since it was featured in *Purab aur Pachchim* (East and West, 1970). This song evokes a connection between *Purab aur Pachchim* and *Kuch Kuch Hota Hai* that is too coincidental not to be deliberate. In *Purab aur Pachchim*, a decadent West and even more decadent expatriate Indians living in the West were chastised by the hero Bharat (the Sanskrit name for India), who meets the Westernized Preeti in London. Preeti travels to India with Bharat and unlearns her Westernization to be a true Indian woman and a fitting partner for Bharat. In Johar's 1998 film, it was the expatriate's turn to be more Indian than the actual residents of India.

While the 1970s version of populist patriotism harped on stereotypes such as the glories of ancient Indian civilization and India's spiritual superiority over the materialistic West, the 1990s patriotism propagated a neoconservative approach, presenting Indianness as a perfect marriage between tradition and a capitalist global modernity.

It was not just ideology but a market-driven campaign that turned patriotism into accessible capital. The young rebels from the past were replaced by young men and women who did not fight against state, family, or patriarchy in any form. They were poster children for "shining India." The secular socialist sentimentality of the postcolonial decades was replaced by a neoconservative pro-wealth outlook in the 1990s when India's GDP began to show record growth following the implementation of new economic policies. The image of affluence in earlier all-India films from the 1950s through the 1980s was unreal, created as a lower-middle-class fantasy.[42] In contrast, the post-liberalization Bollywood has been partial to the seemingly endless exhibition of brand names and merchandise that entered India in the 1990s.

Kuch Kuch Hota Hai draws special attention in this regard. Anupama Chopra has written how the director, Karan Johar, went to London on a special shopping trip before shooting began. The parade of labels in the film ended up as excessive, almost as if Johar were trying to justify his expensive trip to his father (the film's producer). Everyone's clothes, especially those of the three main characters—Rahul, Anjali, and Pooja, played by Shah Rukh Khan, Kajol, and Rani Mukherjee respectively—"prominently displayed their foreign-designer origins. Several had labels emblazoned across the chest. Anjali's first shot has her playing basketball in a DKNY tracksuit. Rahul, more sartorially evolved than his earlier screen avatars, is partial to Polo Sport and Gap."[43] Whatever Johar's immediate motives were, the international designer labels worked out in multiple ways. In the pre-global era, the all-India film had influenced hairstyles and fashion off-screen: the big hairdo with a bun at the back in the 1960s; the haircuts worn by Dilip Kumar, Dharmendra, and Amitabh Bachchan; the variations in the length of women's tunics and the width of the bottoms; the "Bobby print" in 1973 after the eponymous character in *Bobby*. But "brand placement" was categorically different in a controlled market economy. As the Indian markets opened to foreign brands, however, "brand placement" exploded on the big screen. In another telling of the story, "Bollywood" itself became a brand, the face of India in overseas markets. In her book, Chopra writes of the Oxford Street Gap store in London that ran out of logo-emblazoned orange sweatshirts after Shah Rukh Khan's character was seen wearing one in *Kuch Kuch Hota Hai.* Johar's use of brands in this film was, according to Chopra, trendsetting, offering a new way of defining identity. This directly reversed the notion of Indian identity that Raj Kapoor's character could sing of in *Shree 420*:

My shoes are Japanese
My trousers are English
My red hat is Russian
Still, my heart is Indian.

The Indianness of the heart in the post-global representation is not just complementary to an international vestmental ensemble. Indian bodies were now entitled to all the globality that money could buy. New stars such as Shah Rukh Khan, Kajol, and Aamir Khan as well as older stars such as Amitabh Bachchan "sold a new India to the world, at the same time that it sold an accessible, buyable world to the newly affluent Indians."[44]

The most enduring effect of the above interface involved bridging the gap between resident Indians and expatriates, thus contributing to the already popular idea of a global India. Recalling the expatriate Baldev Singh's reference in *DDLJ* to the Non-Resident Indian as "the proverbial washerman's dog, who belongs neither to the ghar [house] nor the ghat [riverbank]," Anupama Chopra points out the ideological feat that Bollywood performed in vindicating the expatriate Indian:

They [the expatriate Indians] did belong. Living in the West had not robbed them of their roots; Indian values were portable and malleable. They could straddle both worlds, just as the characters in *DDLJ* and *Kuch Kuch Hota Hai* did. Both films offered non-resident Indians a palatable India. The poverty, corruption, injustice—all reasons for leaving home, perhaps—were carefully edited out. Instead these films fed a nostalgia for an imagined homeland in which beautiful homes were filled with large, loving families, rituals and traditions remained intact, and children, despite their cool posturing, were happily subservient to their parents.[45]

While the films' foregrounding of the nonresident Indian celebrated Indian family values across the globe, one remarkable exception chose an Indian locale, albeit no less Disneyfied than the London or Los Angeles of Bollywood: *Hum Aapke Hai Koun* (Who Am I to You?, 1994, henceforth *HAHK*), Suraj Barjatya's second blockbuster after *Maine Pyaar Kiya*, a melodrama solely about two weddings and the subsequent familial interactions. In *HAHK*, Salman Khan essays almost the same role he had in *Maine Pyaar Kiya*, playing Prem, the scion of a wealthy business family. The heroine Madhuri Dixit, by now an established and experienced female star, carries over her dominant screen image from *Khalnayak* and *Beta* to this film. Her presence fills the screen so much that it is supposed to have inspired the painter M. F. Hussain to make his film *Gaja Gamini* (2000), an incoherent and derivative allegory on art and its muse. In *HAHK*, Dixit's character, Nisha, is a computer engineer, a fact that is never established cinematically, as in the film she is depicted doing everything but work on a computer. Although she is not the quiet, demure maiden (it is her elder sister who is more like *Maine Pyaar Kiya*'s Suman), Nisha, like Suman, is willing to sacrifice all for the sake of the family's happiness. Nikhat Kazmi's reading of *HAHK* confirms the message of the film that was not even subtle or coded:

> Here was an unbridled celebration of the *Bharatiya parampara* [Indian tradition] that was being saluted and sanctified by the BJP as the Indian way of life. . . . In such a set-up, class, caste and communal differences do exist. Nevertheless, everyone—the lower class, the minority community—are all happily adjusted due to the benevolence of the ruler-masters: the upper class and the dominant community. In *HAHK*, there is . . . the happy servant and the Muslim doctor couple who join the familial bonhomie time and again. Simply because they do not clamour about separateness and distinct identities. [*sic*][46]

The somewhat arbitrary success of *HAHK* is significant in that it became a watershed moment for production of a parallel resident-national spectacle that could complement the emergent cinematic spectacle of the Indian diaspora. While there are no significant films that followed the same formula, *HAHK*'s enduring influence could be felt in the spectacularization of rituals and celebrations within the familial space. An entire gamut of television serials, including *Kyunki Saas Bhi Kabhi Bahu Thi* (Because a Mother-in-Law Was Once a Daughter-in-Law, Too, 2000–2008), modeled themselves on *HAHK*'s spectacle.

HAHK's was not the only form of spectacle that was adapted to suit India's growing television programming needs. A cinematic revisioning of patriotism, packaged specifically for metropolitan young viewers, was happening on television at the same time young resident and expatriate Indians were defining a new, more globalized Indianness on-screen. The aesthetic logic of the song "Om Jai Jagdish Hare" in *Kuch Kuch Hota Hai* or "I Love My India" in *Pardes* (Foreign Country, 1997) finds resonance in what Vamsee Juluri calls "youth-oriented and globally positioned music video nationalism." Two non-film audio-video productions are highlighted by Juluri in this context: (1) Alisha Chinai's *Made in India* (1996), which "was the first India pop album to be sold on a scale comparable to Hindi film music albums, and the music video for the title song was among the first popular Indian music videos," and (2) the music video that accompanied A. R. Rahman's "Maa Tujhe Salaam," which was part of an album produced by Sony, *Vande Mataram* (the album is based on a nineteenth-century nationalist song, and Rahman's song is a Hindi/Urdu rendition of the same).[47]

An extrinsic element that contributed to the sea change was the arrival of Star TV, a network based in Hong Kong and owned at that time by Rupert Murdoch. Coincident with the macro-economic shifts mandated by the World Bank, the advent of Star TV caused an explosion in the Indian television viewer's everyday relationship with new configurations of capitalism. The rapid expansion of Star TV between 1991 and 1993 was fueled in part by the government's inexperience with private enterprise. But it was India's first Hindi cable channel, Zee TV, that "accomplished what Star TV alone could not; 'with its relentless entertainment agenda,' Zee cut into portions of Doordarshan's 'hitherto untouched mass national audience.'"[48] Films and film music became the primary content of all emergent private cable channels and of the network Doordarshan as well. According to Juluri, the battle between private and state-run television in Indian languages "came down to a battle of film music countdowns."[49]

With television providing seemingly unlimited opportunities for broadcasting film music, principles behind the "picturization" of songs underwent a profound change, as did the style of music. The cassette industry had already crowded the market with more music, singers, and musical styles; increased television exposure demanded a song to be more like an MTV-style music video; and a rhythm-based fusion music—noted exponents included composers such as Ilaiyaraaja and A. R. Rahman—came into being. These three factors—audiocassettes, television channels, and fusion music—became the cornerstones of the music of Bollywood. Rahman, whose early work was in television advertisements, began as Ilaiyaraaja's assistant and developed his distinct style. Ashok Da Ranade describes how Rahman's departure from the circular movement of the traditional Indian rhythm and his unexpected use of choral elements made his songs particularly suitable for MTV-style picturization:

> [The] chorality may sometimes become background music through vocalizing or sometimes it may appear to function as chance contributory elements adding tonal colour. The collectivity is, of course, not confined to melody or song. As a part of his musical imagination it spills over to collective movement which stops short of becoming a stylized or codified dance. Instead, the collectivity becomes hypnotically repetitive and a simple kinesthetic pattern which may intermittently suggest dance but mostly remains satisfied by making rhythmic frameworks more catchy and appealing to all. In "Chhaiyan chhaiyan" (in *Dil Se*) we have the train-

roof-top dance-song which has strong clap-rhythm, all kinds of energetic, collective and rather jerkily collective movements with tonal framework of *raga* Sarang, the most worked-over *raga*-frame in the categories of Indian folk and religious music.[50]

Formative innovations such as these completed the long death not just of genres of film music but of the entire industry that had dominated Indian popular culture from the 1940s. The path for the new film music to be ushered in had been cleared in the mid-1980s with the advent of cassette-based production. "In effect, the cassette revolution had definitively ended the hegemony . . . of the corporate music industry in general, of film music, of the Lata [Mangeshkar]-Kishore [Kumar] duocracy, and of the uniform aesthetic which the Bombay film-music producers had superimposed on a few hundred million listeners over the preceding forty years," writes Peter Manuel.[51] There are still not more than a handful of studies on the enormous shift that Indian film music has experienced in the recent years. Manuel's groundbreaking work on the cassette industry in India provides the most useful contextual background of that shift.[52]

Bollywood, Corporatization, and the Spectacle of Consumption

Bollywood emerged in the twenty-first century out of such radical changes in the world of Indian cinema and media as described in the last section. Ideologically, the crucial shift to Bollywood entailed the rise of a liberal, right-leaning worldview, combining a diminished symbolic importance for the state, on the one hand, and a contrasting increase in symbolic importance for the citizen-subject, on the other. The 1990s phenomena of the positively valenced NRI and the increasingly aggressive tenor of nationalism were sustained and naturalized in the new millennium, with overtones of an ever-increasing global ambition.

Guru (2007), a thinly veiled biopic of Dhirubhai Ambani, the founder of Reliance Industries, was unabashedly critical of the Nehruvian nation-state. The film conflates corporate interests with national pride, presenting the capitalist as a hero whose unscrupulous but profitable business practice fights a just war against a sluggish, controlling government. Gurukant Desai, the Ambani figure in *Guru*, creates wealth for the public by making money, an end that justifies his illegal means. The government, by espousing a regulatory socialist model, keeps the public in perpetual poverty. *Guru* thus recasts in a neoliberal mold the narrative of the individual citizen's dreams and aspirations vis-à-vis the nation-state that Bombay cinema had espoused since *Shree 420*, pitting the freedom that capital promises and delivers against the "false" security of the nation-state's laws. Karan Johar's *My Name is Khan* (2010) cast the Bollywood superstar Shah Rukh Khan in the mold of the cosmopolitan global citizen propagating a global version of the American dream. As a general trend, while the Non-Resident Indian remained ubiquitous and nearly beyond reproach, the image of the Indian resident subject was transformed beyond recognition. The relationship between reformist social heroism and the imagined community it sought to reform was interpellated by a composite individualism, created out of a pastiche of rhetoric and imagery from mostly Hollywood and earlier Bombay-based Hindi cinema.

An extrinsic factor that influenced film production and played a role in the rise of Bollywood was the physical compartmentalization of the market. The phenomenon of multiplexes, often an extension of air-conditioned shopping malls (themselves a post-global phenomenon in India), brought the urban middle-class to the theater in record numbers.[53] Big-budget films promising all-around entertainment and superior cinematography and sound were produced specifically for this urban affluent viewership; the same category of films was exported globally to cater to the diaspora. Even though these films came to represent Bollywood—which became a readily recognizable stand-in nickname for Indian popular cinema—in India and the world, there have been several hundred commercial films produced in Hindi and all the regional languages that aimed at selling tickets at lower prices in theaters outside of the metropolises and then collecting revenue from cable telecasts and DVD sales.

Opinions vary on the "newness" of Bollywood's current era. Derek Bose, a journalist who has written extensively on Bollywood, has conjectured that "growing film literacy and exposure to overseas cinematic trends through the electronic media" have transformed at least a section of the audience. This, combined with the "maturing" of the industry "to a point where it holds the capacity to handle any kind of film, of whatever magnitude and budget to match the very best in the world," has resulted in "the death of the formula."[54] Bose's statement, representative of a broad spectrum of popular opinion, is applicable not to formula in general but partly to the all-India film form that was prevalent for over four decades. A section of the globalized Indian audience was certainly more enlightened and more demanding; its taste in films had departed from the pre-global generation's taste so far that the formula had to be dismantled in favor of a new adaptive format. The enlightened section of the audience, owing to class-based privilege and consequent access to resources, had also grown further from the masses. This, in addition to the physical compartmentalization of distribution, has created new generic divisions within the popular industry. Films are increasingly made for target sectors of viewership, the two most common mutually exclusive sectors being the middle-class metropolitan Indian and the expatriates on the one hand, and the suburban and rural viewers on the other. Another prevalent view, expressed mostly by directors and producers, is that it is simply not possible to make the all-India film anymore.

The alleged disappearance or decline of the all-India film in the twenty-first century seems to contradict the rise of the "Hindi modernity" discussed earlier. While Hindi became a viable mode for the new "national modern" in the 1980s, there are fissures within that "modern" that are made apparent in any ethnolinguistic study of Indian cinema. According to Verma and Tripathy, while certain "regional or sub-national identities," such as Bengali, Maharashtrian, or Tamil, have acquired obvious differentiation through long periods of social or political history, the Hindi-speaking states/peoples have always "had trouble finding a distinct and separate identity under the huge umbrella of Hindi, even though the prominent dialects of Hindi indicate clear dividing lines all over."[55] The sudden increase in production of Bhojpuri films at the turn of the twenty-first century obviously catered to a need that Hindi films with their synthesized Hindi/Indian identity could not fulfill.

As grounded as Bollywood's filmmaking is in the star-centric system that grew in the late 1940s, its economic world is far removed from the ad hoc mode of operation of the 1950s. India's mainstream film industry, now increasingly transparent under the watchful eyes of innumerable private media agencies, appears to have a kind of stability that was unthinkable in the pre-global era. The stability is visible in the limits on time and resources deployed in production, as well as in organized marketing and ticketing. "Instead of months and years, films are being wrapped up within weeks on start-to-finish schedules," writes Bollywood historian Mihir Bose.[56] The sense of order is not just a matter of impression. The synchronized release of films in urban multiplexes in India, foreign premieres, sale of merchandise, airing of commercials and songs on cable television, and organized sponsorships and advertisements all point to the structural changes in the industry that have contributed to the new order. First, the government's granting of industry status to film production in 1998 led to an organizing in the funding process for films.[57] This was further improved when the Indian Reserve Bank opened up the loan process to commercial cinema in 2001: "Like any entrepreneur applying for an industrial loan, a film-maker had to go through a drill of preparing project blueprints and spread sheets, submitting audited accounts and income tax returns, obtaining insurance cover, presenting collaterals and such other documents to the bank. . . . Meanwhile, angel investors and venture capitalists showed up. Watching them, some corporate houses also jumped on to the film-making bandwagon."[58]

This was precisely the process that all art cinema or "New Cinema" productions had to go through with the Film Finance Corporation and the National Film Development Corporation, beginning in the late 1960s. The loans and collaterals associated with the production of commercial cinema, especially in the twenty-first century, is on a scale so colossal as to make any comparison with FFC or NFDC funding for New Cinema almost irrelevant. The logical extension of this is the advent of corporatization, which according to Bose is the second important structural change in the economics of Indian cinema: "Leading production houses like Mukta Arts (owned by Subhash Ghai) and Pritish Nandy Communications went public. This reduced the personal liability of the producer-promoter and, at the same time, gave him access to large sums of the shareholders' money to play with. Consequently, the stranglehold of the proverbial Shylocks, including the underworld dons, loosened. More importantly, fresh directorial talent, which earlier did not have a chance to experiment with unconventional ideas and forms, were now able to see their dreams take shape under corporate banners."[59]

Film production unit Reliance Industries has emerged as a corporate player in the restructured film industry.[60] The number of companies that have operations in multiple sectors of the entertainment industry has increased, and these companies have frequently produced/financed films for various sectors of viewers. For instance, UTV was the primary financier of *Welcome to Sajjanpur* (2008), directed by Shyam Benegal, one of India's pioneering New Cinema directors. This is a phenomenon separate from the corporate sponsoring of films; the latter grew out of the implosion of product placement in the late 1990s. Coca-Cola, for example, has been involved in direct or indirect financing of feature films. One of the first films it financed was the Dreamz Unlimited production of *Phir Bhi Dil Hai Hindustani* (Still, the Heart Is Indian, 2000). Shah Rukh Khan, the star of the film, was also a cofounder and co-owner of the company and assumed full control of it in 2002, transforming it into Red Chillies Entertainment. Red Chillies has grown to be the umbrella company for Shah Rukh Khan's business empire, with stakes in advertising, television programming, film editing, and most notably the private cricket league (it is the primary stakeholder in Kolkata Knight Riders, the Indian Premier League team based in Calcutta). Coca-Cola has also used Aamir Khan extensively in its television advertisements and organized an Internet campaign to tie in its products with *Rang De Basanti* (Paint It Saffron, 2006). The field of advertising and the subsequent earnings for Indian cinema stars have widened significantly in the twenty-first century with media convergence. The popular discourse on stardom in India was made possible through the traditional network connecting cinema, television, and the press. The rise and phenomenal growth of media convergence in India has radically expanded and transformed the scope of star images. According to Valentina Vitali, "The personae of contemporary Hindi action heroes have internalized the advertising potential that came to be associated with Shah Rukh Khan. Actors such as John Abraham and Hrithik Roshan look like the anonymous figures of fashion shows. . . . Hrithik Roshan displays 'a physique so perfect, it seems somehow unreal and plastic.' Action heroes such as those interpreted by Roshan have muscles and show them, but their somewhat 'unreal plasticity' owes much to the fact that they do not use them."[61] The tableau of bodies that is expansive enough to allow such comparisons would have been unthinkable in the Cold War era, when Indian access to media was limited to state-controlled radio and television networks.

The corporate success of stars such as Aamir Khan and Shah Rukh Khan can be contrasted with the failure of Amitabh Bachchan's company ABCL, which went bankrupt in the late 1990s and became part of the overall narrative of decline in Bachchan's career and image. The next two phases that transformed him from the hero with a glorious past into a star whose global recognition is comparable with Shah Rukh Khan's could only have been possible in a post-global India. Susmita Dasgupta, who wrote her doctoral dissertation on Amitabh Bachchan (the first dissertation on popular stardom to be written in India), explains how incredible it was that, after his dismal downturn in film, politics, and business, he was suddenly the most popular star again in 1999. He was voted the star of the millennium in a BBC poll, and Madame Tussaud's museum inaugurated his wax statue, the first for an Indian star. The recasting of Bachchan began in 2000 with his hosting *Kaun Banega Crorepati* (*KBC*), a game show on Star TV, modeled on the British show *Who Wants to Be a Millionaire*. *KBC* "beamed" the legendary star into individual households, the effect of which was quite different from that of viewing him in a film. In the brave new world of Indian game shows, Amitabh Bachchan was attributed an edge over everyone else:

In all quiz shows . . . the contestant pits his wit against the quizmaster. It is the interrogator who knows the answers and has power over the players. . . . The genius of Amitabh Bachchan lay in the manner he changed the rules of the power game. . . . A contestant in *KBC* is not trying to outguess Bachchan. Instead, he and Bachchan are allies who try to outwit "Computerji" together. . . . Bachchan redefined his role so that he was on the contestant's side. [The other quiz shows] failed—despite larger prize money—because the anchors did not come across as the sort of allies you wanted in a life-changing experience. . . . That is probably why none of the other stars—Madhuri Dixit, Karishma Kapoor and Sridevi, all superstars of cinema in the 1990s—who ventured into television in the wake of Amitabh Bachchan made any impact whatsoever in the audience.[62]

Such observations notwithstanding, it is not possible to analyze, in retrospect, the success of Amitabh Bachchan as the first memorable host of *KBC*. *KBC*, by virtue of being part of the *Who Wants to Be a Millionaire* franchise, was unlike any other quiz show that the Indian viewer, raised on the diet of state-run Doordarshan, had ever seen. It was the perfect coming together of the "new world" quiz and the "old world" superstar, and Amitabh Bachchan's impeccable performance did not hurt. He is well known in the industry for his professionalism and his striving for perfection. The magic of the moment was not lost upon the advertisement industry. He was recruited for a series of television advertisements for a wide variety of products, mostly mundane, such as Nerolac Paints, Parker pens, ICICI Bank, Dabur Anardana, Pepsi, and Cadbury. The ultimate reorientation of his star image began with *Mohabbatein* (Love Stories, 2000), where he appeared with Shah Rukh Khan for the first time. *Mohabbatein* was directed by Aditya Chopra (the director of *DDLJ*), and Shah Rukh Khan and Amitabh Bachchan received Filmfare Awards, for Best Actor and Best Supporting Actor respectively. *Mohabbatein* cast Bachchan as the perfect combination of a Victorian headmaster and a neo-Hindu patriarch, a far cry from the young rebel that was his established screen persona in the earlier decades. He reprised this patriarchal role in his next film, Karan Johar's *Kabhi Khushi Kabhie Gham* in 2002. This was the great return or reinvention of Amitabh Bachchan, complete with a changed visage—always bearded, except for the role of a boy suffering from progeria in *Pa* (2009)—and a global recognition in the media worldwide. He was chosen to be a member of the relay team carrying the 2012 Olympic torch the day before the opening ceremony in London. In 2013, he made his Hollywood debut as Meyer Wolfsheim in the latest adaptation of *The Great Gatsby* (2013, dir. Baz Luhrmann).

Shah Rukh Khan—often referred to as King Khan on the web and in popular publications—has emerged as the only icon remotely comparable to Amitabh Bachchan in terms of star power and name recognition. The two other Khans—Aamir and Salman—have claimed powerful niche markets, distinguishably separated from the Shah Rukh sphere of influence. While Shah Rukh Khan rose through the ranks, having begun his career in a television series, both Aamir's and Salman's careers were "launched" in films produced by close members of their respective families. It is worthwhile to follow the very different choices that the young stars Aamir and Salman made, in the aftermath of their successful "launch," in *QSQT* and *Maine Pyaar Kiya* respectively. Aamir Khan chose to make one film at a time and in the process managed to act in only twenty films in the next fifteen years; twelve of them were big successes, giving him a rare success rate of 60 percent.[63]

Both Aamir and Salman Khan underwent extraordinary changes in appearance and roles in the twenty-first century. Salman Khan, who focused on action-based comedy dramas, has had the rare distinction of starring in five successive blockbusters that grossed INR 100 crore (1 billion): *Dabangg* (Audacious) in 2010, *Ready* and *Bodyguard* in 2011, and *Ek Tha Tiger* (There Was a Tiger) and *Dabangg 2* in 2012. Aamir Khan has alternately played in films with narratives that were unusual or had large degrees of political symbolism. Both categories were nevertheless well financed and successful. Off-beat films such as *Dil Chahta Hai* (2001), *Fanaa* (2006), and *3 Idiots* (2009) and patriotic melodramas such as *Lagaan: Once upon a Time in India* and *Mangal Pandey: The Rising* (2005) all contributed to the star image of Aamir Khan, who in 2012 launched his television talk show, *Satyamev Jayate* (Truth Alone Prevails, inscribed on the base of the "Lion Capital" image, which is the official logo of the Indian government), highlighting controversial social and political issues. Its first episode was on female feticide, a serious problem in India that has largely been glossed over by mainstream media. Aamir Khan has also starred in action thrillers such as *Ghajini* (2008) and *Talaash* (The Answer Lies Within, 2012).

In the summer of 2013, Salman Khan led the "100-Crore Club," with five films that had each grossed INR 100 crore after taxes. Shah Rukh Khan and Ajay Devgan trailed close behind with four films each. The actresses who have been inducted into the 100-Crore Club are Kareena Kapoor, Asin Thottumkal, and Sonakshi Sinha with four films each; Priyanka Chopra and Deepika Padukone are close behind with three films each. In 2013, the 100-Crore Club seemed a mere qualifier for top-grossing films, as half a dozen films had already moved on to earn 200 crore and 300 crore, with *3 Idiots* and *Chennai Express* (2013) at the 400-crore threshold. The first film to cross the 100-crore line was *Ghajini*, starring Aamir Khan as a mild-mannered business magnate who is transformed into a ruthless avenger after an assault by organized criminals leaves his fiancée murdered and him severely injured. The attack damaged his brain, causing a specific form of amnesia. The film made "short-term memory loss" a popular phrase in India, quickly picked up by comedians and politicians alike. *Ghajini* was a remake of a 2005 Tamil film with the same title (the villain's first name), starring Surya Sivakumar. The idiosyncratic element in the revenge drama—a subgenre that became prevalent in the 1970s and rose in popularity in the 1980s—was the specific form of amnesia, used memorably as a narrative tool in Christopher Nolan's *Memento* (2000).

Manjunath Pendakur and Jyotsna Kapur have provided a detailed account of how, with the advent of Bollywood, the macro-ideology of the nation shifted in Indian cinema's dominant representation of the nation to its own citizens and the world. This new representation simultaneously disavowed imperialism in the present while reclaiming the nationalism from the past by erasing labor and class from the picture. In so doing, Bollywood mirrored popular imagination of India's place in the world through hallmarks such as "military might (nuclear power), economic strength (computer education and information technology), and cultural dynamism (Indian beauty queen, authors, and Bollywood suddenly in fashion)."[64] A direct effect of these changes in the mise-en-scène of recent films has been the "disappearance of Bombay" from the city in Bollywood, replaced with a generic South Asian city, synthetic in texture. The Indian state of Goa, known for its beaches and tropical vegetation, has been frequently replaced by the island nation of Mauritius, including in *Golmaal: Fun Unlimited* (2006) and all its sequels.[65] But replacement of Bombay with a synthetic city creates an uncanny effect in films that are marketed as "realistic," such as *A Wednesday* (2008), a thriller police drama involving the city's chief of police and a suspected terrorist who turns out to be a middle-class elderly citizen disillusioned with the government's ability to protect its citizens.

It is possible to think of the replacement of actual cities and other particularities of lived reality with a synthesized screen as symptomatic of a larger reconfiguration of Indian cinema. There is increasing international marketing of Bollywood via online streaming (discussed in the epilogue), which, added to the pressure of international funding, can create demands for films that present a universal synthetic realism with local color. A successful example of such as cinematic narrative can be seen in *The Lunchbox* (2013, dir. Ritesh Batra), where the male and female lead characters communicate through the lunchbox delivery system ubiquitous in the metropolis of Bombay/Mumbai. Though the key moments in the film—the letters written and read by the two protagonists and passed through the lunchbox—belong indoors, a realist exotic tenor is established in the film through effective use of limited outdoor shots, made to accentuate the strangeness of the metropolitan scene in a city of the global south where intense loneliness can exist in crowded spaces. In *Delhi Belly* (2011, dir. Abhinay Deo), the sprawling city of Delhi provides the background of a fast-paced comic noir, abundant in mistaken identities and drug deals gone wrong. *The Lunchbox* and *Delhi Belly* are targeted for a niche cosmopolitan viewership both in India and abroad: there is more use of continuity-style editing than montages, and music videos are shot and marketed separately, thus keeping the use of non-diegetic music in the actual films minimal. Both films are funded by corporate bodies in collaboration with local star-owned enterprises, exemplifying the kind of fluid investment and professionalization that Bollywood wants to be associated with.

A crucial shift caused by a large number of such niche productions is the disappearance of contemporary political issues from urban cinema as they were prevalent in the New Cinema or parallel cinema of the 1960s and 1970s. It is no small irony that parallel cinema sponsored and subsidized by the government in the decade preceding globalization—from Mrinal Sen's *Kharij* (The Case Is Closed, 1982) to Govind Nihalani's *Ardh Satya* (Half-Truth, 1983)—delivered scathing indictments of the state and its laws from a leftist liberal perspective. Parallel cinema and the all-India film have been dual casualties of the simultaneous rise of Bollywood spectacles and corporate-funded niche cinema.

EPILOGUE

Cinema, Media, and Global Capital in an Unruly Democracy

Cinema's explosive global spread as the first truly universal medium occurred at the end of the age of empire—the twentieth century's first decade and into the early years of the next, which was also the final segment in what Eric Hobsbawm has called the long nineteenth century (1875–1914). The role of transnational empires in the history of cinema's early years is incontrovertible. Even as we follow the trajectories of national cinemas—French, Italian, Japanese, Indian—vis-à-vis local, regional, and global influences throughout the twentieth century or take cues from the Eurocentric film studies curricula, a study of cinema on a global scale in the twenty-first century calls for a renewed perspective. While globalization, the historical end to the shorter twentieth century (1914–91), made the telecommunications revolution possible, it quickly became dependent on the latter. Telecommunication and globalization now feed each other in a circle of accelerated motion. Audio-visuality in the twenty-first century is the established universal currency of communication, exchanged digitally.

That cinema would be affected by this global digital flow seems predictable, almost natural. It is important, however, to be cognizant of the fine yet discernible line running between the heady, diffused impression that global media confluence makes, on the one hand, and the concrete operations of capital, labor, and profit that can still be analyzed using nineteenth- and twentieth-century paradigms, on the other. Indian cinema's global currency is a resulting function of both digitality and physical in-/outsourcing. In 2007 *Saawariya*, the first Indian film to be produced by a non-Indian studio, Sony Pictures Entertainment, was released. Since then, several Hollywood studios have financed productions in India. Disney and India's YashRaj Studios have signed an agreement for co-productions, and 20th Century Fox has produced films through its Fox-Star Productions. In what can be viewed as a flow in an opposite direction, the Indian business giant Reliance ADA Group acquired majority share of the American company DreamWorks in 2009. However, Reliance's ownership of DreamWorks might have little or no effect on the creative aspect of Dream-Works, just as the Japanese conglomerate Sony's purchase of Columbia Pictures in 1984 affected only the corporate operations of the studio. In contrast, the flow of international capital into Indian cinema and other programming comes with the distinct possibility of changing the medium. The *India Film Guide* of 2015 that was distributed in Cannes signaled the post-global Indian government's positive attitude toward film marketing and foreign investments. The changed attitude of the Indian government, in combination with a renewed global expansion of Hollywood, has cleared the way for an upsurge in the numbers of Hollywood productions of "Bollywood films." Since 2015, Indian films have found new outlets in online media companies such as Netflix, Amazon Studios, and YouTube. In 2018 Netflix inaugurated its Indian production line with *Sacred Games*, a series based on Vikram Chandra's novel of the same name.[1] Later in 2018, Ted Sarandos, one of the executive officers of Netflix, attended the Mumbai Film Festival and announced a new slate of films and series produced in India and distributed globally. Amazon Studios had preceded Netflix in its Indian ventures; it began offering its Prime Video Streaming Services in India and in 2017 produced and streamed its first Indian show, *Inside Edge*, based on cricket, the most popular sport in India.[2] In a growing trend that began after Google's acquisition of YouTube in 2006, both established stars and aspiring young actors have appeared in short features produced specifically for YouTube. The global distribution of these films, along with those streamed by Netflix and Amazon, offers international exposure to Indian actors, singers, and directors that only a small minority of celluloid stars could attain in the first decade of the twenty-first century.

The flow of global capital from Sony/Columbia, Disney, Universal Pictures, Netflix, and Amazon to physical sites of Indian film production and the outward flow thereafter of Indian programming on a global scale have noticeably changed the content of such programming and the government's control over it. Indian viewers gained access to unrestricted content characteristic of premium American television channels such as HBO and Showtime beginning only in the first decade of the 2000s. Netflix and Amazon have extended such access to mobile users (a significant expansion, since more Indian consumers access media content through mobile devices than through cable television). Amazon's first Indian series, *Inside Edge*, opens with a close-up of a couple engaged in intercourse, something that Bollywood's inherited prohibitional code would not allow. However, notwithstanding the explosion of online streaming entertainment in India via Netflix and Amazon, Indians have continued to watch movies in theaters in record numbers, defying a worldwide trend of decline in moviegoing practices. The centrality of cinema, and by extension Bollywood, therefore remains relevant.

What is impossible to predict is how the onslaught of streaming media is going to affect the form and content of Indian mainstream cinema. In 1931, a politically powerless Indian cinema of the colonized won the battle against Hollywood's dominance over the market by creating a unique musical form that Hollywood could not or did not care to replicate. In the 1990s, Bollywood's reimagination of a global/national film form kept the revival of Hollywood in India via dubbed versions at bay. But what will the outcome be if Hollywood is able to make a Bollywood movie after all?[3] Or better still, if Netflix and Amazon can produce and distribute series and films at a fraction of the cost of a Bollywood film? Will Bollywood's entrenched star-centric system be displaced by a global corporate mode of production? Since Indian cinema was legalized as an "industry" in 1998, it is in theory vulnerable to takeovers and acquisitions like any other industry. Examples of such acquisitions abound. When Coca-Cola reentered the Indian market in 1993, it purchased Thums Up, the indigenous brand of cola that had served Indian consumers between 1978 and 1993. Flipkart, the online Indian company built in 2007 on the Amazon model, fell behind Amazon India and was eventually purchased by Walmart in 2018.[4] Even as the Indian government promoted manufacture through its "Make in India" campaign, India has consistently relied on imports for most of its defense and consumer technology. The neoliberal lifestyle foregrounded in Bollywood films and the middle-class's changed patterns of consumption engendered by the deregulation of India's markets in 1991 are fed by imported consumer goods, ranging from washing machines to cars. The telecommunications revolution that increased Indians' access to phones from 14.5 million connections in 1997 to 1.15 billion in 2017 has been profitable for all major phone manufacturers across the globe, ranging from the global giants such as Apple and Samsung to Oppo, a Chinese company relatively unknown in the global north.

Notwithstanding these cautionary examples, clues to possible futures for Indian cinema have eluded us so far through the second decade of the twenty-first century. While it may be tempting to predict changes to the business model, there are political and cultural forces strong enough to influence markets and economics. Indian cinema has continued to evolve and morph, and not in a linear and predictable fashion. Simultaneously with the encroachment of global corporate media, a new generation of big-budget films has ignited the possibility of a return of the all-India film. Between 2015 and 2017, films foregrounding spectacles of a mythical or mythologized past have appeared in the top echelons of the box office. Two Bollywood films featuring Deepika Padukone and Ranveer Singh, *Bajirao Mastani* (2015) and *Padmaavat* (2018), and a two-part Telugu film, *Baahubali* (2015–17), revived the historical/mythological genre that had in the 1930s been displaced by the rise of the social genre.

The director of both *Bajirao Mastani* and *Padmaavat* is Sanjay Leela Bhansali, whose 2002 film *Devdas* had premiered at Cannes. Schooled in filmmaking at the Film and Television Institute of India, Bhansali specialized in making visually spectacular melodrama, replete with elaborate costumes and sets, so much so that the narrative of Devdas, a melancholic alcoholic who commits slow suicide, was transformed in his version into a loud musical exposition of unrequited love. In an article published in 2017, Ajay Gehlawat discusses how Bhansali's *Bajirao Mastani*, based on a minor historical episode of a love affair between Maratha Hindu ruler Bajirao and Muslim courtesan Mastani, was a thinly veiled eulogy of Hindu chivalry and significant for its timeliness in the aftermath of the election of the first ever Hindu nationalist government of India in 2014.[5] More egregious in its expression of Hindu nationalism, Bhansali's next film, *Padmaavat*, glorified the mass honor suicide of women led by a Hindu queen to escape a rapacious Muslim invader. First appearing in a Sufi romance, the story of Alauddin Khalji, sultan of Delhi, and his lust for Padmini, a Rajput queen, had entered historical discourses through James Tod's *Annals and Antiquities of Rajasthan* (1832), which then became the source of nationalist history texts written in the late nineteenth and early twentieth centuries. The film was originally entitled *Padmavati* in 2017, when the incendiary subject of women's self-immolation and an Islamophobic depiction of Khalji incited a lengthy debate. When the film was finally released in 2018, the name of the film was changed to *Padmaavat* after the title of the sixteenth-century Sufi text by Malik Muhammad Jaysi, and the film began with a declaration of the narrative's source in legends and not in history. Reaching the "100-Crore Club" mark in a week, *Padmaavat* was praised for its lavish costumes and sets and spectacular battle scenes aided by CGI. The film's denouement, shot in slow motion, shows the queen leading a host of women into a firepit, and, as her profile fades into the fire, the palace door closes on Khalji, whose jubilant mood quickly changes into frustration as he fails to enter the grounds to claim his prize.

In contrast with the mythologized historical narratives of *Bajirao Mastani* and *Padmaavat*, S. S. Rajamouli's two-part *Baahubali*, shot in Telugu and dubbed in Tamil and Hindi, purported to present a fictionalized account of a Hindu kingdom and its neighbors caught in a drama of succession and political intrigue. A fantasy action melodrama with CGI-intensive scenes reminiscent of Hollywood films such as *300* (2006), *Transformers* (2007), and *Thor* (2011), *Baahubali* invoked nostalgia for a martial and opulent Hindu past without the gore and profanity of films such as *300*. And while the costumes and dialogue were reminiscent of the first generation of televised Hindu epics from the late 1980s, *Baahubali* was imbued with distinct regional markers. The names were Sanskritic and therefore northern, but the characters as seen on-screen were visibly darker in skin tone as if to underscore a southern identity, which was further enhanced by distinct styles of jewelry and hairdo, as well as the drape of the sari. Prabhas, the male lead, presented a dark-skinned, muscular persona with a hairstyle from the temple art, and the villain as well as the lead supporting actress equally stood apart from the established north Indian physiognomy that Bombay-based Hindi cinema had naturalized as pan-Indian. Once released, the first film of the series, *Baahubali: The Beginning*, superseded the "100-Crore Club" to be the first member of the "400-Crore Club." The second part, *Baahubali: The Conclusion*, had a much-anticipated national release in 2017 and became the first film to earn 800 crore. Special effects and battle scenes, especially in the second film, pushed the limits of Indian cinema's CGI standards and were complex enough to compete with the year's Hollywood releases with similar fantasy themes such as *The Mummy* (2017). To underscore the CGI—and almost to justify the resources spent on it—most of the scenes, both of battle and dramatic events, played in slow motion, thus stretching a relatively simple narrative—of the return of a prince to claim the throne and demand justice—to a melodrama with a run-time of nearly three hours.

The *Baahubali* series, besides producing a new benchmark for success at the box office, is indicative of a new turn in Indian cinema's engagement with the global, the national, and the regional. The films were made and marketed globally as part of a transmedia campaign, covering comics, games, fashion lines, and action figures.[6] They occupy a special spot among Indian films listed on the iTunes catalog and have been available for rent and purchase in Hindi, Tamil, and Telugu. The first *Baahubali* (2015) was the first film from South India since Mani Ratnam's *Roja* to be dubbed in Hindi. The sequel was released nationally, and it far outperformed any Indian film ever produced on its initial release. From the perspective of an intranational history of Indian cinema, *Baahubali* was a bridge to two discrete pasts: the mythologicals of the silent era that disappeared from the mainstream once sound was introduced and the social genre became dominant in the 1930s, and the revival of mythologicals in Telugu cinema in the 1970s, exemplified in the career of N. T. Rama Rao, who used his star power to create a powerful political party and was elected twice as the chief minister of Andhra Pradesh. Between 2005 and 2018, the Film Federation of India has reported the number of Telugu films as the second or third highest among all Indian films, including Hindi films produced in Bombay, though most Telugu films are accessible only to viewers in the states of Andhra Pradesh and Telangana in India, as well as to the Indian diaspora via portable media and online streaming. In the arenas of transmedia marketing and CGI, *Baahubali* accomplished what two sci-fi films had attempted with limited success: the Bollywood film *Ra-One* (2011), starring Shah Rukh Khan, and the Tamil film *Endhiran* (Robot, 2010), starring Rajinikanth. *Baahubali*'s interpellation of an imagined Hindu past as opposed to the futuristic worlds depicted in *Ra-One* and *Endhiran* makes it more accessible and adaptable to a transmedia mode of dissemination, owing to the established Indian market of media such as the comic book publication *Amar Chitra Katha*, which specializes in mythology and history. The future of such mythologicals and their resonance with the continued surge of a muscular neoliberal Hindu nationalism will be a crucial determinant in the next chapter of Indian cinema's history.

The future of Indian cinema, however, remains difficult to extrapolate. The first wave of globalization in the 1990s led to Bombay cinema's reconfiguration as Bollywood, while the second wave at the turn of the twenty-first century engendered the unique phenomenon of Bollywood cinema produced by Hollywood studios. The encroachment of Netflix, Amazon, YouTube, and social media, along with the total digitization of filmmaking, has further complicated the picture. While Indian cinema has been persistently unruly, the unruliness of online real-time media may be the most disruptive force yet.

A Google search for "Bollywood" in January 2019 yielded 0.5 billion results, compared with 7.6 million results for "Indian cinema."[7] Bollywood films have assumed a nationalistic significance on a global, grander scale, unprecedented in the long history of Indian cinemas. More than any other form, genre, or period of Indian cinema, twenty-first-century Bollywood's global footprint is prominently visible in the news media archives. A select few Bollywood stars have international recognition and popularity; their personal fame quotient is often greater than the popularity of their films. These stars often appear as India's unofficial cultural ambassadors, representing the "new," pro-global India. Foreign dignitaries include them in their schedule; the Duke and Duchess of Cornwall and Apple's Tim Cook, for example, attended receptions at Bollywood stars' homes during their visits to India in 2016. Amitabh Bachchan, India's most recognizable film star, participated in the torch relay at the 2012 London Olympics. Shah Rukh Khan received an honorary doctorate from Edinburgh University in 2015 and was Chubb Fellow at Yale in 2012. Both Bachchan and Shah Rukh Khan are recipients of the French civilian award Legion d'honneur. Word of such international honors is reported widely in the Indian news media, boosting national pride and reflecting the air of respect that India accords popular cinema and its artists.[8] Nationally, Bollywood stars run in elections, campaign for politicians, and are frequently elected to the upper and lower houses of the parliament.[9] Their endorsements are sought by multinational companies that entered the Indian market for the first time in the 1990s. Lever has long used Indian film stars in advertisements for its Lux soap. PepsiCo, the first foreign brand of soft drink to enter India after the forced exit of Coca-Cola in 1977, pioneered ads featuring the youngest generation of stars such as Juhi Chawla, Aamir Khan, and Aishwarya Rai in the 1990s. A most unique engagement of Bollywood stars in extra-cinematic realms has been in the world of sports. In 2008, with the inauguration of the Indian Premier League, a private system of clubs for cricket (India's most popular sport), Bollywood stars became capital investors and owners of a number of clubs.[10] The stars' presence and Bollywood-style entertainment at the beginning and in the half-time show add to the exhibitory value of the league games. While Bollywood is everywhere on the Internet, its affective power in India is palpable in the larger-than-life star images in every arena of popular culture, from advertisements of consumer goods to fashion magazines and live entertainment.

Cultural branding, in either a regulatory state or in a pro-capitalist society, is rarely what it seems on the surface, and Bollywood is no exception. If the half-billion search results for Bollywood is a marvel of keyword-driven data structures, its physical ubiquity in India's popular cultural sphere is a delicately sutured layer, convincing only on the surface. Bollywood's relationship with Indian political power structures is not as facile as it appears. The star power and the money obfuscate the distrust and deep anxiety that have always characterized popular cinema's relationship with the state in India. Notwithstanding the overwhelming popularity that Bollywood stars enjoy in India—a distant second place is held by cricket players—the status of cinema as an industry and an art form in twenty-first century India remains complicated.

Notes

Introduction

1. Both Tamil and Telugu produce as many films as does Hindi. Other industries include Bengali, Malayalam, Kannada, Bhojpuri, and nearly forty other languages and dialects. The studios are located in nine separate locations across India.

2. The Reorganisation of States Act (1956) configured the division of states within the nation along linguistic lines, each state with its majority language: Tamil in Tamil Nadu, Malayalam in Kerala, Kannada in Karnataka, Bengali in West Bengal.

3. Thus, a person living in the southern state of Kerala in the 1970s would have access to films in Malayalam (the majority language of Kerala), Hindi, and English (through imports from Hollywood).

4. The bifurcation of the market for two kinds of Indian cinema can be traced to the mid-1950s. Satyajit Ray's debut film *Pather Panchali* (Song of the Road), screened at Cannes in 1955, marked Indian cinema's entry into the highly selective realm of world cinema of the Cold War era. The first Indian Film Festival in Moscow in 1954, on the other hand, opened up the USSR and the Eastern Bloc to Indian entertainment cinema, primarily the Hindi films produced in Bombay.

5. Ramchandra Gopal Torney's *Shree Pundalik* (1912) has recently been recognized as the first full-length feature film made by an Indian filmmaker; earlier official histories refer to D. G. Phalke's *Raja Harishchandra* (1913) as the first Indian feature film. The first sound films (or talkies) were made in Bombay and Calcutta, including Imperial Studios' *Alam Ara*, in 1931.

6. MIB 1954.

7. The committee, in its report (*Report of the Indian Cinematograph Committee*, 1928), discussed in chapter 1, recommended patronage of Indian indigenous cinema and dismissed the idea of "empire cinema" as nonviable.

8. The "Salt March," led by M. K. Gandhi and other Congress leaders in March–April 1930 in protest against taxation of salt production and import, was one of the central events of the civil disobedience movement against British rule in India.

9. This situation is discussed in detail in chapter 1.

10. Benegal 1981, 54.

11. Benegal 1981, 54.

12. Swadeshi = *swa* (self) + *deshi* (of the land). The term, meaning *indigenous*, gained political currency with the swadeshi movement in Bengal, which was the first mass movement led by the middle-class against the British administration.

13. Bhowmik 1995.

14. Rajadhyaksha 1993.

15. Chakrabarty 2008. I follow Chakrabarty in using the term *subaltern* to mean the opposite of *bourgeois*.

16. The destabilization of film studios by the inflow of illegal financing during World War II and the loss of a significant part of the market due to the partition of British India (into India and Pakistan) in 1947 are discussed in the concluding section of chapter 1.

17. Government of India 1951.

18. The song, composed by Shailendra and set to music by Shankar-Jaikishan, was voted the most popular song of 1955 by listeners of *Binaca Geet Mala*, Radio Ceylon's popular program of Hindi film songs. The first stanza, which has been repeated and evoked in numerous pre-Bollywood and Bollywood films, can be translated as

My shoes are Japanese
My trousers are English
My red hat is Russian
Still, my heart is Indian. [My translation.]

19. It was included, almost as an afterthought, in Sangeet Natak Akademi (Academy of Music and Drama), but the programs and artists supported by the Sangeet Natak Akademi had no space for cinema or film artists.

20. Majumdar 2009. Satyajit Ray's 1948 characterization of the disorderly and inferior standards of Indian popular cinema—"starting a production without adequate planning, some-times even without a shooting script; a penchant for convolutions of plot and counter-plot rather than the strong, simple unidirectional narrative; the practice of sandwiching musical numbers in the most unlyrical situation"—was applicable to popular cinema even when it had found its postcolonial moorings in the 1950s and was frequently reiterated by film critics. According to Neepa Majumdar, the query of Satyajit Ray's article "What's Wrong with Indian Film?" represented the orientation of an entire genre of Indian film criticism (2009, 52).

21. See Kaul and Sen 2014.

22. As most of the raw stock for movie cameras was imported, control and distribution of the import of stock could have a direct effect on the process of film production.

23. The international market for Indian cinema consisted of Asian, African, and East European countries and was divided into several circuits. See Dharap 1975, appendix, for a list of the circuits as compiled by Dharap.

24. Films such as *Faulad* (Steel, 1963) and *Aaya Toofan* (Storm Arrives, 1964), featuring Dara Singh, the wrestler in macho-heroic roles, circulated in rural areas in the Hindi belt. Dara Singh performed his own stunts, like Fearless Nadia did in the 1940s.

25. Rajagopal 2001. The role of television in modulating the expectations and demands of the film-viewing public is significant, and a detailed study of the confluence of the effects of cinema and television is yet to be done. For the purpose of retaining focus on cinema, I have not covered any aspect of television programming in this book.

26. Pendakur 1985. Pendakur offers an in-depth study of the rules, conditions, coercion, and diplomacy that guided Hollywood studios' transactions with India.

27. Rajagopalan 2008. *Love Story* (1981) and *Disco Dancer* (1982) were both attempts to break away from the "revenge and retribution" theme. *Love Story*, featuring teenage debutant actors Kumar Gaurav and Vijayata Pandit in the lead roles, projected "love" as a form of rebellion against established norms represented by the family. Mithun Chakraborty, recipient of a National Film Award for best actor in Mrinal Sen's *Mrigayaa* (The Royal Hunt, 1976), trained as a dancer to play the title role in *Disco Dancer*. The film made Chakraborty a popular star in the Soviet Union.

28. Wolpert 1997. Rajiv Gandhi was elected as the prime minister when, following his mother Indira Gandhi's assassination, her fraction of the Congress Party, Congress (I), won a record number of parliamentary seats in a "sympathy wave." During his first term (1984–89), Rajiv Gandhi formed a cabinet and advisory committee of a pro-business elite and proposed a series of reforms to take India into the twenty-first century.

29. R. Mehta 2010, 2.

30. Vernallis 2013.

31. The Apu trilogy consists of *Pather Panchali, Aparajito* (The Unvanquished, 1956), and *Apur Sansar* (The World of Apu, 1959).

32. Rajadhyaksha and Willemen 1999, 41.

33. Giridharadas 2007.

34. Athique 2012; Punathambekar 2013; Gehlawat 2010 and 2015.

Chapter 1. Colonial Indian Cinema

1. After the advent of the Lumière brothers' *cinématographe* in 1895, Pathé Frères, the French company, had established outposts far and wide, thus creating an extensive system of distribution. London had grown into a hub for distribution of films into the colonies and beyond by leveraging the global infrastructure of trade and transport of the British empire.

2. Film Daily 1930. The success of sound technology from the perspective of American

films is the dominant theme of the 1930 edition of *The Film Daily Year Book*. It also has reports on the difficulties faced by some European countries, especially Germany, to adapt to sound due to ongoing patent conflicts.

3. Thompson 1986, 145.

4. Thompson 1986, 165–66. Thompson notes that these two were also the nonsocialist countries to become major producers of films.

5. Thompson 1986, 145.

6. Film Daily 1938, 1227.

7. Film Daily 1940, 1109

8. While the post-1947 Indian government, seeking to preserve its foreign currency reserves during the Cold War era, had stringent regulations on imports, it did little to encourage commercial cinema. The success and growth of Bollywood cinema in the 1990s, in the era of open imports, speak for the change in the dynamic between government and cinema.

9. Creekmur and Mokdad 2012, 1: "Indeed, in a country like India . . . popular music is film music; the hit song that does not derive from a film, and simultaneously ensure the film's success, is rare." What they write of Indian cinema is particularly applicable to Bombay-based Hindi cinema.

10. Quoted in Ramachandran, Burra, and Chandran 1981, 78.

11. In his own work of the 1940s and 1950s, Damle would use loud background music with little nuance, and it is therefore interesting to hear his apprehensions about the "single-shot" song sequence.

12. Rushdie 1981, 162 (italics mine).

13. Ray 1976, 74: "Once in a long while, through sheer accident, the singing voice may match with the speaking one, but it is never expected to. To one not familiar with the practice the change of timbre usually comes as a jolt. But for the audience here the jolt would probably come if they did not recognize one of their six favorites in the playback."

14. Ray 1976, 5–6.

15. Flinn 2016.

16. Hobsbawm 1987.

17. Whitman 1872.

18. Mahadevan 2015, 35.

19. Dada Torney, one of India's early filmmakers, purchased equipment and raw stock from Bourne and Shepherd for his 1912 film *Shree Pundalik*, which has been the contender for the first indigenous feature film, made a year before Phalke's *Raja Harishchandra*. Some film historians, such as Ranita Chatterjee and Rosie Thomas, have found evidence of full-length films made in Calcutta that predated both Phalke's and Torney's work.

20. Mahadevan 2015, 31.

21. Mahadevan 2015, 34–35.

22. Chabria 1994, 3.

23. Ranade 2011, 75.

24. Sharma 1968.

25. Chabria 1994, 5.

26. Thoraval 2000, 3–4: "Often instead of money for payment, they received food or something that they had to sell in order to survive. Sometimes they also had to serve as commentators on what was happening on screen."

27. Chabria 1994, 6.

28. Thoraval 2000, 4.

29. Vasudev 1978, 4.

30. Radjou, Prabhu, and Ahuja 2012; Nelson 2018; Rai 2019.

31. Mahadevan 2015, 64.

32. Michelutti 2008. Michelutti's is an excellent study of Indian political niches grown in the recent decades.

33. Mahadevan 2015, 64.

34. Dass 2016, 4.

35. Andrew 2010, 59.

36. Gramsci 1988, 363–70.

37. Bhaumik 2010, 137.

38. Burra 1981, 12.

39. Thoraval 2000, 2.

40. Kohli-Khandekar 2003, III.

41. Baskaran 2009, 18.

42. Baskaran 2009, 19. The march organized by M. K. Gandhi to Dandi to protest the Salt Tax was the most filmed event up to that point in Indian film history, since "a number of agencies, Indian and foreign, filmed this event and all the films were banned by the British government including the one titled *Mahatma Gandhi's March to Freedom* by Sarada Film company." In the case of the Mapla Rebellion, the British initiated a documentary filming of the colonial quelling of the "uprising among the Mapla Muslims of Malabar in Madras Presidency." It was as if the British authorities "felt the need to explain, both to the Indian and the international public," the rationale behind the repressive measures. "Shot by H. Doveton, a cinematographer based in Calcutta, this two-reel film showed the refugees, captured rebels and their weapons."

43. Quoted in Burra 1981, 13.

44. Sinha 2013, 52.

45. Sinha 2013, 52.

46. Bhowmik 1995, 42.

47. Bhowmik 1995, 42.

48. Chakravarty 1993, 36.

49. Thomas 2015, 8–9.

50. Raj 2010, 13.

51. Vasudev and Lenglet 1983, 20.

52. The W. Evans report is discussed later in this chapter.

53. Ramachandran, Burra, and Chandran 1981, 34.

54. Barnouw and Krishnaswamy 1980, 65–66.

55. Chabria 1994, 13.

56. Chabria 1994, 14.

57. Chabria 1994, 10.

58. Wadia 1981, 111.

59. Quoted in Vasudev 1978, 62.

60. Burra 1981, 21.

61. Vasudev 1978, 6.

62. Garga 1983, 20.

63. Rajadhyaksha 1993.

64. Vasudev 1978, 14 (italics mine): "No person shall give an exhibition by means of a cinematograph elsewhere than in a place licensed under the Act" (section 3). "Licences were to be granted by the District Magistrate or by the Commissioner of Police" (section 4). "No film should be exhibited unless it had first been certified by the prescribed authority as suitable for public exhibition" (section 5[2]). "The Governor-General in Council would[,] by notification in the Gazette of India, constitute *as many authorities as he might think fit* for examining and certifying films with the certificate of such an authority to be valid in areas specified in the notification" (section 7[1]). "However, the exhibition of a film could be suspended and its certificate annulled in any Province, on the authority of the District Magistrate or Commissioner of Police, pending the order of the Provincial Government, which could uncertify the film for the whole or part of the province" (sections 7[5] and [6]). "If an authority refused to certify a film, the person applying for the certificate could appeal within 30 days of the decision, for consideration of the matter by the Local Government" (section 7[3]).

65. Verma 2000, 17.

66. MIB 1954. The pamphlet for the first national awards ceremony in 1954 described the colonial system as "provincial censorship," to distinguish it from the Central Board of Censorship that was created by the postcolonial government in 1950.

67. Vasudev 1978, 15–16:

The Bombay Board consisted of (1) the Commissioner of Police, who was the President ex-officio, (2) the Collector of Customs, (3) a member of the Indian Educational Service, (4) a prominent Hindu citizen of Bombay, (5) a prominent Muslim citizen, and (6) a prominent Parsi citizen. All members were appointed by the Government of Bombay. . . . The Calcutta Board consisted of (1) the Commissioner of Police, President ex-officio, (2) the Station Staff Officer, (3) a European lady representative, (4) and (5) one representative each of the Bengal Chamber of Commerce, and the Calcutta Trades Association, (6) a Jewish merchant, (7) a Muslim representative of the Education Department, and (8) a Hindu lawyer, representing the Calcutta Corporation. . . . At Madras too, the ex-officio president was the Commissioner of Police. The Board consisted of one military representative and four Indian gentlemen of whom one had to be Muslim. . . . The Censor Board at Rangoon was composed of (1) the Commissioner of Police, as President ex-officio, (2) the Assistant Commissioner of Police, ex-officio, who also acted as the Secretary, (3) a military representative, (4) a European medical man who represented the Vigilance Society, and (5) three Burmese gentlemen and one Burmese lady.

68. The electoral politics of religion, caste, and other forms of communities has had an interesting correspondence with Indian cinema. Tamil cinema's role in the rise of the Dravidian political parties in the 1950s and the eruption of rural caste politics in Hindi cinema during the 1980s are two of many instances that are outside the scope of this book.

69. W. Evans, "Cinema Publicity in India 1921," in Letter No. 1237, Law (G) 12.5, 1921, Tamil Nadu Archives.

70. Evans, "Cinema Publicity."

71. Jaikumar 2006, 42.

72. Jaikumar 2006, 46.

73. Dharap 1975, 487. The totals are missing the films that were examined by the Rangoon board.

74. Barnouw and Krishnaswamy 1980, 44.

75. ICC 1928, xii.

76. ICC 1928, 1–2.

77. ICC 1928, 13–14:

The number of Questionnaires issued was 4,325. . . . The number of replies received was 320. The total number of witnesses examined was 291 (counting a group of witnesses examined jointly as one). The total number altogether was 353. Of those examined, 114 were Europeans, Anglo-Indians, or Americans, and 239 Indians of whom 157 were Hindus and 82 non-Hindus. Of the non-Hindus, 38 were Muslims, 25 Parsis, 16 Burmese, 2 Sikhs, and 1 Christian. Altogether 35 ladies were examined, of whom 16 were Europeans and 19 Indians, Parsis, and Burmese. Among the witnesses were 26 members of the Legislatures, 101 officials, and 98 persons connected with the cinema trade. Of the 353 witnesses, 59 appeared at Bombay, 13 at Karachi, 35 at Lahore, 13 at Peshawar, 18 at Lucknow, 72 at Calcutta (of whom 2 were from Bihar and Orissa and 1 from Assam), 53 at Madras, 38 at Rangoon, 11 at Mandalay, 1 at Jamshedpur, 14 at Nagpur, and 26 at Delhi. The Committee visited some 45 cinemas and witnessed, in addition to a number of short-length or educational films, about 57 feature films, of which 21 were Indian or Burmese productions. Thirteen producing studios were inspected. The total distance travelled was approximately 9,400 miles.

78. Quoted in Verma 2000, 21.

79. ICC 1928, 3.

80. ICC 1928, 99.

81. ICC 1928, 102.

82. ICC 1928, 102.

83. Jaikumar 2006, 91–92.

84. Prasad 2009, 14.

85. Ramachandran, Burra, and Chandran 1981, 34.

86. J. Desai 2004, 48–49.

87. Rajadhyaksha 1993, 64–65.

88. See chapter 3.

89. Karanjia 1981.

90. Ganti 2004, 11–12.

91. The States Reorganisation Act, 1956.

92. Luthra 1986, 268–69.

93. Quoted in Luthra 1986, 270.

94. A. Sircar 2011, 76.

95. Pillai 2010, 104–5.

96. Hughes 2009.

97. Pillai 2010, 106.

98. Manuel 1993, 49. Manuel writes, "While drawing liberally from traditional folk and light-classical genres, [Indian film music] is a studio-bred art to which live performances are unimportant. It is true, of course, that folk musicians often borrow from film melodies, but on the whole, only elaborate 'orchestras' playing for upper-class festivities even attempt to reproduce the ensemble timbres and style of film songs."

99. Manuel 1993, 50–51.

100. Baskaran 2009, 24.

101. Dasgupta 1980a, 12–13.

102. Balraj Sahni 1979, 55.

103. B. Chopra 1981.

104. Lahoti 1981, 100–102.

105. Lahoti 1981, 102.

106. MIB 1954, 6.

107. Vasudev 1978, 67 (italics mine).

108. MIB 1981, 59.

109. MIB 1981, 59.

Chapter 2. Shadow Nationalism

1. R. Ray 1956, 21–22. Nehru, who had a law degree just as Dr. Rajamannar did, had also been elected as the president of the Sahitya Akademi (Academy of Literature).

2. Nehru 1958, 411.

3. Nehru 1958, 408.

4. The transition from the studio system to the star-centric system of production in Indian cinema during the World War II years is discussed in chapter 1.

5. Nehru 1958, 1–4. This speech was later paraphrased by Arundhati Roy as "dams are the temples of modern India" in her essay "The Greater Common Good," (1999).

6. Government of India 2015, 324.

7. B. Anderson 1983. Anderson's concept of nation as an "imagined community" is used throughout this book.

8. Althusser 1971.

9. Government of India 1951, 13. The Film Enquiry Committee (Patil Committee) report contains all necessary statistics relevant to the 1940s.

10. S. Sarkar 1983, 4. The Indian Civil Services was renamed the Indian Administrative Services.

11. Nehru 1979, 61.

12. A. Jain 2013; "About Us," Films Division (website), accessed December 17, 2017, http://filmsdivision.org/about-us.html. The Films Division website names the originary mission of the Films Division as an endeavor to "articulate the energy of a newly independent nation." See Anuja Jain's 2013 article for a concise history of the Films Division evolution from its colonial predecessors such as Information Films of India and Indian News Parade.

13. *Times of India*, September 9, 1947.

14. *Times of India*, January 15, 1948.

15. This act was listed as Central Act No. 37 of 1952.

16. In theory, the board had the simple task of issuing a license and one of three kinds of ratings: "UA" for a film for public or unrestricted exhibition, "A" for a film for restricted exhibition, and "S" for a film for exhibition restricted to members of any profession or any class. The third category applied mostly to informational and training films that were not marketed via the regular channels and therefore lay outside public scrutiny or discussion on censorship.

17. Reddi 1983, 97–98.

18. Prasad 1993, 71–86.

19. Reddi 1983, 152–53.

20. Ganti 2004, 12.

21. Kaul 1998, 40.

22. Quoted in Kaul 1998, 41.

23. Chakravarty 1993, 307.

24. See the introduction for an account of the recurring references to the song "Mera Joota Hai Japani."

25. Tharoor 1997; Nilekani 2009. Both offer mainstream, centrist readings of India's postcolonial experience.

26. Vasudevan 2011, 89–90.

27. Madhu Jain 2005.

28. Ramachandran 1983, 131.

29. Ramachandran 1983, 131

30. Chakravarty 1993, 133.

31. Chakravarty 1993, 133–34.

32. For more on city symbolisms, see my discussion below on film noir.

33. Rajadhyaksha and Willemen 1999.

34. *Jis Desh Mein Ganga Behti Hai* was produced by Raj Kapoor and directed by Radhu Karmakar, the cinematographer of *Awaara*.

35. Vasudevan 2011, 94–95.

36. Vasudevan 2011, 88.

37. B. Sarkar 2007.

38. Vasudevan 2011, 89.

39. N. Kazmi 1998, 92.

40. N. Kazmi 1998.

41. L. M. Desai 2004, 60.

42. Quoted in Vasudev 1978, 58.

43. "Duniya Na Mane" literally means "The World Does Not Allow/Agree," and "Kunku" refers to the red dot on the forehead worn by Hindu women in most parts of India.

44. Majumdar 2009, 52.

45. Burra 1981, 133.

46. Majumdar 2005, 510–27. Majumdar offers an insightful discussion on Satyajit Ray's *Pather Panchali* in the context of the neorealist moment in Indian cinema.

47. MIB 1965, 72.

48. MIB 1954, 2.

49. MIB 1954, 3.

50. MIB 1954, 7.

51. MIB 1954, 8.

52. MIB 1955b, 4.

53. Chatterji 1987, 49.

54. Punathambekar 2010, 195.

55. Punathambekar 2010, 192.

56. Keskar 1967, 74–75.

57. Quoted in Brodbeck 2011.

58. K. Kumar 2003, 2176. Keskar also introduced slots for folk music and experimented with the idea of developing folk music and performances for propaganda. In 1958, an annual festival called Songs of Nation Builders was organized in which "folk musicians and dancers from different parts of India presented songs with a developmental content."

59. K. Kumar 2003, 2176.

60. Television was officially launched in India in 1959, but daily service was available in select metropolitan areas only from 1965 onward. Countrywide expansion occurred only in 1975.

61. *Times of India* 1954, 9.

62. Rajagopalan 2008, 2.

63. Rajagopalan 2008, 57.

64. MIB 1965, 103. During the Cold War era, beyond South Asia, Indian films were exported to the USSR and, via the USSR, to a few countries in the Eastern Bloc. The Indian government had established exports with (1) countries in regions that had a siz-

able Indian diaspora such as East Africa, West Indies, Fiji, Mauritius, and Malaysia, and (2) regions where the "local population had cultivated interest in certain types of Indian films," such as the Middle East and North and West Africa.

65. B. Anderson 1991.

66. YouTube videos of Hindi film songs performed on various television talent shows in the countries that were part of either the USSR or the Eastern Bloc are mainly of songs from the 1950s through the 1980s. These songs are often erroneously referred to as Bollywood songs.

67. Quoted in Roth-Ey 2011. This book is an excellent study on how media and the Soviet state influenced each other.

68. Lipkov 1994, 191.

69. Raghavendra 2011, 35–38.

70. Raha 1974, 180.

Chapter 3. Culture Wars and Catharses

1. Robinson 1989, 327. Robinson reports the interview from its original appearance in the October 1980 issue of *Probe India*. Robinson also quoted from the letter that the Forum for Better Cinema addressed to Nargis Dutt: "The Modern India that you speak of is the India of dams, of scientists, steel plants and agricultural reforms. Do you honestly believe that it is this India that is portrayed in the so-called commercial films of Bombay? In fact, the world of commercial Hindi films is peopled by thugs, smugglers, dacoits, voyeurs, murderers, cabaret dancers, sexual perverts, degenerates, delinquents and rapists, which can hardly be called representative of Modern India" (328).

2. *Times of India* 1979b.

3. Lakshmi 1980, 957. The newly appointed members of the board included G. P. Sippy (the producer of *Sholay*), Gul Anand (exporter), N. K. Goel (industrialist), Aruna Vasudev (writer), and Bhaktavatsala (producer based in Tamil Nadu).

4. The Film Institute of India was established in Pune in 1960 and was renamed the Film and Television Institute of India in 1971. Television programs were produced in Mandi House in New Delhi until 1971. Between 1971 and 1974, all operations of the television wing moved from Mandi House in New Delhi to the Film and Television Institute in Pune. The National Film Archives was established in 1964. The Film Finance Corporation provided financial support to parallel filmmakers until the National Film Development Corporation subsumed it in 1980. The International Film Festival, first organized in 1952, was brought under an apex body called the Directorate of Film Festivals, which was also given responsibility for organizing the National Film Awards and promoting Indian films abroad through various events showcasing a diverse selection of films. An oft-repeated event through the years was called "Indian Panorama."

5. The privately owned Filmfare Awards, instituted in 1958 by the publishers of the *Filmfare* magazine, was more of a platform for commercial cinema, with Hindi cinema and its stars occupying the central stage.

6. *Times of India* 1979a; "Nandan" in Calcutta was born out of this effort.

7. A notable exception was Shyam Benegal, who made his debut film, *Ankur* (Seedling, 1974), with funding from a leading advertisement company, Blaze, for which he worked before he began making feature films.

8. The five films selected for the 1954 festival were *Do Bigha Zamin, Baiju Bawra, Aandhiyan, Awaara,* and *Rahi.* See *Times of India* 1954.

9. See Box Office India, http://www.boxofficeindia.com/showProd.php?itemCat =164&catName=MTk1OA, accessed January 14, 2019.

10. Pendakur 1985. Pendakur offers a detailed account of the history of Hollywood's market in India.

11. The progressive niche within the Hindi film industry belonged to the lyricists and screenplay writers, a significant number of whom were Urdu poets with clear communist/socialist leanings. K. A. Abbas, who wrote screenplays for Raj Kapoor's films, and lyricists such as Sahir Ludhianvi and Majrooh Sultanpuri interpolated themes and motifs of protest and social justice into mainstream melodrama.

12. Rushdie 1995. In Rushdie's novel, the star couple Nargis Dutt and Sunil Dutt, who played the heroic mother and the errant son in *Mother India,* appear in a cameo, at a party attended by throngs of Bombay intellectuals. Chiding other guests on their lighthearted reference to *Mother India,* Nargis, the "Living Mother Goddess," says, "How you people wallow-pollow in negative images! In our picture we put stress on the positive side. Courage of the masses is there, and also the dams." In response, Miranda makes a wordplay on "dam"/"damn," and Sunil erupts, "Bleddy dumbo! Not oathery, but new technology is being referred to: to wit, the hydro-electric project, as inaugurated by my goodwife in the opening scene." When Miranda is left unimpressed, Nargis drags her husband away. "Sunil, come. . . . If this godless anti-national gang is the world of art, then I-tho am happy to be on commercial side" (138).

13. The top grossing films in 1970–79 were *Sholay, Bobby* (1973), *Muqaddar Ka Sikandar* (Conqueror of Destiny, 1978), *Roti Kapada Aur Makaan* (Food, Clothing, and Shelter, 1974), *Amar Akbar Anthony* (1977), *Dharam-Veer* (The Righteous, 1977), *Johny Mera Naam* (My Name Is Johny, 1970), *Jai Santoshi Maa* (Victory to the Goddess Santoshi, 1975), and *Sanyasi* (Mendicant, 1975). The top grossing films in 1980–89 were *Kranti* (Revolution, 1981), *Maine Pyaar Kiya* (I Fell in Love, 1989), *Ram Teri Ganga Maili* (Ram, Your Ganga Has Become Impure, 1985), *Coolie* (Porter, 1983), *Vidhaata* (Providence, 1982), *Naseeb* (Destiny), *Meri Awaaz Suno* (Listen to My Voice, 1981), *Qurbani* (Sacrifice, 1980), *Mard* (Macho, 1985), and *Laawaris* (Orphan, 1981).

14. See note 1.

15. Prabhat Studios in Pune had closed production in 1956, marking only the official end of the studio-system; other major studios had already long discontinued production.

16. Raj Kapoor was the oldest of the three sons of the actor Prithviraj Kapoor to act in the lead role in dozens of films. His other two brothers, Shammi Kapoor and Shashi Kapoor, were also stars in dozens of films. Raj Kapoor produced *Kal Aaj Aur Kal* (Yesterday, Today, Tomorrow, 1971), directed by his son Randhir Kapoor. Raj Kapoor

was also the director of *Bobby*, which "launched" the career of his second son, Rishi Kapoor, whose son Ranbir Kapoor in turn had his debut in *Saawariya* in 2007, the first Bollywood film produced by a Hollywood studio. Randhir Kapoor's children, Karisma Kapoor and Kareena Kapoor, were likewise launched as lead actresses in the late 1990s. Rajiv Kapoor, Raj Kapoor's youngest son, was given the lead role in Raj Kapoor's *Ram Teri Ganga Maili*.

17. Rajadhyaksha 1993.

18. Two South Indian cinemas, Telugu and Kannada, were able to assert their independence from their dominant Tamil counterpart with the rise of the Telugu star N. T. Rama Rao and the Kannada star Rajkumar.

19. Raj 2004. Raj defines "the post-classical phase of Hindi cinema (1966–1985)" by "a qualitative change in the content, texture, treatment and presentation, music and overall social appeal. Indian cinema now began to build a quasi-modernist image . . ., which was based on . . . a simplification. To come out of the shadow of the classical film, the post-classical cinema based itself on: (1) A complete redefinition of film aesthetics and appearance, making the hero and heroine . . . gorgeous, far more provoking with their gestures and flashy costumes; elaborate gaudy indoors and extensive use of the outdoors, particularly the hill stations, to create a sense of freeness and abundance; (2) A simplification of the interpretation of love, by . . . making it more sensuous and glamorous; and (3) A renewed emphasis on a new genre of flashy and fast romance combined often with a crime plot (which had a secondary status in the classical period), employing the basic model developed by Guru Dutt Films and Navketan in the early 1950s" (799).

20. P. Chatterjee 1993. The first conflict between a premodern tradition and colonial modernity was resolved ideologically in the Indian novel, which was born in the late nineteenth century. By the time Indian nationalism was formulated, also in the late nineteenth century, a cultural framework was already established via literature. Indian cinema, especially the social genre, drew its ideological coherence from the world of the Indian novel. Chatterjee offers a detailed discussion on Indian nationalism and the evolution of cultural spheres.

21. Raha 1974.

22. A. Sircar 2011, 121.

23. Quoted in R. Ray 1956, 258–59.

24. Quoted in R. Ray 1956, 259.

25. See chapter 2 for a detailed account of the impasse between Hindi film music and All India Radio.

26. Morcom 2007, 28–29.

27. Morcom 2007, 28.

28. Morcom 2007, 28.

29. Raha 1974, 168.

30. Raha 1974, 168.

31. Raha 1974, 167.

32. Sanjay Srivastava 2004, 2021.

33. I am using loosely Sigmund Freud's use of *heimlich* and *unheimlich* in *The Uncanny* (2003), 123–62.

34. Benegal 1981, 54.

35. Benegal 1981, 54.

36. S. Ray 1981, 47.

37. Karanth 1981, 70.

38. Dasgupta 1969, 28.

39. Dasgupta 1969, 34.

40. Raha 1974, 168.

41. Raha 1974, 169.

42. Vitali 2008.

43. K. Sarkar 1975, 129.

44. K. Sarkar 1975, 131.

45. This is discussed in detail in the first chapter.

46. Rajadhyaksha 1993, 56–57.

47. Rajadhyaksha 1993, 58–59.

48. Ramachandran 1983, 21. The Khosla Committee's observation (see Government of India 1969) is confirmed by J. B. H. Wadia of Wadia Movietone, who recalled in a memorial volume on Indian cinema that "kissing and love-making were not taboo." He cited several examples of films, such as "a film in which the heroine (Laita Pawar) kissed her leading man without inhibition. In a film called *Pati Bhakti* (1920), produced by Madans of Calcutta, the camp played by a voluptuous Italian actress (Sinora Minelli) wore revealing costumes, which were considered indecent later on. In *A Throw of Dice* (1929), Charu Roy kissed Sita Devi on the lips. In an early talkie *Zarina* (1932), which Ezra Mir had directed on his return from the Hollywood Studios, the hero (Jal Merchant) and the heroine (Zubeida) expressed their 'true love' by kissing each other quite often." Wadia attributed this not to the enlightened wisdom of the filmmakers but to the laxity of censorship, which, in his experience, "was quite liberal in all respects except for political films. . . . The British regime in India did not bother to interfere in filmmaking so long as there was no overt attack on the Imperial rule" (Wadia 1981, 112).

49. Prasad 1993, 72.

50. Prasad 1993, 77.

51. Roberge 1974, 172.

52. MIB 1965, 87–88.

53. Mrinal Sen 1977, 11–12.

54. Mrinal Sen 1977, 14.

55. Mrinal Sen 1977, 91.

56. B. Chopra 1981, 66.

57. Directorate of Film Festivals 1981, 12.

58. Quoted in Directorate of Film Festivals 1981, 12.

59. Quoted in Directorate of Film Festivals 1981, 13.

60. Murthy 1981, 82.

61. Murthy 1981, 82.

62. Murthy 1981, 82.

63. Murthy 1981, 82.

64. Murthy 1981, 82.

65. Ramachandran 1983, 259.

66. Dharap 1975. Dharap cites the innovative efforts of Harish S. Booch, a film journalist, who discovered a private collection of early films by D. G. Phalke and persuaded the authorities to reprocess the films. On December 19, 1956, at the inauguration of the Talkie Silver Jubilee at Liberty Cinema, Bombay, the collection of Phalke's films was exhibited. In Dharap's account, the film archive movement was made possible by a set of rules introduced in 1955 by the National Awards Committee that "made it obligatory on producers to deposit with the Government prints of award-winning films. It was these films, deposited with the Government year after year, that formed the nucleus of the Indian film archive. For almost a decade, all such prints were lodged between the Films Division and the Central Board of Film Censors and were considered to be a part of the 'National Film Library,' as it was then known" (529).

67. Quoted in Jeffrey 2009, 181.

68. P. Chatterji 1987, 147.

69. P. Chatterji 1987, 63–64.

70. P. Chatterji 1987, 104.

71. Jeffrey 2009, 179.

72. Quoted in P. Chatterji 1987, 104–5.

73. Dharap 1975, viii.

74. Rajadhyaksha 2009, 234–35.

75. Rajadhyaksha 2009, 233.

76. Rajadhyaksha 2009, 233–34.

77. Rajadhyaksha 2009, 234.

78. Rajadhyaksha 2009, 236–37.

79. Wolpert 1997, 399–400.

80. Quoted in Vasudev 1978, 163.

81. Quoted in K. Kumar 2003, 2177.

82. Vasudev 1978, 153–54.

83. Rajadhyaksha 2009, 233.

84. Vasudev 1978, 160.

85. Rampell, Anderson, and Rubenstein 1983, 37.

86. Gopinath 2013, 117.

87. Rajadhyaksha and Willemen 1999, 420.

88. N. Kazmi 1998, 124–25.

89. Mishra 2002, 138.

90. Vitali 2008, 24.

91. Kabir 2002, 43–44.

92. Kabir 2002, 45.

93. Vitali 2008, 220.

94. Susmita Dasgupta 2011, 21.

95. M. Bose 2006, 287.

96. N. Kazmi 1998, 104–5.

97. Susmita Dasgupta 2006, 55–56. Dasgupta writes, "by 1978, Amitabh Bachchan was one of the busiest actors in the industry. Ever since *Zanjeer*, he'd had on an average six releases a year. Surprisingly, and unlike the case with other stars with multiple releases, Amitabh's films did very good business even when they followed each other in quick succession, thus turning on its head the logic of spacing out releases. In fact, 1978 turned out to be the golden year in Amitabh's career. Of the six films in which he starred that year, five were released over a period of two months, and they all went on to celebrate jubilee runs—an unimaginable achievement seen in the light of box-office performances of even the most successful stars today."

98. Chaudhuri 2005, 99.

99. M. Bose 2006, 289.

100. Chaudhuri 2005, 98. It was directed by Nasir Hussain, Amir Khan's uncle and producer of *Qayamat Se Qayamat Tak*.

101. Rajadhyaksha and Willemen 1999, 424. *Jai Santoshi Maa* made a little-known mother goddess into one of the most popular icons especially among the urban working-class women who started observing the goddess's ritual fast on 12 consecutive Fridays and made offerings of chick-peas. The foremost earthly disciple of the deity Santoshi is Satyavati. When Satyavati marries the itinerant Birju, the wives of the celestial trio Brahma, Vishnu, and Shiva feel envious and create a series of problems intended to test Satyavati's devotion. After Santoshi has made the heavens literally rock with rage, Satyavati emerges from her trials with her faith untarnished and so allows Santoshi to be accepted into the cosmic pantheon.

102. Roberge 1974, 210–12.

103. M. Mehta 2012, 112.

104. M. Mehta 2012, 115.

105. Quoted in Ramachandran 1983, 128.

106. Ramachandran 1983, 99.

Chapter 4. India's Long Globalization and the Rise of Bollywood

1. Kollywood is Tamil cinema, named after Kodambakkam in Chennai. Sandalwood is the Kannada film industry based in Bangalore, named after the Sandalwood trees in the region. Mollywood refers to the Malayalam film industry based in Kerala. Lollywood is named after Lahore in Pakistan, and Dhallywood is the Bengali film industry based in Dhaka, Bangladesh.

2. Tollywood, for Calcutta's Tollygunge, predates Bollywood as a neologism. See note 4.

3. Film Federation of India, "Indian Feature Films Certified During the Year 2017," Film Federation of India, accessed February 1, 2019, http://www.filmfed.org/IFF2017 .HTML.

4. Prasad 2003. I am not elaborating on the origins of the word "Bollywood," which are contested. The reference to Tollygunge, the area in Calcutta where most studios were located, as "Tollywood" predates the use of "Bollywood" for Bombay cinema.

5. Chakravarty 1993.

6. Stenport and Traylor 2015. Stenport and Traylor offer a useful discussion on the strategic advantage of unique words or phrases in the context of the film *The Girl with the Dragon Tattoo* (2011), changed from *Men Who Hate Women* in the original Swedish.

7. MIB 2015, 35.

8. Punathambekar 2013, 26.

9. Aishwarya Rai acted in *The Last Legion* (2007) and *Pink Panther 2* (2009) and has been brand ambassador for L'Oréal Paris and Longines.

10. The first Indian film produced and financed by a Hollywood studio (Sony/Columbia) was the 2007 *Saawariya* (translated variously as Beloved or My Love, dir. Sanjay Leela Bhansali). Yash Raj Productions signed a "coproduction" deal with Disney Animation; their first production was *Roadside Romeo* (2009).

11. Prabhakar 2012. *Ghajini* (both the Tamil and Hindi versions were directed by Murugadoss, in 2005 and 2008 respectively) derives from the idea of "anterograde amnesia" and a protagonist seeking to avenge his partner's murder who tattoos his body with facts relevant to his mission.

12. Cain 2015.

13. Weinraub 1991.

14. A. Roy 1997, 28.

15. Dahlburg 1994.

16. P. Chatterji 1987, 21–22. Chatterji writes, "Public sector enterprises produce such diverse products as arms and defence equipment, aircraft, atomic energy, plant machinery, steel, coal, aluminum, copper, heavy and light engineering products, petroleum products, locomotives, ships, telephones and telephone cables, telegraph and wireless apparatus. Important minerals fall within the exclusive sphere of the public sector. In the sphere of joint operations come minerals, other than those confined to the public sector, machine tools, ferrous alloys, drugs, antibiotics, fertilisers, plastics and synthetic rubber."

17. Sanders 1977.

18. Vasudevan 2011, 156.

19. N. Kazmi 1998, 195.

20. N. Kazmi 1998, 195.

21. A. Sircar 2011, 124.

22. A. Sircar 2011, 125–26.

23. N. Kazmi 1998, 54.

24. M. Mehta 2012, 161.

25. M. Mehta 2012, 161.

26. Gopal 2012. I borrow the specific usage of "conjugation" from Gopal.

27. Vasudevan 2011, 157.

28. Vitali 2008, 235–36.

29. Verma and Tripathy 2010, 104.

30. A. Sircar 2011, 76.

31. Manuel 1991, 191.

32. Filkins 1997.

33. Nilekani 2009.

34. Koshy and Radhakrishnan 2008, 16.

35. Koshy and Radhakrishnan 2008, 17–18.

36. Wolpert 1997, 447.

37. Bharucha 1998, 126.

38. Bharucha 1998, 136.

39. Pendakur 2003, 110.

40. A. Chopra 2011, 25–26.

41. R. Mehta 2010, 1–2.

42. Nandy 2011. I am playing on Nandy's coinage, "Slum's Worldview of Indian Politics," with reference to popular cinema in India.

43. A. Chopra 2011, 28.

44. A. Chopra 2011, 28–29.

45. A. Chopra 2011, 28–29.

46. N. Kazmi 1998, 191–92.

47. Juluri 2003, 96.

48. Juluri 2003, 30.

49. Juluri 2003, 31.

50. Ranade 2011, 326–27.

51. Manuel 1993, 63.

52. Manuel 1993.

53. Athique and Hill 2007. Athique and Hill offer a comprehensive study of the multiplex phenomenon in India.

54. D. Bose 2006, 46.

55. Verma and Tripathy 2010, 96–97.

56. M. Bose 2006, 22.

57. Sanjeev Srivastava 2001.

58. M. Bose 2006, 22.

59. M. Bose 2006, 23.

60. The founder of Reliance Industries was Dhirubhai Ambani, whose fictionalized biopic, Mani Ratnam's *Guru*, is discussed earlier in this chapter.

61. Vitali 2008, 240.

62. Susmita Dasgupta 2006, 118.

63. M. Bose 2006, 324.

64. Pendakur and Kapur 2007, 45.

65. Looch 2017.

Epilogue

1. Rahman 2018.

2. See Bhushan 2018.

3. Giridharadas 2007.

4. ET Bureau 2018.

5. Gehlawat 2017.

6. Escobedo 2017.

7. Both accessed on January 18, 2019.

8. Bollywood stars are also easily maligned in popular media for their political inclinations; Shah Rukh Khan and Aamir Khan have been criticized for their comments on rising intolerance in India after the 2014 elections.

9. Indian film stars have been involved in politics since the 1950s; examples include Sanjay Dutt, the Tamil stars M. G. Ramachandran and Jayalalitha, and the Telugu star Nandamuri Taraka Rama Rao. Bollywood stars' involvement in politics is therefore a well-charted territory.

10. Shah Rukh Khan, Preity Zinta, and Shilpa Shetty are co-owners of Kolkata Knight Riders, Kings XI Punjab, and Rajasthan Royals. For a study on the intermingling of the Indian Premier League and Bollywood, see Rasul and Proffitt 2011.

Bibliography

Abbas, Ackbar, John Nguyet Erni, and Wimal Dissanayake. 2005. *Internationalizing Cultural Studies: An Anthology.* Malden, MA: Blackwell.

Acland, Charles R. 2000. "Cinemagoing and the Rise of the Megaplex." *Television and New Media* 1 (4): 375–402.

———. 2003. *Screen Traffic: Movies, Multiplexes, and Global Culture.* Durham: Duke University Press.

Agrawal, Binod C. 1984. "Indianness of the Indian Cinema." In *Continuity and Change in Communication Systems: An Asian Perspective*, edited by W. Dissanayake and G. Wang, 181–91. Norwood, NJ: Ablex.

Alasuutari, Pertti, ed. 1999. *Rethinking the Media Audience: The New Agenda.* London: SAGE.

Alessandrini, Anthony C. 2001. "'My Heart's Indian for All That': Bollywood Film between Home and Diaspora." *Diaspora: A Journal of Transnational Studies* 10 (3): 315–40.

Althusser, Louis. 1971. "Ideology and Ideological State Apparatus (Notes toward an Investigation)." In *Lenin and Philosophy*, 126–87. New York: Monthly Review Press.

Anderson, Benedict. 1983. *Imagined Communities: Reflections on the Origin and Spread of Nationalism.* London: Verso.

Anderson, Perry. 2012. *The Indian Ideology.* Gurgaon: Three Essays Collective.

Andrew, Dudley. 2010. "Time Zones and Jetlag: The Flows and Phases of World Cinema." In *World Cinemas, Transnational Perspectives*, by Nataša Ďurovičová and Kathleen Newman, 59–89. New York: Routledge.

Appadurai, Arjun. 1996. *Modernity at Large: Cultural Dimensions of Globalization.* Minneapolis: University of Minnesota Press.

————, ed. 2001. *Globalization.* Durham: Duke University Press.

Aranya, R. 2003. "Globalisation and Urban Restructuring of Bangalore, India." Paper presented at the 39th ISOCARP Congress. Cairo, Egypt, October 17–22, 2003.

Armes, Roy. 1987. *Third World Filmmaking and the West.* Berkeley: University of California Press.

Arora, V. N. 1986. "Popular Songs in Hindi Films." *Journal of Popular Culture* 20 (2): 143–66.

Ashokamitran. 2002. *My Years with Boss at Gemini Studios.* New Delhi: Orient Longman.

Athique, Adrian Mabbott. 2008a. "The Global Dynamics of Indian Media Piracy: Export Markets, Playback Media and the Informal Economy." *Media, Culture and Society* 30 (5): 699–717.

————. 2008b. "A Line in the Sand: The India-Pakistan Border in the Films of J. P. Dutta." *South Asia: Journal of South Asian Studies* 31 (3): 472–99.

————. 2009. "From Monopoly to Polyphony: India in the Era of Television." In *Television Studies after TV: Understanding Television in the Post Broadcast Era*, edited by Graeme Turner and Jinna Tay, 159–67. London: Routledge.

————. 2012. *Indian Media.* Cambridge, UK: Polity Press.

Athique, Adrian Mabbott, and Douglas Hill. 2007. "Multiplex Cinemas and Urban Redevelopment in India." *Media International Australia, Incorporating Culture and Policy*, no. 124: 108–18.

Bahadur, Satish. 1976. "The Context of Indian Film Culture." In *Film Miscellany*, edited by Jagar Murari, 90–107. Pune: Film and Television Institute of India.

Banerjee, Arpan. 2010. "Political Censorship and Indian Cinematographic Laws: A Functionalist-Liberal Analysis." *Drexel Law Review* 2:557–626.

Banerjee, Haimanti. 1985. *Ritwik Kumar Ghatak: A Monograph.* Pune: National Film Archive of India.

Bannerjee, Shampa, ed. 1982. *New Indian Cinema.* New Delhi: National Film Development Council.

Barlet, Olivier. 2010. "Bollywood/Africa: A Divorce?" *Black Camera* 2 (1): 126–43.

Barnouw, Erik, and Subrahmanya Krishnaswamy. 1980. *Indian Film.* New York: Oxford University Press.

Baskaran, S. Theodore. 1981. *The Message Bearers: The Nationalist Politics and the Entertainment Media in South India 1880–1945.* Madras: Cre-A.

————. 2009. *History through the Lens: Perspectives on South Indian Cinema.* Hyderabad: Orient Blackswan.

Benegal, Shyam. 1981. "Wanted: A Cinema of Our Times." In Ramachandran, Burra, and Chandran 1981, 54–55.

Bhabha, Homi K. 1994. *The Location of Culture.* New York: Routledge.

Bharat, Meenakshi, and Nirmal Kumar. 2007. *Filming the Line of Control: The Indo-Pak Relationship through the Cinematic Lens.* New Delhi: Routledge.

Bharucha, Rustom. 1998. *In the Name of the Secular: Contemporary Cultural Activism in India.* New Delhi: Oxford University Press.

Bhattacharjya, Nilanjana. 2009. "Popular Hindi Film Song Sequences Set in the Indian Diaspora and the Negotiating of Indian Identity." *Asian Music* 40 (1): 53–82.

Bhattacharya, Malini. 1983. "The IPTA in Bengal." *Journal of Arts and Ideas*, January–March, 5–22.

Bhattacharya, Nandini. 2004. "A 'Basement' Cinephilia: Indian Diaspora Women Watch Bollywood." *South Asian Popular Culture* 2 (2): 161–84.

Bhaumik, Kaushik. 2010. "At Home in the World: Cinema and Cultures of the Young in Bombay in the 1920s." In *Towards a History of Consumption in South Asia*, edited by Douglas E. Haynes, Abigail McGowan, Tirthankar Roy, and Haruka Yanagisawa, 136–54. Oxford: Oxford University Press.

Bhowmik, Someswar. 1995. *Indian Cinema: Colonial Contours*. Calcutta: Papyrus.

Bhushan, Nyay. 2018. "Amazon Prime Video India Boss on Peak TV, Competing with Netflix." *Hollywood Reporter*, September 21, 2018. https://www.hollywoodreporter .com/news/amazon-prime-video-india-boss-peak-tv-competing-netflix-q-a-1145659.

Binford, Mira Reym. 1983a. "The New Cinema of India." *Quarterly Review of Film and Video* 8 (4): 47–61.

———. 1983b. "State Patronage and India's New Cinema." *Critical Arts* 2 (4): 33–46.

———. 1987. "The Two Cinemas of India." In *Film and Politics in the Third World*, edited by John D. H. Downing, 145–66. New York: Praeger.

———. 1988. "Innovation and Imitation in the Indian Cinema." In *Cinema and Cultural Identity: Reflections on Films from Japan, India, and China*, edited by Wimal Dissanayake, 77–92. Lanham, MD: University Press of America.

Binford, Mira Reym, Robert W. Lucky, and Sumita Chakravarty. 1989. "Indian Cinema: An Annotated Bibliography." *Quarterly Review of Film and Video* 11 (3): 83–92. http://dx.doi .org/10.1080/10509208909361317.

Birla, Ritu. 2009. *Stages of Capital: Law, Culture, and Market Governance in Late Colonial India*. Durham: Duke University Press.

Booth, Greg. 2005. "Pandits in the Movies: Contesting the Identity of Hindustani Classical Music and Musicians in the Hindi Popular Cinema." *Asian Music* 36 (1): 60–86.

Bose, A. B. 1963. "Mass Communication: The Cinema in India." *Indian Journal of Social Research* 4:80–88.

Bose, Brinda. 2008. "Modernity, Globality, Sexuality, and the City: A Reading of Indian Cinema." *Global South* 2 (1): 35–58.

Bose, Derek. 2006. *Brand Bollywood: A New Global Entertainment Order*. New Delhi: SAGE.

Bose, Mihir. 2006. *Bollywood: A History*. Stroud, UK: Tempus.

Bose, Nandana. 2009. "The Hindu Right and the Politics of Censorship: Three Case Studies of Policing Hindi Cinema, 1992–2002." *Velvet Light Trap*, no. 63: 22–33.

———. 2010. "The Central Board of Film Certification Correspondence Files (1992–2002): A Discursive Rhetoric of Moral Panic, 'Public' Protest, and Political Pressure." *Cinema Journal* 49 (3): 67–87.

Brass, Paul R. 1990. *The Politics of India since Independence*. Cambridge: Cambridge University Press.

Breckenridge, Carol Appadurai, ed. 1995. *Consuming Modernity: Public Culture in a South Asian World*. Minneapolis: University of Minnesota Press.

Brodbeck, Sam. 2011. "Famous Last Words." sambrodbeck.com, October 29, 2011. Accessed March 15, 2013. http://sambrodbeck.com/2011/10/29/famous-last-words/ (site discontinued).

Brosius, Christiane, and Melissa Butcher. 1999. *Image Journeys: Audio-Visual Media and Cultural Change in India*. New Delhi: SAGE.

Burra, Rani, ed. 1981. *Looking Back, 1896–1960*. New Delhi: Directorate of Film Festivals, Ministry of Information and Broadcasting.

Butcher, Melissa. 2003. *Transnational Television, Cultural Identity and Change: When STAR Came to India*. New Delhi: SAGE.

Cain, Rob. 2015. "India's Film Industry—A $10 Billion Business Trapped in a $2 Billion Body." *Forbes*, October 23, 2015. https://www.forbes.com/sites/robcain/2015/10/23/indias-film-industry-a-10-billion-business-trapped-in-a-2-billion-body/#30bba2ea70d2.

Chabria, Suresh. 1994. *Light of Asia: Indian Silent Cinema 1912–1934*. New Delhi: National Film Archive of India.

Chakrabarty, Dipesh. 2008. *Provincializing Europe*. Princeton: Princeton University Press.

Chakravartty, Paula. 2008. "In or as Civil Society: Workers and Subaltern Publics in India's Information Society." In *Global Communications: Towards a Transcultural Political Economy*, edited by Paula Chakravartty and Yuezhi Zhao, 285–308. New York: Rowan and Littlefield.

Chakravarty, Sumita S. 1993. *National Identity in Indian Popular Cinema, 1947–1987*. Austin: University of Texas Press.

———. 2000. "Fragmenting the Nation: Images of Terrorism in Indian Popular Cinema." In *Cinema and Nation*, edited by Mette Hjort and Scott Mackenzie, 222–37. London: Routledge.

Chakravorty, Mrinalini. 2012. "Picturing the Postmaster: Tagore, Ray, and the Making of an Uncanny Modernity." *Framework: The Journal of Cinema and Media* 53 (1): 117–46.

Chandra, Bipan, Mridula Mukherjee, and Aditya Mukherjee. 2000. *India since Independence*. New Delhi: Penguin Books.

Chandra, Nandini. 2010. "Young Protest: The Idea of Merit in Commercial Hindi Cinema." *Comparative Studies of South Asia, Africa and the Middle East* 30 (1): 119–32.

Chatterjee, Bankimchandra. 2005. *Anandamath, or The Sacred Brotherhood*. Edited by Julius Lipner. New York.

Chatterjee, Partha. 1986. *Nationalist Thought and the Colonial World: A Derivative Discourse*. London: Zed Books.

———. 1993. *The Nation and Its Fragments: Colonial and Postcolonial Histories*. Princeton: Princeton University Press.

Chatterji, P. C. 1987. *Broadcasting in India*. New Delhi: SAGE.

Chatterji, Shoma A. 2004. *Ritwik Ghatak: The Celluloid Rebel*. New Delhi: Rupa.

———. 2008. *P. C. Barua*. New Delhi: Wisdom Tree.

Chaudhuri, Shantanu Ray. 2005. *Icons from Bollywood*. New Delhi: Puffin Books.

Chopra, Anupama. 2011. "Shah Rukh Khan: A Global Icon." In *The Greatest Show on Earth: Writings on Bollywood*, edited by Jerry Pinto, 25–34. New Delhi: Penguin Books.

Chopra, B. R. 1981. "Are We United." In Ramachandran, Burra, and Chandran 1981, 64–68.

Chowdhry, Prem. 2000. *Colonial India and the Making of Empire Cinema: Image, Ideology and Identity*. Manchester: Manchester University Press.

Cooper, Darius. 1988. "The Hindi Film Song and Guru Dutt." *East-West Film Journal* 2 (2): 49–65.

Cort, David. 1952. "The Biggest Star in the World." *Theatre Arts* 24–26:95.

Crawford, Reavis. 2002. "Bullets over Bombay: Exposing the Underworld of Hindi Cinema (Both Onscreen and Offscreen)." *Film Comment*, May-June 2002, 53–55.

Creekmur, Corey, and Linda Y. Mokdad, eds. 2012. *The International Film Musical*. Edinburgh: Edinburgh University Press.

Cubitt, Sean. 1999. "Phalke, Melies, and Special Effects Today." *Wide Angle* 21 (1): 115–30.

Cullity, Jocelyn, and Prakash Younger. 2004. "Sex Appeal and Cultural Liberty: A Feminist Inquiry into MTV India." *Frontiers: A Journal of Women Studies* 25 (2): 96–122.

Czach, Liz. 2004. "Film Festivals, Programming, and the Building of a National Cinema." *Moving Image* 4 (1): 76–88.

Dahlburg, John-Thor. 1994. "India Finds 'Jurassic Park' a Real Scream." *Los Angeles Times*, May 21, 1994. http://articles.latimes.com/1994-05-21/entertainment/ca-60417_1_hindi-film-north-india-new-delhi.

Das, Gucharan. 2002. *India Unbound: From Independence to the Global Information Age*. New Delhi: Penguin Books.

Dasgupta, Chidananda. 1969. "Indian Cinema Today." *Film Quarterly* 22 (4): 27–35.

———. 1980a. *Cinema of Satyajit Ray*. New Delhi: Vikas Publishing House.

———. 1980b. "New Directions in Indian Cinema." *Film Quarterly* 34 (1): 32–42.

———. 1981. *Talking about Films*. New Delhi: Orient Longman.

———. 1986. "Indian Cinema: Dynamics of Old and New." In *India 2000: The Next Fifteen Years*, edited by James R. Roach, 81–95. New York City: Riverdale Press.

———. 1991. *The Painted Face: Studies in India's Popular Cinema*. New Delhi: Roli Books.

Dasgupta, Chidananda, and J. Hoberman. 1987. "Pols of India." *Film Comment*, June 1987, 20–24.

Dasgupta, Shamita Das. 1986. *"All that Glitters . . .": An Assessment of Feminist Consciousness in Hindi Films*. East Lansing: Michigan State University Press.

———. 1996. "Feminist Consciousness in Woman-Centered Hindi Films." *Journal of Popular Culture* 30 (1): 173–89.

Dasgupta, Susmita. 2006. *Amitabh: The Making of a Superstar*. New Delhi: Penguin Books.

———. 2011. "The Birth of Tragedy." In *The Greatest Show on Earth: Writings on Bollywood*, edited by Jerry Pinto, 14–24. New Delhi: Penguin Books.

Dass, Manishita. 2004. "Outside the Lettered City: Cinema, Modernity, and Nation in India." Diss., Stanford University.

———. 2016. *Outside the Lettered City: Cinema, Modernity, and the Public Sphere in Late Colonial India.* New York: Oxford University Press.

Datt, Gopal. 1984. *Indian Cinema, the Next Decade.* New Delhi: Indian Film Directors' Association.

David, C. R. W. 1983. *Cinema as Medium of Communication in Tamil Nadu.* Madras: Christian Literature Society.

De, Amalendu. 1995. "The Social Thoughts and Consciousness of the Bengali Muslims in the Colonial Period." *Social Scientist* 23 (4/6): 16–37.

Deprez, Camille. 2013. "The Films Division of India, 1948–1964: The Early Days and the Influence of the British Documentary Film Tradition." *Film History: An International Journal* 25 (3): 149–73.

Desai, Jigna. 2002. "Homo on the Range: Mobile and Global Sexualities." *Social Text* 20 (4): 65–89.

———. 2004. *Beyond Bollywood: The Cultural Politics of South Asian Diasporic Film.* London: Routledge.

Desai, Lord Meghnad. 2004. *Nehru's Hero: Dilip Kumar.* New Delhi: Roli Books.

Desai, Rachana. 2005. "Copyright Infringement in the Indian Film Industry." *Vanderbilt Journal of Entertainment Law and Practice* 7 (2): 259–78.

Dharap, B. V. 1975. *Indian Films.* Poona: Motion Picture Enterprises.

Dhondy, Farrukh. 1985. "Keeping Faith: Indian Film and Its World." *Daedalus* 114 (4): 125–40.

Directorate of Film Festivals. 1981. *The New Generation: 1960–1980.* New Delhi: Ministry of Information and Broadcasting.

Dissanayake, Wimal. 1986. "Art, Vision, and Culture: Satyajit Ray's Apu Trilogy Revisited." *East-West Film Journal* 1 (1): 69–83.

———, ed. 1993. *Melodrama and Asian Cinema.* New York: Cambridge University Press.

Dissanayake, Wimal, and Sahai Malti. 1992. *Sholay: A Cultural Reading.* New Delhi: Wiley Eastern.

Dudrah, Rajinder. 2002. "Vilayati Bollywood: Popular Hindi Cinema-Going and Diasporic South Asian Identity in Birmingham (UK)." *Javnost* 9 (1): 19–36.

Dwyer, Rachel. 2000. "'Indian Values' and the Diaspora: Yash Chopra's Films of the 1990's." *West Coast Line* 32 (2): 6–27.

Dwyer, Rachel, and Divia Patel. 2002. *Cinema India: The Visual Culture of the Hindi Film.* London: Reaktion Books.

Escobedo, Joe. 2017. "Transmedia Will Shape the Future of Hollywood and Fortune 500 Firms." *Forbes,* July 1, 2017. https://www.forbes.com/sites/joeescobedo/2017/07/01/meet-the-man-behind-hollywood-and-fortune-500-firms-transmedia-success/#2c2996ef33da.

ET Bureau. 2018. "Walmart Flipkart Acquisition: Walmart Acquires Flipkart for $16 billion

in World's Largest eCommerce Deal." *Economic Times,* May 10. https://economictimes
.indiatimes.com/small-biz/startups/newsbuzz/walmart-acquires-flipkart-for-16-bn
-worlds-largest-ecommerce-deal/articleshow/64095145.cms.

Fernandes, Leela. 2000. "Nationalizing 'The Global': Media Images, Cultural Politics
and the Middle Class in India." *Media Culture and Society* 22 (5): 611–28.

Filkins, Dexter. 1997. "In India's Film World, Violence Is Very Real." *Los Angeles Times,*
November 21, 1997. http://articles.latimes.com/1997/nov/21/news/mn-56037.

The Film Daily. 1930. *The Film Daily Year Book of Motion Pictures.* New York: The Film
Daily.

———. 1938. *The Film Daily Year Book of Motion Pictures.* New York: The Film Daily.

———. 1940. *The Film Daily Year Book of Motion Pictures.* New York: The Film Daily.

Flinn, Caryl. 2016. "The Music of Screen Musicals." In *The Cambridge Companion to
Film Music,* by Mervyn Cooke and Fionna Ford, 231–46. Cambridge: Cambridge
University Press.

Freud, Sigmund. 2003. *The Uncanny.* Translated by David McLintock. London: Penguin.

Friesen, Dwight. 2008. "Showing Compassion and Suggesting Peace in *Karunamayudu,*
an Indian Jesus Film." *Studies in World Christianity* 14 (2): 125–41.

Gandhy, Behroze, and Rosie Thomas. 1991. "Three Indian Film Stars." In *Stardom Industry
of Desire,* edited by Christine Gledhill, 111–35. London: Routledge.

Gangar, Amrit. 2014. *The Music That Still Rings at Dawn, Every Dawn.* Bombay: Goethe
Institut.

Ganti, Tejaswini. 2002. "And Yet My Heart Is Still Indian: The Bombay Film Industry
and the (H)Indianization of Hollywood." In *Media Worlds: Anthropology on New Ter-
rain,* edited by Faye Ginzburg, Lila Abu-Lughod, and Brian Larkin, 281–300. Berkeley:
University of California Press.

———. 2004. *Bollywood: A Guidebook to Popular Hindi Cinema.* New York: Routledge.

———. 2012. *Producing Bollywood: Inside the Contemporary Hindi Film Industry.* Durham: Duke University Press.

Garga, B. D. 1983. "The History: A Diachronic Perspective." In *Indian Cinema Superbazaar,* edited by Aruna Vasudev and Philippe Lenglet, 19–27. Delhi: Vikas Publishing House.

Geeta, J. 2003. "Bollywood Ending." *Sight and Sound* 13 (6): 31–32.

Gehlawat, Ajay. 2010. *Reframing Bollywood: Theories of Popular Hindi Cinema.* New
Delhi: SAGE.

———. 2015. *Twenty-First Century Bollywood.* New York: Routledge.

———. 2017. "The Metatext of Bajirao Mastani: Intolerance in the Time of Modi."
South Asian History and Culture 8 (3): 338–48.

Ghosh, Avijit. 1996. "India's Journey with Amitabh Bachchan." *Pioneer,* November
24, 1996.

Ghosha, S. C. 1981. *Twelve Indian Directors.* Calcutta: People's Book Publications.

Gill, Aastha. 2013. "Bollywood Turns 100—a Long Journey for Indian Cinema." Ministry of External Affairs, Government of India. May 30, 2013. http://mea.gov.in/

articles-in-foreign-media.htm?dtl/21775/Bollywood+turns+100++a+long+journey+for
+Indian+cinema.

Giridharadas, Anand. 2007. "Can Hollywood Make a Bollywood Movie?" *New York Times*,
August 7, 2007. http://www.nytimes.com/2007/08/07/business/worldbusiness/07iht
-bollywood.1.7017281.html?pagewanted=all&_r=0.

Gokulsing, K. Moti, and Wimal Dissanayake. 1998. *Indian Popular Cinema: A Narrative
of Cultural Change*. Stoke-on-Trent, Eng.: Trentham Books.

Gondhalekar, Nandini, and Sanjoy Bhattacharya. 1999. "The All-India Hindu Mahas-
abha and the End of British Rule in India, 1939–1947." *Social Scientist* 27 (7/8): 48–74.

Gooptu, Sharmistha. 2003. "The Glory That Was: An Exploration of the Iconicity
of New Theatres." *Comparative Studies of South Asia, Africa and the Middle East* 23
(1–2): 286–300.

Gopal, Sangita. 2012. *Conjugations: Marriage and Form in New Bollywood Cinema*. Chicago: University of Chicago Press.

Gopalan, Lalitha. 2003. *Cinema of Interruptions: Action Genres in Contemporary Indian
Cinema*. New Delhi: Oxford University Press.

Gopinath, Praseeda. 2013. *Scarecrows of Chivalry: English Masculinities after Empire*.
Richmond: University of Virginia Press.

Government of India. 1951. *Report of the Film Enquiry Committee*. New Delhi: Government of India.

———. 1969. *Report of the Enquiry Committee on Film Censorship*. Simla: Government
of India Press.

———. 2015. *Constitution of India*. New Delhi: Ministry of Law and Justice.

Govil, Nitin. 2007. "Bollywood and the Frictions of Global Mobility." In *Media on
the Move: Global Flow and Contra-flow*, edited by Daya Thussu, 76–88. London:
Routledge.

———. 2013. "Recognizing 'Industry.'" *Cinema Journal* 52 (3): 172–76.

Gramsci, Antonio. 1988. *The Gramsci Reader: Selected Writings, 1916–1935* . Edited by
David Forgacs. New York: New York University Press.

Griffith, Alison. 1996. "A Moving Picture in Two Senses: Allegories of the Nation in
1950s Indian Melodrama." *Continuum* 9 (2): 173–84.

Gupta, Sourav. 2013. "The Deprived Technologist: Hiralal Sen and Bioscope." *Journal
of Bengali Studies* 2 (2): 8–16.

Gupta, Udayan. 1975. "A Cinema in a Revolutionary Society." *Jump Cut*, no. 8: 15–19.

———. 1982. "New Visions in Indian Cinema." *Cinéaste* 12 (1): 18–24.

Gupta, Udayan, and Satyajit Ray. 1982. "The Politics of Humanism: An Interview with
Satyajit Ray." *Cinéaste* 12 (1): 24–29.

Gupta, Udayan, Mrinal Sen, Girish Karnad, and Ketan Mehta. 1982. "New Visions
in Indian Cinema: Interviews with Mrinal Sen, Girish Karnad, and Ketan Mehta."
Cinéaste 11 (4): 18–24.

Guy, Randor. 2004. "First Film to Talk in Kannada." *The Hindu*, December 31, 2004.
http://hindu.com/thehindu/fr/2004/12/31/stories/2004123102420300.htm.

———. 2010. "He Brought Cinema to South." *The Hindu*, April 30, 2010.

Hardgrave, Robert L., Jr. 2008. "Politics and the Film in Tamil Nadu: The Stars and the DMK." In *Tamil Cinema: The Cultural Politics of India's Other Film Industry*, edited by Selvaraj Velayutham, 59–76. New York: Routledge.

Hardgrave, Robert L., Jr., and Anthony C. Neidhart. 1975. "Films and Political Consciousness in Tamil Nadu." *Economic and Political Weekly*, January 11, 27–35.

Hariharan, K. 1999. "Revisiting Sholay, a.k.a. Flames of the Sun." *Asian Cinema* 10 (2): 151–54.

Hassam, Andrew, and Makarand Paranjape. 2010. *Bollywood in Australia: Transnationalism and Cultural Production*. Perth: UWA Press.

Hatcher, Brian. 2008. *Bourgeois Hinduism, or Faith of the Modern Vedantists: Rare Discourses from Early Colonial Bengal*. New York: Oxford University Press.

Heuze, Gerard. 2000. "Populism, Religion, and Nation in Contemporary India: The Evolution of the Shiv Sena in Maharashtra." *Comparative Studies of South Asia, Africa and the Middle East* 20 (1–2): 3–43.

Higson, Andrew, and Richard Maltby, eds. 1999. *"Film Europe" and "Film America": Cinema, Commerce and Cultural Exchange, 1920–1939*. Exeter: University of Exeter Press.

The Hindu. 2015. "Furore as Leela Samson Quits." *The Hindu*, January 17, 2015. http://www.thehindu.com/news/national/censor-board-chief-leela-samson-decides-to-quit/article6792822.ece?css=print.

Hobsbawm, Eric J. 1987. *The Age of Empire, 1875–1914*. New York: Pantheon Books.

Hofneyr, Isabel, Preben Kaarsholm, and Bodil Folke Frederiksen. 2011. "Introduction: Print Cultures, Nationalisms and Publics of the Indian Ocean." *Africa: The Journal of the International African Institute* 81 (1): 1–22.

Hogan, Patrick Colm. 2008. *Understanding Indian Movies: Culture, Cognition, and Cinematic Imagination*. Austin: University of Texas Press.

Hudson, Dale. 2009. "Undesirable Bodies and Desirable Labor: Documenting the Globalization and Digitalization of Transnational American Dreams in Indian Call Centers." *Cinema Journal* 49 (1): 82–102.

Hughes, Stephen Putnam. 2009. "Tamil Mythological Cinema and the Politics of Secular Modernism." In *Aesthetic Formations: Media, Religion, and the Senses*, by Birgit Meyer, 93–116. New York: Palgrave Macmillan.

ICC. 1928. *Report of the Indian Cinematograph Committee, 1927–1928*. Calcutta: Government of India Central Publication Branch.

Inden, Ronald. 1999. "Transnational Class, Erotic Arcadia and Commercial Utopia in Hindi Films." In *Image Journeys: Audio-Visual Media and Cultural Change in India*, edited by Christiane Brosius and Melissa Butcher, 41–68. New Delhi: SAGE.

India Today. 2015. "Pahlaj Nihalani New Censor Board Chief, Nine New Members Appointed." *India Today*, January 19, 2015. http://indiatoday.intoday.in/articlePrint.jsp?aid=414156.

Iyengar, Rishi. 2017. "Netflix Steps Up Its Battle with Amazon in India." *CNN Tech*.

August 4, 2017. http://money.cnn.com/2017/08/04/technology/netflix-india-original
-series-amazon/index.html.

Jacob, Preminda. 2009. *Celluloid Deities: The Visual Culture of Cinema and Politics in South India.* Lanham, MD: Lexington Books.

Jaikumar, Priya. 2003. "More Than Morality: The Indian Cinematograph Committee Interviews (1927)." *Moving Image* 3 (1): 82–109.

———. 2006. *Cinema at the End of Empire: A Politics of Transition in Britain and India.* Durham: Duke University Press.

———. 2009. "A Throw of Dice (Prapancha Pash)" (review). *Modernism/Modernity* 16 (4): 845–48.

Jain, Anuja. 2013. "The Curious Case of the Films Division: Some Annotations on the Beginnings of Indian Documentary Cinema in Postindependence India, 1940s-1960s." *Velvet Light Trap*, no. 71: 15–23.

Jain, M. 1990. "The 80s Cinema: Triumph Trauma and Tears." *India Today*, January 15, 1990, 44–49.

Jain, Madhu. 2005. *The Kapoors: The First Family of Indian Cinema.* New Delhi: Penguin.

Jeffrey, Robin. 2009. "The Mahatma Didn't Like the Movies and Why It Matters: Indian Broadcasting Policy, 1920s-1990s." In *The Indian Public Sphere: Readings in Media History*, edited by Arvind Rajagopal, 171–87. Delhi: Oxford University Press.

Jha, Priya. 2003. "Lyrical Nationalism: Gender, Friendship, and Excess in 1970s Hindi Cinema." *Velvet Light Trap*, no. 51: 43–53.

Johar, Karan. 2017. "Karan Affairs: In Defence of My Nepotism by Karan Johar." NDTV. March 29, 2017. http://www.ndtv.com/opinion/karan-affairs-in-defence-of-my-nepotism-1674657.

Jolly, Gurbir Singh, Zenia B. Wadhwani, and Deborah Barretto. 2007. *Once upon a Time in Bollywood: The Global Swing in Hindi Cinema.* Toronto: TSAR.

Jones, Geoffrey, Namrata Arora, Surachita Mishra, and Alexis Lefort. 2005. "Can Bollywood Go Global?" Harvard Business School Case 806–040.

Joshi, Puran Chandra. 1974. *Balraj Sahni: An Intimate Portrait.* Delhi: Vikas Publishing House.

Juluri, Vamsee. 2003. *Becoming a Global Audience: Longing and Belonging in Indian Music Television.* New York: Peter Lang.

Kaarsholm, Preben. 2004. *City Flicks: Indian Cinema and the Urban Experience.* Calcutta: Seagull Books.

Kabir, Nasreen Munni. 1999. *Talking Films: Conversations on Hindi Cinema with Javed Akhtar.* New York: Oxford University Press.

———. 2002. *Bollywood: The Indian Cinema Story.* London: Channel 4 Books.

Kabir, Nasreen Munni, and Rauf Ahmed. 1985. *Les Stars du cinéma indien.* Paris: Centre Georges Pompidou.

Kapse, Anupama. 2013. "Melodrama and Method." *Framework: The Journal of Cinema and Media* 54 (2): 146–51.

Kapur, Geeta. 1987. "Mythic Material in Indian Cinema." *Journal of Arts and Ideas*, nos. 14–15: 79–107.

Karanjia, B. K. 1981. "Survival Not Enough: Self-Respect, Self-Confidence a Must for Film-Makers." In Ramachandran, Burra, and Chandran 1981, 19–21.

———. 1986. *A Many-Splendoured Cinema*. Bombay: New Thacker's Fine Art Press.

Karanth, B. V. 1981. "There's More to Sound Than Music." In Ramachandran, Burra, and Chandran 1981, 70–71.

Karim, Karim H., ed. 2003. *The Media and Diaspora*. London: Routledge.

Kaul, Arun, and Mrinal K. Sen. 2014. "Manifesto of the New Cinema Movement." In *Film Manifestos and Global Cinema Cultures: A Critical Anthology*, edited by Scott MacKenzie, 165–68. Los Angeles: University of California Press.

Kaul, Gautam. 1998. *Cinema and the Indian Freedom Struggle*. New Delhi: Sterling.

Kaur, Raminder, and Ajay J. Sinha, eds. 2005. *Bollyworld: Popular Indian Cinema through a Transnational Lens*. New Delhi: SAGE.

Kaur, Ravinder. 2002. "Viewing the West through Bollywood: A Celluloid Occident in the Making." *Contemporary South Asia* 11 (2): 199–209.

Kavoori, Anandam, and Aswin Punathmbekar. 2008. *Global Bollywood*. New York: New York University Press.

Kazmi, Fareed. 1999. *The Politics of India's Conventional Cinema: Imaging a Universe, Subverting a Multiverse*. New Delhi: SAGE.

Kazmi, Nikhat. 1996. *Ire in the Soul: Bollywood's Angry Years*. New Delhi: Harper Collins India.

———. 1998. *The Dream Merchants of Bollywood*. New Delhi: UBSPD.

Kesavan, Mukul. 1994. "Urdu, Awadh, and the Tawaif: The Islamicate Roots of Hindi Cinema." In *Forging Identities: Gender, Communities, and the State*, edited by Zoya Hassan, 244–57. New Delhi: Kali for Women.

Keskar, B. V. 1967. *Indian Music: Problems and Prospects*. Bombay: Popular Prakashan.

Khosla, G. D. 1986. "Why We Need Film Censorship." *Times of India: Miscellany*, February 9, 1986.

Kohli-Khandekar, Vanita. 2003. *The Indian Media Business*. New Delhi: Response Books.

Koshy, Susan, and R. Radhakrishnan. 2008. *Transnational South Asians: The Making of a Neo-Diaspora*. New Delhi: Oxford University Press.

Krishen, Pradip. 1980. "Indian Popular Cinema: Myth." *India International Centre Quarterly* 8 (1): 57–76.

———. 1981. "The Heady Thirties." In Ramachandran, Burra, and Chandran 1981, 40–44.

Krishna, Govind. 2013. *Law Relating to Cinema Video and Cable Television*. Allahabad: Hind Publishing House.

Kumar, Kanchan. 2003. "Mixed Signals: Radio Broadcasting Policy in India." *Economic and Political Weekly* 38 (22): 2173–82.

Kumar, Ramesh. 2013a. "The Making of the National Film Archive of India: Notes from the Archive of the Archive." *Moving Image* 13 (1): 98–128.

————. 2013b. "On Scavenging and Salvaging: NFAI and Early Indian Cinema." *Framework: The Journal of Cinema and Media* 54 (2): 152–57.

Lahoti, Devendra Pratap. 1981. "Stars—Then and Now." In Ramachandran, Burra, and Chandran 1981, 100–103.

Lakshmi, C. S. 1980. "Quiet Take-Over of NFDC." *Economic and Political Weekly* 15 (22): 957–58.

Langer, Jessica. 2012. "Endhiran (Robot)" (review). *Science Fiction Film and Television* 5 (1): 147–51.

Larkin, Brian. 2003. "Itineraries of Indian Cinema: African Videos, Bollywood and Global Media." In *Multiculturalism, Postcoloniality and Transnational Media*, edited by Ella Shohat and Robert Stam, 406–40. New Brunswick: Rutgers University Press.

Lent, John. 1983. "Heyday of the Indian Studio System: The 1930s." *Asian Profile* 11 (5): 467–74.

Lipkov, Alexander. 1994. "India's Bollywood in Russia." *India International Centre Quarterly* 21 (2/3): 185–94.

Looch, Cassam. 2017. "Here's Why So Many Bollywood Films Are Shot in Mauritius." *Culture Trip*, April 7, 2017. https://theculturetrip.com/africa/mauritius/articles/heres -why-so-many-bollywood-films-are-shot-in-mauritius/.

Lorenzen, Mark, and Ram Mudambi. 2013. "Clusters, Connectivity and Catch-Up: Bollywood and Bangalore in the Global Economy." *Journal of Economic Geography*, no. 13: 501–34.

Luthra, H. R. 1986. *Indian Broadcasting*. New Delhi: Ministry of Information and Broadcasting, Government of India.

Mahadevan, Sudhir. 2009. "The Traffic in Technologies: Early Cinema and Visual Culture in Bengal, 1840–1920." Diss., New York University.

————. 2013. "Early Cinema in South Asia: The Place of Technology in Narratives of Its Emergence." *Framework: the Journal of Cinema and Media* 54 (2): 140–45.

————. 2015. *A Very Old Machine: The Many Origins of the Cinema in India*. Albany: SUNY Press.

Mahmood, Hameeduddin. 1974. *The Kaleidoscope of Indian Cinema*. New Delhi: East-West Press.

Majithia, Sheetal. 2015. "Rethinking Postcolonial Melodrama and Affect." *Modern Drama* 58 (1): 1–23.

Majumdar, Neepa. 2005. "*Pather Panchali*: From Neo-realism to Melodrama." In *Film Analysis: A Norton Reader*, edited by Jeffrey Geiger and R. L. Rutsky, 510–27. New York: W. W. Norton.

————. 2009. *Wanted Cultured Ladies Only! Female Stardom and Cinema in India, 1930s-1950s*. Urbana: University of Illinois Press.

————. 2013. "What Is 'Early' Cinema?" *Framework: The Journal of Cinema and Media* 54 (2): 136–39.

Malcolm, Derek. 1986. "India's Middle Cinema." *Sign and Sound* 55 (Summer): 172–74.

Manuel, Peter. 1991. "The Cassette Industry and Popular Music in North India." *Popular Music* 10 (2) (May 1991): 189–204.

———. 1993. *Cassette Culture: Popular Music and Technology in North India*. Chicago: University of Chicago Press.

Mazumdar, Ranjani. 2011. "Terrorism, Conspiracy, and Surveillance in Bombay's Urban Cinema." *Social Research: an International Quarterly* 78 (1): 143–72.

McKernan, Luke. 2009. "'The Modern Elixir of Life': Kinemacolor, Royalty and the Delhi Durbar." *Film History: An International Journal* 21 (2): 122–36.

Mehta, Monika. 2009. "Reframing Film Censorship." *Velvet Light Trap*, no. 63: 66–69.

———. 2012. *Censorship and Sexuality in Bombay Cinema*. Delhi: Permanent Black.

Mehta, Nalin, ed. 2008. *Television in India: Satellites, Politics and Cultural Change*. New York: Routledge.

Mehta, Rini Bhattacharya. 2010. "Bollywood and Globalization: An Incomplete Introduction." In *Bollywood and Globalization: Indian Popular Cinema, Nation, and Diaspora*, edited by Rini Bhattacharya Mehta and Rajeshwari V. Pandharipande, 1–14. London: Anthem.

———. 2014. "Screening/Meaning: Hollywood's Long Career in India." *Comparative American Studies: An International Journal* 12 (1–2): 93–98.

Mehta, Vinod. 1972. *Meena Kumari: The Classic Biography*. New Delhi: HarperCollins.

Menon, Raghava R. 1978. *K. L. Saigal, the Pilgrim of the Swara*. Delhi: Clarion Books.

MIB (Ministry of Information and Broadcasting). 1954. *State Awards for Films, 1954*. Brochure. New Delhi: Government of India Publications Division.

———. 1955a. *India: A Reference Annual (1955)*. Delhi: Government of India Publications Division.

———. 1955b. *State Awards, 1955*. Brochure. New Delhi: Government of India Publications Division.

———. 1965. *Indian Cinema*. New Delhi: Ministry of Information and Broadcasting, Government of India Publications Division.

———. 1981. *State Awards*. New Delhi: Government of India Publications Division.

———. 2015. *India Film Guide*. Delhi: Government of India.

Michelutti, Lucia. 2008. *The Vernacularisation of Democracy: Politics, Caste, and Religion in India*. New Delhi: Routledge.

Mishra, Vijay. 1985. "Towards a Theoretical Critique of Bombay Cinema." *Screen* 26 (3–4): 133–46.

———. 2002. *Bollywood Cinema: Temples of Desire*. New York: Routledge.

Mittal, Ashok. 1995. *Cinema Industry in India: Pricing and Taxation*. New Delhi: Indus Publishing.

Mohan, Jag. 1984. *S. Sukhdev, Film-Maker: A Documentary Montage*. National Film Archive of India.

Morcom, Anna. 2007. *Hindi Film Songs and the Cinema*. Hampshire, UK: Ashgate.

Moullier, Betrand. 2007. "Whither Bollywood? IP Rights, Innovation, and Economic Growth in India's Film Industries." Study, George Washington University Law School.

Mujawar, Isak. 1969. *Maharashtra: Birthplace of Indian Film Industry*. New Delhi: Maharashtra Information Centre.

Mukharjee, Arpita. 2002. *India's Trade Potential in Audio-Visual Services and the GATS.* New Delhi: Indian Council for Research on International Economic Relations.

Mukhopadhyay, Urvi. 2011. "Addressing the Masses': Gandhi's Notion of 'the People' and Indian Cinema's Popular Market." *South Asian History and Culture* 2 (3): 417–30.

Murthy, N. K. 1981. "Training for Cinema." In Ramachandran, Burra, and Chandran 1981, 81–82.

Nandy, Ashis. 1995. "An Intelligent Critic's Guide to Indian Cinema." In *The Savage Freud and Other Essays on Possible and Retrievable Selves,* 196–236. Bombay: Oxford University Press.

———. 1999. *The Secret Politics of our Desires: Innocence, Culpability and Indian Popular Cinema.* London: Zed Books.

———. 2011. "Modernity and the Sense of Loss, or Why Bhansali's *Devdas* Defied Experts to Become a Box Office Hit." *Inter-Asia Cultural Studies* 12 (3): 445–53.

Nehru, Jawaharlal. 1958. *Nehru's Speeches.* Vol. 3. New Delhi: Publications Division.

———. 1979. *Selected Works.* Edited by S. Gopal. Vol. 7. New Delhi: Orient Longman.

Nelson, Dean. 2018. *Jugaad Yatra: Exploring the Indian Art of Problem Solving.* New Delhi: Aleph.

Nilekani, Nandan. 2009. *Imagining India: The Idea of a Renewed Nation.* New York: Penguin.

Oommen, M. A., and Kumbattu Varkey Joseph. 1981. *Economics of Film Industry in India.* Gurgaon, India: Academic Press.

Padmanabhan, Anil. 2005. "Cinema Scope." *India Today International Edition,* February 28, 2005, 25–28.

Pande, Mrinal. 2006. "'Moving beyond Themselves': Women in Hindustani Parsi Theatre and Early Hindi Films." *Economic and Political Weekly* 41 (17): 1646–53.

Pandian, Anand. 2011. "Landscapes of Expression: Affective Encounters in South Indian Cinema." *Cinema Journal* 51 (1): 50–74.

Pandian, M. S. S. 1992. *The Image Trap: M. G. Ramachandran in Film and Politics.* New Delhi: SAGE.

Parrain, Philippe. 1969. *Regards sur le cinema indien.* Paris: Editions du Cerf.

Patel, Sujata, and Alice Thorner, eds. 1995. *Bombay: Mosaic of Modern Culture.* Bombay: Oxford University Press.

———, eds. 1996. *Bombay: Metaphor for Modern India.* Bombay: Oxford University Press.

Pathy, P. V., and Jag Mohan. 1972. *Dr. P. V. Pathy: Documentary Film Maker (1906–1961).* Poona: National Film Archive of India, Ministry of Information and Broadcasting, Government of India.

Pendakur, Manjunath. 1985. "Dynamics of Cultural Policy Making: The U.S. Film Industry in India ." *Journal of Communication,* Autumn, 52–72.

———. 1990. "India." In *The Asian Film Industry,* edited by John Lent, 229–52. Austin: University of Texas Press.

———. 1996. "India's National Film Policy: Shifting Currents in the 1990s." In *Film Policy: International, National, and Regional Perspectives,* edited by Albert Moran, 148–71. London: Routledge.

———. 2003. *Indian Popular Cinema: Industry, Ideology and Consciousness*. Broadway, NJ: Hampton Press.

Pendakur, Manjunath, and Jyotsna Kapur. 2007. "The Strange Disappreance of Bombay from Its Own Cinema." *Democratic Communiqué* 21 (1): 43–59.

Pendakur, Manjunath, and Radha Subramanyam. 1996. "Indian Cinema beyond National Borders." In *New Patterns in Television: Peripheral Vision*, edited by John Sinclair, Elizabeth Jacka, and Stuart Cunningham, 67–100. Oxford: Oxford University Press.

Pfleiderer, Beatrix, and Lothar Lutze. 1985. *The Hindi Film: Agent and Re-agent of Cultural Change*. New Delhi: Manohar.

Pillai, Swarnavel Eswaran. 2010. "Tamil Cinema and the Major Madras Studios." PhD diss., University of Iowa.

Prabhakar, Binoy. 2012. "Business of Rs 100-cr Films: Who Gets What and Why." *Economic Times*, August 26, 2012. http://economictimes.indiatimes.com/industry/media/entertainment/business-of-rs-100-cr-films-who-gets-what-and-why/printarticle/15700710.cms.

Prasad, M. Madhava. 1993. "Cinema and the Desire for Modernity." *Journal of Arts and Ideas*, nos. 25–26: 71–86.

———. 1998. *Ideology of the Hindi Film: A Historical Construction*. New Delhi: Oxford University Press.

———. 2003. "This Thing Called Bollywood." Seminar 525 online. Accessed June 17, 2017. http://www.india-seminar.com/2003/525/525%20madhava%20prasad.htm.

———. 2009. "The Natives Are Looking: Cinema and Censorship in Colonial India." In *Narratives of Indian Cinema*, edited by Manju Jain, 3–18. Delhi: Primus.

Punathambekar, Aswin. 2010. "Ameen Sayani and Radio Ceylon: Notes towards a History of Broadcasting and Bombay Cinema." *BioScope: South Asian Screen Studies* 1 (2): 189–97.

———. 2013. *From Bombay to Bollywood: The Making of a Global Media Industry*. New York: New York University Press.

Qureshi, Irna. 2013. "Bollywood's 100th Birthday Celebrated at Bradford International Film Festival." *The Guardian*, April 10, 2013. http://www.theguardian.com/film/the-northerner/2013/apr/10/bollywood-indian-cinema-bradford-film-festival.

Radjou, Navi, Jaideep Prabhu, and Simone Ahuja. 2012. *Jugaad Innovation: Think Frugal, Be Flexible, Generate Breakthrough Growth*. San Francisco: Jossey-Bass.

Raghavendra, M. K. 2011. *Bipolar Identity: Region, Nation, and the Kannada Nation Film*. New Delhi: Oxford University Press.

Raha, Kironmoy. 1974. "Indian Cinema." In *Chitra Bani: A Book on Film Appreciation*, edited by Gaston Roberge, 163–82. Calcutta: Chitra Bani.

———. 1991. *Bengali Cinema*. Calcutta: Nandan.

Rahman, Abid. 2018. "Ted Sarandos on Netflix India Plans." *Hollywood Reporter*, October 28, 2018. https://www.hollywoodreporter.com/news/ted-sarandos-netflix-india-plans-1155745.

Rai, Alok. 2000. *Hindi Nationalism*. New Delhi: Orient Longman.

Rai, Amit. 2009. *Untimely Bollywood: Globalization and India's New Media Assemblage.* Durham: Duke University Press.

———. 2019. *Jugaad Time: Ecologies of Everyday Hacking in India.* Durham: Duke University Press.

Raina, M. L. 1986. "'I'm All Right Jack': Packaged Pleasures of the Middle Cinema." *Journal of Popular Culture* 20 (2): 131–41.

Raj, Ashok. 2004. "The Curse of Globalised Culture: The Fall of Indian Cinema Foretold." *Futures* 36:797–809.

———. 2010. *Hero: The Silent Era to Dilip Kumar.* London: Hay House.

Rajadhyaksha, Ashish. 1982. *Ritwik Ghatak: A Return to the Epic.* Bombay: Screen Unit.

———. 1986. "Neo-traditionalism: Film as Popular Art in India." *Framework* 32 (33): 20–67.

———. 1993. "Epic Melodrama: Themes of Nationality in Indian Cinema." *Journal of Arts and Ideas,* nos. 25–26: 55–70.

———. 2000. "Realism, Modernism, and Post-colonial Theory." In *World Cinema: Critical Approaches,* edited by John Hill and Pamela Gibson, 29–41. Oxford: Oxford University Press.

———. 2003. "The 'Bollywoodisation' of the Indian Cinema: Cultural Nationalism in a Global Arena." *Inter-Asia Cultural Studies* 4 (1): 25–39.

———. 2009. *Indian Cinema in the Time of Celluloid: From Bollywood to the Emergency.* Bloomington: Indiana University Press.

Rajadhyaksha, Ashish, and Paul Willemen. 1999. *Encyclopaedia of Indian Cinema.* 2nd ed. Chicago: Routledge.

Rajagopal, Arvind. 2001. *Politics after Television: Religious Nationalism and the Reshaping of the Indian Public.* Cambridge: Cambridge University Press.

———, ed. 2009. *The Indian Public Sphere: Readings in Media History.* Delhi: Oxford University Press.

Rajagopalan, Sudha. 2008. *Indian Films in Soviet Cinemas: The Culture of Movie-Going after Stalin.* Bloomington: Indiana University Press.

Raju, Zakir Hussain. 2008. "'Bollywood in Bangladesh': Transcultural Consumption in Globalizing South Asia." In *Media Consumption in Everyday Life in Asia,* edited by Youna Kim, 155–66. London: Routledge.

———. 2012. "Indigenization of Cinema in (Post)Colonial South Asia: From Transnational to Vernacular Public Spheres." *Comparative Studies of South Asia, Africa and the Middle East* 32 (3): 611–21.

Ram, N. 2011. "The Changing Role of the News Media in Contemporary India." *Proceedings of the Indian History Congress* 72 (2): 1289–1310.

Ramachandran, T. M., ed. 1983. *70 Years of Indian Cinema (1913–1983).* Bombay: Cinema India-International.

Ramachandran, T. M., Rani Burra, and Mangala Chandran, eds. 1981. *Fifty Years of Indian Talkies, 1931–1981: A Commemorative Volume.* Bombay: Indian Academy of Motion Picture Arts and Sciences.

Rampell, E., Lindsay Anderson, and Lenny Rubenstein. 1983. "Revolution Is the Opium of the Intellectuals: An Interview with Lindsay Anderson." *Cinéaste* 12 (4): 36–38. http://www.jstor.org/stable/41686217.

Ranade, Ashok Da. 2011. *Hindi Film Song: Music beyond Boundaries.* New Delhi: Promilla and Co.

Ranganathan, Maya, and Usha Rodrigues. 2010. *Indian Media in a Globalised World.* New Delhi: SAGE.

Rangoonwalla, Firoze. 1973. *Guru Dutt, 1925–1965: A Monograph.* Poona: National Film Archive of India, Government of India.

———1979. *A Pictorial History of Indian Cinema.* London: Hamlyn.

———. 1980. *Satyajit Ray's Art.* New Delhi: Clarion.

———. 1983. *Indian Cinema: Past and Present.* New Delhi: Clarion.

Rangoonwalla, Firoze, and Vishwanath Das. 1970. *Indian Filmography: Silent and Hindi Films (1897–1969).* Bombay: Rangoonwalla and Udeshi.

Ransom, Amy J. 2014. "Bollywood Goes to the Stadium: Gender, National Identity, and Sport Film in Hindi." *Journal of Film and Video* 66 (4): 34–49.

Rasul, Azmat, and Jennifer M. Proffitt. 2011. "Bollywood and the Indian Premier League (IPL): The Political Economy of Bollywood's New Blockbuster." *Asian Journal of Communication* 21 (4): 373–88.

Ray, Manas. 2001. "Bollywood Down Under: Fiji-Indian Cultural History and Popular Assertion." In *Floating Lives: The Media and Asian Diasporas*, edited by Stuart Cunningham and John Sinclair, 136–79. Lanham, MD: Rowan and Littlefield.

Ray, R. M. 1956. *Indian Cinema in Retrospect.* New Delhi: Sangeet Natak Akademi.

Ray, Satyajit. 1976. *Our Films, Their Films.* Bombay: Orient Longman.

———. 1981. "My Work and My Philosophy." In Ramachandran, Burra, and Chandran 1981, 45–50.

———. 1982. "Under Western Eyes." *Sight and Sound* 51 (Autumn): 268–74.

Reddi, Rama P. 1983. *The Indian Cinematograph Code.* Hyderabad: Cinematograph Laws Research Institute.

Roberge, Gaston. 1974. *Chitra Bani: A Book on Film Appreciation.* Calcutta: Chitra Bani.

———. 1984. *Another Cinema for Another Society.* Calcutta: Seagull Books.

Robinson, Andrew. 1989. *Satyajit Ray: The Inner Eye.* Berkeley: University of California Press.

Roth-Ey, Kristin Joy. 2011. *Moscow Prime Time: How the Soviet Union Built the Media Empire that Lost the Cultural Cold War.* Ithaca: Cornell University Press.

Roy, Arundhati. 1997. *God of Small Things.* New York: HarperCollins.

———. 1999. "The Greater Common Good." *Outlook*, May 24, 1999. http://www.outlookindia.com/article/the-greater-common-good/207509.

Roy, Rajat. 1983. *Filmography of Sixty Eminent Indian Movie-Makers: Along with Their Short Biographical Notes.* Mosaboni: Cine Society.

Roy, Tapti. 1995. "Disciplining the Printed Text: Colonial and Nationalist Surveillance of

Bengali Literature." In *Texts of Power: Emerging Disciplines in Colonial Bengal*, edited by Partha Chatterjee, 30–62. Minneapolis: University of Minnesota Press.

Rushdie, Salman. 1981. *Midnight's Children*. Delhi: Penguin.

———. 1988. *The Satanic Verses*. New York: Random House.

———. 1995. *The Moor's Last Sigh*. New York: Pantheon.

Sahai, Malti. 1987. "Raj Kapoor and the Indianization of Charlie Chaplin." *East-West Film Journal* 2 (1): 62–76.

Sahni, Balraj. 1979. *Balraj Sahni: An Autobiography*. Translated by Ramesh Deshpande. Delhi: Hind Pocket Books.

Sahni, Bhisham. 1981. *Balraj, My Brother*. New Delhi: National Book Trust, India.

Salazkina, Masha. 2010. "Soviet-Indian Coproductions: Alibaba as Political Allegory." *Cinema Journal* 49 (4): 71–89.

Salgia, Deepesh. 2005. "Mughal-e-Azam: Restoration-cum-Colorization for 35mm Release." *Moving Image* 5 (1): 128–35.

Sanders, Sol W. 1977. "India: Ending the Permit-License Raj." *Asian Affairs* 5 (2): 88–96.

Sarkar, Bhaskar. 2007. "Shah Rukh's Hair, Saif's Abs: Towards a Theory of Cosmoplastics." Paper presented at South Asia Studies Center Colloquium, University of Texas at Austin, April 2007.

Sarkar, Kobita. 1975. *Indian Cinema Today: An Analysis*. New Delhi: Sterling.

———. 1982. *You Can't Please Everyone! Film Censorship, the Inside Story*. New Delhi: IBH.

Sarkar, Sumit. 1959. *Modern India: 1857–1947*. Delhi: Macmillan.

———. 1983. *Modern India: 1885–1947*. Madras: Macmillan India.

Sarkar, Tanika. 2001. *Hindu Wife, Hindu Nation: Community, Religion, and Cultural Nationalism*. Bloomington: Indiana University Press.

Sathe, V. P. 1981. "Advance of the Sound FIlm." In Ramachandran, Burra, and Chandran 1981, 34–39.

Schaefer, David J., and Kavita Karan. 2010. "Problematizing Chindia: Hybridity and Bollywoodization of Popular Indian Cinema in Global Film Flows." *Global Media and Communication* 6 (3): 309–16.

———. 2011. "Bollywood Cinema at the Crossroads: Tracking the Dimensions of Globalization in Postcolonial Popular Hindi Cinema." *Mass Communication and Society* 14 (6): 700–719.

Scott, A. O. 2007. "Dostoyevsky with Bollywood Style." *New York Times*, November 9, 2007. http://www.nytimes.com/2007/11/09/movies/09saaw.html.

Sen, Meheli. 2013. "Beyond Bollywood?" *Cinema Journal* 52 (4): 155–80.

Sen, Mrinal. 1977. *Views on Cinema*. Calcutta: Ishan.

Seshagiri, Urmila. 2003. "At the Crossroads of Two Empires: Mira Nair's Mississippi Masala and the Limits of Hybridity." *Journal of Asian American Studies* 6 (2): 177–98.

Shah, Panna. 1981. *The Indian Film*. Westport, CT: Greenwood Press.

Shahani, Kumar. 1986. "Dossier: Kumar Shahani." *Framework*, nos. 30–31: 68–111.

Shantaram, Kiran, and Sanjit Narwekar. 2003. *V. Shantaram: The Legacy of the Royal Lotus*. New Delhi: Rupa and Co.

Sharma, Mohan Lal. 1968. "Mark Twain's Passage to India." *Mark Twain Journal* 14 (2): 12–14.

Shastri, Sudha. 2011. "'The Play's the Thing, Wherein I'll Catch the Conscience of the King': Intertextuality in *Om Shanti Om*." *Journal of Film and Video* 63 (1): 32–43.

Shoesmith, Brian. 1987. "From Monopoly to Commodity: The Bombay Studios in the 1930s." In *History on/and/in Film*, edited by Tom O'Regan and Brian Shoesmith, 68–75. Perth: History and Film Association of Australia.

Shrinivas, Lakshmi. 2002. "The Active Audience: Spectatorship, Social Relations and the Experience of Cinema in India." *Media, Culture and Society* 24:155–73.

Sinha, Babli. 2009. "'Lowering Our Prestige': American Cinema, Mass Consumerism, and Racial Anxiety in Colonial India." *Comparative Studies of South Asia, Africa and the Middle East* 29 (2): 291–305.

———. 2013. *Cinema, Transnationalism, and Colonial India: Entertaining the Raj*. New York: Routledge.

Sircar, Ajanta. 2011. *Framing the Nation: Languages of "Modernity" in India*. Calcutta: Seagull.

Sircar, Jawhar. 2014. "Vividh Bharati's Role in 'Unifying' the Indian Nation." jawharsircar.com, January 29, 2014. http://jawharsircar.com/assets/pdf/Vividh_Bharati's_Role_in_'Unifying'_the_Indian_Nation_Jawhar_Sircar.pdf.

Sivathamby, Karthigesu. 1971. "Politicians as Players." *Drama Review* 15 (2): 212–20.

———. 1981. *The Tamil Film as a Medium of Political Communication*. Madras: New Century Book.

Skillman, Teri. 1986. "The Bombay Hindi Film Song Genre: A Historical Survey." In *Yearbook for Traditional Music*, edited by Dieter Christensen, 133–44. New York: International Council for Traditional Music.

Souter, Kay, and Ira Raja. 2008. "Mothering Siblings: Diaspora, Desire and Identity in *American Born Confused Desi*." *Narrative* 16 (1): 16–28.

Srinivasan, Supraja. 2017. "Amazon Prime Video India Launches First India Original Series *Inside Edge*." *Economic Times*, June 16, 2017. http://economictimes.indiatimes.com/industry/media/entertainment/media/amazon-prime-video-india-launches-first-india-original-series-inside-edge/articleshow/59181039.cms.

Srivastava, Sanjay. 2004. "Voice, Gender and Space in Time of Five-Year Plans: The Idea of Lata Mangeshkar." *Economic and Political Weekly* 39 (20): 2019–28.

Srivastava, Sanjeev. 2001. "Cash Boost for Bollywood." BBC News, July 25, 2001. http://news.bbc.co.uk/2/hi/entertainment/1456962.stm.

Stenport, Anna Westerstahl, and Garrett Traylor. 2015. "The Eradication of Memory: Film Adaptations and Algorithms of the Digital." *Cinema Journal* 55 (1): 74–94.

Sundar, Pavitra. 2007. "Meri Awaaz Suno: Women, Vocality, and Nation in Hindi Cinema." *Meridians: Feminism, Race, Transnationalism* 8 (1): 144–79.

Tagore, Rabindranath. 1986. *Rabindra-Racanabali, Volume 12.* Calcutta: Visvabharati.

Tharoor, Shashi. 1997. *India: From Midnight to the Millennium.* New York: Arcade.

Thomas, Rosie. 1985. "Indian Cinema: Pleasures and Popularity." *Screen* 26 (3–4): 116–31.

———. 1987. "Mythologies and Modern India." In *World Cinema since 1945*, edited by William Luhr, 301–29. New York: Ungar.

———. 2015. *Bombay before Bollywood: Film City Fantasies.* Albany: SUNY Press.

Thompson, Kristin. 1986. *Exporting Entertainment: America in the World Film Market, 1907–1934.* London: BFI.

Thoraval, Yves. 2000. *The Cinemas of India.* Delhi: Macmillan.

Thorne, Susan. 1999. "Missionary-Imperial Feminism." In *Gendered Missions: Women and Men in Missionary Discourse and Practice*, by Mary Taylor Huber and Nancy C. Lutkehaus, 39–66. Ann Arbor: University of Michigan Press.

Times of India. 1954. "Film Delegation to Russia: No Govt. Nominees." August 31, 1954, 9.

———. 1979a. "FFC Move to Finance Cinema Halls." January 16, 1979.

———. 1979b. "Karanth to Head Working Group on Film Policy." May 8, 1979.

TRAI. 2017. "A Twenty Year Odyssey: 1997–2017." Telecom Regulatory Authority of India. Accessed February 8, 2019. https://main.trai.gov.in/sites/default/files/A_Twenty Year_Odyssey_1997_2017.pdf.

Tripathi, Salil. 2001. "Gangsters Grab the Limelight in Bollywood." *New Statesman*, March 21, 2001, 32–33.

Tully, Mark. 2007. "The Business of Broadcasting." *India International Centre Quarterly* 33 (3/4): 254–61.

Tyrrell, Heather. 1999. "Bollywood versus Hollywood: Battle of the Dream Factories." In *Culture and Global Change*, by Tracey Skelton and Tim Allen, 260–66. London: Routledge.

Uberoi, Patricia. 1998. "The Diaspora Comes Home: Disciplinng Desire in DDLJ." *Contributions to Indian Sociology* 32 (2): 305–36.

Vasudev, Aruna. 1978. *Liberty and Licence in the Indian Cinema.* New Delhi: Vikas Publishing House.

———. 1986. *The New Indian Cinema.* New Delhi: Macmillan India.

———, ed. 1995. *Frames of Mind: Reflections on Indian Cinema.* Bombay: UBS Publishers.

Vasudev, Aruna, and Philippe Lenglet, eds. 1983. *Indian Cinema Superbazaar.* Delhi: Vikas Publishing House.

Vasudevan, Ravi. 1989. "The Melodramatic Mode and the Commercial Hindi Cinema: Notes on Film History, Narrative, and Performance in the 1950s." *Screen* 30 (3): 29–50.

———. 1994. "Dislocations: The Cinematic Imagining of a New Society in 1950s India." *Oxford Literary Review* 16 (1): 93–124.

———. 1995. "Addressing the Spectator of a 'Third World' National Cinema: Bombay 'Social' Film of the 1940s and 1950s." *Screen* 36 (4): 312–13.

———. 1996. "Shifting Codes, Dissolving Identities: The Hindi Social Film of the 1950s as Popular Culture." *Third Text* 10 (34): 59–77.

————, ed. 2000a. *Making Meaning in Indian Cinema*. New Delhi: Oxford University Press.

————. 2000b. "The Politics of Cultural Address in a 'Transitional' Cinema: A Case Study of Indian Popular Cinema." In *Reinventing Film Studies*, edited by Christine Gledhill and Linda Williams, 130–64. London: Arnold.

————. 2010. "In the Centrifuge of History." *Cinema Journal* 50 (1): 135–40.

————. 2011. *The Melodramatic Public: Film Form and Spectatorship in Indian Cinema*. New York: Palgrave Macmillan.

Velayutham, Selvaraj. 2008. *Tamil Cinema: The Cultural Politics of India's Other Film Industry*. London: Routledge.

Verma, R. K. 2000. *Filmography: Silent Cinema, 1913–1934*. Dehra Dun: Saraswati Press.

Verma, Ratnakar, and Jitendra Tripathy. 2010. "Identites in Ferment: Reflections on the Predicament of Bhojpuri Cinema, Music and Language in Bihar." In *Indian Mass Media and the Politics of Change*, edited by Angad Chowdhry, Meena Gaur, Matti Pohjonen Somnath Batabyal, 93–121. New Delhi: Routledge.

Vernallis, Carol. 2013. *Unruly Media: YouTube, Music Video, and the New Digital Cinema*. Oxford: Oxford University Press.

Vincent, Alice. 2013. "100 Years of Bollywood: A Beginner's Guide." *The Telegraph*, May 3, 2013. http://www.telegraph.co.uk/culture/film/bollywood/10033530/100-years-of-Bollywood-A-beginners-guide.html.

Vitali, Valentina. 2008. *Hindi Action Cinema: Industries, Narratives, Bodies*. Bloomington: Indiana University Press.

Wadia, J. B. H. 1981. "Those Were the Days." In Ramachandran, Burra, and Chandran 1981, 110–12.

Waltz, Michael L. 1977–78. "The Indian People's Theatre Association: Its Development and Influences." *Journal of South Asian Literature* 13 (1/4): 31–37.

Watve, Bapu. 1985. *V. Damle and S. Fattelal: A Monograph*. Poona: National Film Archive of India.

Weinraub, Bernard. 1991. "Economic Crisis Forcing Once Self-Reliant India to Seek Aid." *New York Times*, June 21, 1991. http://www.nytimes.com/1991/06/29/world/economic-crisis-forcing-once-self-reliant-india-to-seek-aid.html?pagewanted=print.

Wenner, Dorothee. 2005. *Fearless Nadia: The True Story of Bollywood's Original Stunt Queen*. New Delhi: Penguin.

Whitman, Walt. 1872. "A Passage to India." In *Leaves of Grass*, 4–15. Washington.

Wilkinson-Weber, Clare M. 2006. "The Dressman's Line: Transforming the Work of Costumers in Popular Hindi Film." *Anthropological Quarterly* 79 (4): 581–609.

Willemen, Paul, and Behroze Gandhy. 1980. *Indian Cinema*. London: British Film Institute.

Wlaschin, Ken, and Stephen Bottomore. 2008. "Moving Picture Fiction of the Silent Era, 1895–1928." *Film History: An International Journal* 20 (2): 217–60.

Wolpert, Stanley. 1997. *A New History of India*. 5th ed. New York: Oxford University Press.

Wood, Robin. 1972. *The Apu Trilogy*. New York: Praeger.

Index

RINI BHATTACHARYA MEHTA is an assistant professor of comparative and world literature at the University of Illinois at Urbana-Champaign. She is a coeditor of *Bollywood and Globalization: Indian Popular Cinema, Nation, and Diaspora*.

The University of Illinois Press
is a founding member of the
Association of University Presses.

———————————————

Composed in 10.25/13 Adobe Garamond Pro
with Memphis display
by Jim Proefrock
at the University of Illinois Press
Cover designed by Myra Rivers
Cover illustration: Film strip vector illustration on
white background (My Portfolio/Shutterstock.com);
stamp image (a3701027/Vectorstock.com)
Manufactured by Sheridan Books, Inc.

University of Illinois Press
1325 South Oak Street
Champaign, IL 61820-6903
www.press.uillinois.edu